T0354504

This important work by D.H. Withers is more than just a document giving important and vital truth about Israel and our biblical responsibilities to her. It is indeed a book that is birthed out of her hands on knowledge and experience of Israel. She has lived out all that she teaches and therefore her insights are not only biblical but heart felt and compelling. Such a book is worth reading and will enjoy the favor of God.

-Rev. Malcolm Hedding, former Executive Director
International Christian Embassy Jerusalem

My wife and I had the privilege of hosting a Small Group through our church to learn about Israel. D.H. Withers was our guest teacher for 12 weeks. Her passion for the nation and depth of knowledge was a powerful combination that made a huge impact on our group. The best part was how she could make the complexities simple so we could learn and understand. Having that wisdom in book form is a great gift!

-Pastor Layne Schranz, Associate Pastor Church of
the Highlands, Birmingham, Alabama

Have you ever wondered why Israel is always in the forefront of the news? D.H. examines the question by addressing diverse topics that include the Biblical Feasts, "Aliya," and Islam's rejection of Israel. Read *Unbroken Cord: Israel and the Church* and discover God's prophetic purposes for this Land. The author's knowledge and insight about these subjects, as well as her experience from living in this land, provide unique awareness and understanding to Christians on the timely subject of Israel.

-Gene Little, D. Litt.
House of Peace, Jerusalem, Israel.

Unbroken Cord

Israel and the Church

D. H. Withers

WESTBOW
PRESS®
A DIVISION OF THOMAS NELSON
& ZONDERVAN

Cover Art and Images by Jessica Whitmore
Author photograph by Emily Smith Creatives

This book is a work of non-fiction. Unless otherwise noted, the author and the publisher make no explicit guarantees as to the accuracy of the information contained in this book and in some cases, names of people and places have been altered to protect their privacy.

Unless otherwise marked, Scripture quotations are from The Holy Bible, English Standard Version® (ESV®), copyright © 2001 by Crossway, a publishing ministry of Good News Publishers. Used by permission. All rights reserved.

Scripture taken from the *Amplified Bible*, copyright © 1954, 1958, 1962, 1964, 1965, 1987 by The Lockman Foundation. Used by permission.

Scripture quotations taken from the New American Standard Bible®, Copyright © 1960, 1962, 1963, 1968, 1971, 1972, 1973, 1975, 1977, 1995 by The Lockman Foundation. Used by permission. (www.Lockman.org)

Scripture taken from the Holy Bible, NEW INTERNATIONAL VERSION®. Copyright © 1973, 1978, 1984, 2011 by Biblica, Inc. All rights reserved worldwide. Used by permission. NEW INTERNATIONAL VERSION® and NIV® are registered trademarks of Biblica, Inc. Use of either trademark for the offering of goods or services requires the prior written consent of Biblica US, Inc.

WestBow Press books may be ordered through booksellers or by contacting:

WestBow Press
A Division of Thomas Nelson & Zondervan
1663 Liberty Drive
Bloomington, IN 47403
www.westbowpress.com
1 (866) 928-1240

Because of the dynamic nature of the Internet, any web addresses or links contained in this book may have changed since publication and may no longer be valid. The views expressed in this work are solely those of the author and do not necessarily reflect the views of the publisher, and the publisher hereby disclaims any responsibility for them.

Any people depicted in stock imagery provided by Thinkstock are models, and such images are being used for illustrative purposes only.
Certain stock imagery © Thinkstock.

ISBN: 978-1-5127-5184-0 (sc)
ISBN: 978-1-5127-5185-7 (hc)
ISBN: 978-1-5127-5183-3 (e)

Library of Congress Control Number: 2016912530

Print information available on the last page.

WestBow Press rev. date: 11/28/2016

Contents

Contents

Acknowledgments

Since this book came about as the result of small group meetings, I will always be grateful to the intrepid Robert and Darien Roche; they not only opened their home to the original launch but went on to host several Israel 101 small groups.

And many, many thanks to that special group of friends who generously committed themselves weekly to provide the warm and welcoming atmosphere that so greatly added to each semester's success: Helen James, Kyle and Jan Ware, Tom and Linda Buckner, Theo and Taylor Polstra, Ellen Davis, David and Shannon Jernigan, Diane Olexa, Keith and Carla Rouse, Buddy and Gina Cox, Jeremy and Leah Jones, Layne and Rachel Schranz. For routinely going above and beyond unstinting and magnanimous hospitality to multiple successive groups, I gratefully acknowledge O.Z. and Patty Hall, as well as Lee Fant; you guys are simply amazing. Thank you. Christian Home Educators of Cullman, thank you for giving me the opportunity to share this curriculum with your teens; it was a fun season and kept me on my toes.

I would like to recognize Church of the Highlands, Daystar, and Building Church. Your gracious provision of space accommodations for my groups is much appreciated. Thank you.

I am particularly grateful to Jeff Adams for opening my eyes to the ongoing return of the world's Jews to their ancestral homeland. As incredulous as it seems to me now, I had never heard of *aliyah* until you pointed out and then explained the volume of scripture that foretells the promise of this contemporary phenomenon.

I've been privileged and blessed to learn from some of the best through their books, seminars, and DVDs: Billye Brim, Malcolm Hedding, Lance Lambert, Neil and Jamie Lash, and certainly Derek Prince.

Jeanne Corwin, how can I ever thank you enough for facilitating memorable and life-changing adventures in the Holy Land? The Obed Project has provided *the* dream trip of a lifetime for those we've taken on tours over the years. Thank you for your friendship and for your faithfulness to the keeper of Israel.

Thank you, Lindsey Watson, for your unfailingly cheerful willingness to endure many late nights of reading through early drafts. Parnell, friend and fellow traveler, thank you for offering honest opinions and thoughtful perspective. And, Jeanette Thompson and Kim Frolander, thank you for coming alongside early on in this project with advice and encouragement.

Shannon Jernigan, your suggestions, after reading through the early manuscript, greatly boosted my conviction that putting an expanded version of my small group outline notes onto the pages of a book might actually be a possibility. Thank you for sharing your years of expertise with me. Jessica Whitmore, artist par excellence, I will always admire the grace you unfailingly displayed upon hearing my requests for yet another "tiny change."

My daughters and their husbands will never know just how vital their encouragement has been throughout the writing process, which, at times, felt as though it would never be completed. From the start, you remained a consistently faithful cheering section. Thank you, Allison and Emily, Matt and Josh, for believing in the project and in me. You, along with Greg and Paula Sullivan—my dear covenant friends—have been my mainstays and core support throughout the writing of this book. It is with love and gratitude that I thank you for helping me to be obedient to what I perceive is a mandate from the Lord.

Tishrei 1, 5775

Introduction

Because you're reading this, you're probably interested in Israel or, at the least, a *little* curious about the people who populate the Bible. The following pages are about those people and that book and how both are actively affecting today's world. A few miles east of Jerusalem, I first discovered the unmistakable connection of scripture to modern events and places, and I have come to realize that this seamless, unbroken cord runs throughout both Old and New Testaments. Insights from years of study and travel are best shared from this perspective of continuity, so let's start—from the beginning—in Jerusalem.

I watched as Jerusalem's streets and sidewalks bustled with the early-morning activity of locals already on their way to open-air markets. This was my first trip to the Holy Land, and I was relishing every minute of it from the vantage point of a first-row seat on a comfortable tour bus. Expertly negotiating the noisy, narrow thoroughfares, our driver carefully threaded his way toward the day's destination: the world-renowned Dead Sea. Within a surprisingly short time, the tree-lined streets of the city were behind us as we headed east along Israel's Highway 1. In spite of the early hour, a formidable heat could already be seen rising in waves from the asphalt. Upon leaving Jerusalem, perched high atop the Judean hills, the scenery quickly changed to a starkly-defined mountain/desert landscape of browns and beiges. It seemed surreal that the barren stretch of highway we were traveling still follows the same general route as the ancient path made famous in the parable of the Good Samaritan and that the area on both sides of the road also happens to be the vast and desolate wilderness where Jesus spent forty days being tempted by Satan.

Steadily descending the fifteen miles from Jerusalem's elevation of some twenty-five hundred feet to the nearly eight hundred fifty feet below sea level at Jericho, all of us experienced popping in our ears. Small wonder Jesus had chosen to phrase His parable about the Good Samaritan with the words, "A certain man went *down* from Jerusalem to Jericho." This example of the Bible's devotion to fact and precision would prove to be only the first of many that would follow that same day.

A little east of Jericho, before merging with Highway 90 (the route running directly along the western edge of the Dead Sea), the bus pulled off to the side of the road, and our little group disembarked. The Israeli guide directed our gaze to the mountains east of where we stood and said, "See those mountains way over there, across the Jordan River? That's the modern nation of Jordan. Now imagine that you're living back in the days of the Old Testament, and you're a citizen of Jericho, the beautiful walled city located by a palm-filled oasis. But over there, beneath a pillar of cloud and fire in today's Jordan, sits the camp of the Israelites." Wow. So this was the area where the story of Joshua's victory took place! I was actually looking up into the very sky that Rahab had also looked up into all those years ago. Rahab, the woman who'd hidden the spies on her roof, hung a scarlet ribbon from her window on the wall, and, against all odds, she eventually found a place in the genealogy of the Messiah.

Continuing to address his charges with a steady barrage of rapid-fire information, our Jewish guide flipped through the pages of his Bible, confidently moving from chapter to verse. I learned that this very same location along the Jordan River is the actual staging area from where the priests had carried the Ark of the Covenant across a miraculously dry riverbed prior to the victorious march around Jericho. Much later, it would also become the scene of Elijah's sudden departure from earth when a fiery chariot from heaven burst from out of the sky to carry him away. Then, after another eight hundred years had come and gone, it was here at this same section of the Jordan that the Gospel accounts record the Lord's cousin and forerunner, John, faithfully preaching his message of repentance. Jesus was baptized *here*. While listening to the unfolding story of the area's history, Old Testament dots were starting to connect to the dots of the New Testament, and I could see a clear line of relationship from Genesis straight through to the Gospels and then on into the epistles of the New Testament. Prior to this, any contiguous relationship between BC and AD had always been a bit fuzzy to me.

Sure, I'd read each of these stories before, but seeing the actual places where the events happened put a whole new twist on the retelling. As the Old and New Testaments were merging in a way I'd not seen previously, a new visual energy was quickly animating my Bible's pages. That the old stories were coming alive would have been an understatement, and I was beyond thrilled to be seeing with my own eyes the original locations where they'd actually taken place. Feeling freshly equipped to bring my regular Bible classes to life by providing background and descriptions of the surroundings to favorite stories, I was eager to share everything with people back home. Almost immediately upon my return, friends and family were gathered for a full report of the amazing adventure. In spite of jetlag, I enthusiastically read from the many notes I'd scribbled while bouncing over pockmarked roads up in the Golan or following a morning's poignantly sweet quiet time on a dock at the edge of the Sea of Galilee.

That original trip was the beginning of many subsequent visits to Israel, unique land of the Bible. Some of these travels have been short in duration; others have extended into months. But whether the time has been spent leading tours, attending conferences, or working as a volunteer, I am increasingly aware of an inescapable connection between my Christian faith and this land and its people. It is an unbroken cord of connection.

When I asked my pastor for more sermons about Israel, he encouraged me to pursue my newborn passion with a small group. I should mention that every semester our church offers a brand-new series of these small groups. Organized around mutually-shared interests, lifelong relationships are forged in these gatherings as a broad range of topics is explored. The groups form around such diverse activities as running, Bible study, classes on parenting, weekly dinner groups—anything that a group of friends might enjoy sharing with each other.

It was after that original conversation in the pastor's office, along with support from friends, that the idea was born for an "Israel" small group. One afternoon as I puzzled over the best way to undertake this very broad subject, the Lord impressed me with an easy curriculum of twelve segments that fit conveniently into our semester schedule. The individual topics seemed to be effortlessly downloaded in my mind. I copied them into a spiral notebook and then blocked them out according to a weekly presentation. With no other name for this group in mind, I simply called it "Israel 101," since it would be a basic core study aimed at understanding Israel's place within the context of a modern Christian worldview.

Over the years, I've continued to teach that very same curriculum with the basic outline of twelve lessons. Most semesters, the Israel small group has continued to meet in different towns, inside homes, classrooms, offices, and churches. Along the way, many "graduates" have requested a written compilation of the information we've discussed during the semester. This book grew from those small groups. It is an expanded version of my notes. In addition to footnotes and commentary, study guides appear at the end of each chapter. Use the questions on that page to quiz yourself to see how much more you now understand about that chapter's topic; you'll be amazed! I would imagine that small group leaders would enjoy composing their own study guide questions, as the personality of different groups can vary so much. The book is easily adapted into a twelve-week small group set of meetings. Some people, however, find that two weeks per chapter is a better fit and prefer to stretch the curriculum into twenty-four weeks.

Although the subject of Israel is controversial and has even become a divisive factor among believers, this ought not to be the case. On the other hand, what should a conscientious Christian do with the mountain of conflicting information that perpetually swirls within media reports concerning topics such as BDS (boycott, divestment, and sanctions), the Palestinians, Islam, and so forth? And why do Jews and Arabs remain locked in a seemingly relentless and incessant skirmish over a small plot of land in the Middle East? These are legitimate questions, and they're addressed in the following twelve chapters.

It is my sincere hope that the information shared within these pages will give you a workable framework for understanding the often complex issues that impact Israel and the Middle East, *and* your own relationship to the Bible and with our Savior will be deepened. To that end, each chapter provides details and scripture references and explanations pertinent to the topic. Chapters are organized in a natural sequence, with each one building upon the last. I've had the privilege of sitting under world-class teachers who have dedicated their lives to Biblical studies. Along the way, I've also been blessed with special friends who consistently gave of their time and expertise to explain idioms, regional geography, and history that I never learned from my American Sunday school books. Sharing time with those who have spent their lives in the land of the patriarchs, walking the very paths that Jesus would have followed, has kindled my desire to dig into the scriptures with a real joy.

As you read through the following chapters, I'm hoping they will become like the pages of a trusted handbook, a tool to provide you with a foundational and heretofore untapped realization regarding your personal connection to Israel. Based on the feedback from those who've participated in these Israel small groups, I can guarantee that you'll find many previously confusing, overly complex situations falling into place. Pieces of the puzzle will begin to make sense as you connect the dots and follow along that unbroken cord from Old to New Testament. Having a Christian perspective on Israel will allow news headlines and your personal Bible study begin to make sense as never before. It is my honor to share the lessons and insights within this book. It is my fervent hope that a love for the scriptures will be ignited to blaze forth with each page turned and that a renewed passion for our God and His venerable plan for Israel will be embraced and understood.

Chapter 1

Why Study Israel?

For Christians, the Bible is the foundational text. With much of it written in an ancient Semitic language within another age and culture, this remarkable book originated well over three thousand years ago. With its origin separated from the twenty-first century by more than three millennia, it is no wonder that a measure of disconnection between its beginnings and the current generation developed over time. Specifically, many Christians find themselves devoid of even the most basic understanding of the Old Testament. And yet the first generation of believers in Jesus as Messiah, armed with only the scriptures found in their Hebrew Old Testament, turned the world upside down by winning thousands upon thousands of new converts to the Lord. In an effort to bridge that gap between past and present, it seems reasonable that a contemporary believer might benefit from a simple study tracing New Testament teachings to their origins as found in those first Hebrew scriptures. In doing so, it will become clear that there is, in fact, a seamless flow from Old to New Testament. Along the way, many heretofore vague or difficult to understand passages will begin to fall into place.

Luke 4:1–13. To begin, look at Luke's introduction to Christ's life on earth. The opening verses of Luke 4 give a glimpse into a scenario that took place immediately prior to the beginning of the Lord's formal ministry. It can be seen here that the Holy Spirit intentionally led Jesus into the wilderness where He was then tempted by the devil. As the narrative unfolds, the enemy appears on the scene, and a contest ensues as scriptures from Deuteronomy 8:3, Deuteronomy 6:13, and Deuteronomy 6:16 are quoted. Three separate times Satan seeks to entrap the Lord with enticing propositions, and three separate times Jesus trumps His adversary's intention by answering with a rebuttal that begins, "It is written." Red letter editions of the New Testament will show Jesus's part of the conversation printed in red ink. Yet the words from all three passages cited by the Lord are originally found written in the Torah—that historical Jewish document dictated to Moses during the fifteenth century BC.[1] This means that Jesus wielded a spiritual sword forged from words straight from the ancient Hebrew text. Therefore, it was while dueling with words originating from scriptures written more than a thousand years before He was born that Jesus won this battle mentioned in the third Gospel of the New Testament.

Luke's record of this confrontation, known as Christ's temptation, is not the last time the Savior's words are found to be traced back to the Hebrew scriptures. Three and a half years later, as He was hanging from the cross, Jesus was heard repeating phrases originating directly from David's Psalm 22. During His earthly ministry, the Lord was consistent in explaining that He hadn't come to do away with any of the Old Testament but rather to fulfill it. So Jesus was very clear that He was observant of the law that had been handed down by Moses. He was also a practicing Jew. And lest it be forgotten, the book of Revelation reveals that

---

[1] Torah: the first five books of the Bible, directly given to Moses by God on Mt. Sinai. These five books are the basis of the Jewish law because they are the recorded instructions from God; they are the teachings of God. The word *Torah* can also be used to describe a way of life or lifestyle, as practiced by a devout Jew.

Jesus will return to earth as the lion of Judah. In addition, consider Paul's teaching that Christians have been grafted into the promises of Abraham, a man who lived nearly two thousand years earlier than Paul.[2] These and other examples of the archaic nature of the Bible present many with a challenge when connecting the Old Testament's relevance to modern Christianity.

Jesus Christ. A starting point for reconciling this "disconnect" between Old and New Testaments can be found in the name of the Savior. For the Christian, Jesus is the most precious of names. As the only begotten and perfect Son of God, He was crucified for humanity's sins, was raised from the dead on the third day, and is returning to earth as the victorious king of kings. He is the Christ in Christianity, the Savior and Son of God. Yet although the Hebrew scriptures foretold His birth, life, death, and resurrection, the title *Jesus Christ* is nowhere to be found in any of the books of the Old Testament. The astonishing reason for this is that Jesus Christ was not His first and last name. His mother was not Mary Christ or even Mrs. Christ. Translated into English, "Jesus Christ" is actually His name and title.

Yeshua Ha'Mashiach. The thing is, "Jesus" is the English language version of the Hebrew name *Yeshua* (there is no *J* in Hebrew). The name *Yeshua* is translated from the Hebrew word meaning "salvation." Likewise, *Christ* is derived from the Greek word *Cristos,* meaning "anointed." And "Christos" is the Greek translation of the original Hebrew word *Mashiach.* The meaning of Mashiach is, of course, "anointed." Additionally, the Hebrew Mashiach has been further modified into its Anglicized version,

---

[2] Thomas Robinson, *The Bible Timeline* (Nashville: Thomas Nelson Publishers, 1992). Scholars differ in their opinions as to when Abraham lived; however, the traditional Hebrew Bible (Masoretic Text) places him in the late 1900s BC, and I find this timetable coincides with events that followed, namely, the Exodus, times of the judges, etc. This chronology also makes it easier to mentally round off the millennia so that Abraham = 2000 BC; David = 1000 BC; Jesus = center of the timeline; Crusades = 1000 AD; and finally, the world at present = 2000 AD.

Messiah. Thus, Jesus Christ literally translates to "Salvation the Anointed." Another way of saying it would be, "Jesus, the Anointed One."[3]

Discovering the etymology of His name makes Matthew 1:21 come into clearer focus: "And you shall call his name Jesus, for he will save his people from their sins." When seen from within the context of the original language, there can be no doubt about it; Jesus is the literal personification of the anointed salvation for the human race. His very name—in Hebrew—reveals the deeper levels of unfolding richness from God. And when sifting through the layers, a definite Jewish flavor begins to emerge as one delves into the roots of the Christian faith.

Scriptures that immediately form links to the Jewish roots of Christianity. New Testament writers took it for granted that their readers would understand that all references to *scripture* referred solely to the earlier Old Testament scriptures. Consider the following verses that point directly to an earlier Jewish link:

- Hebrews 9:11–12: Speaks of Jesus as the great high priest, a position known in Hebrew as the *Cohen Gadol*. A Roman Catholic would relate to the concept of a priest, but a Protestant has no point of reference for this scripture unless the role and responsibilities of the priest are studied first from the Old Testament.
- Galatians 3:7: "Know then that it is those of faith who are the sons of Abraham." It is because of Jesus that Christians are sons (and daughters) of God, but this verse defines Christians as offspring of Abraham the Jew.

---

[3] James Strong, *Strong's Exhaustive Concordance of the Bible* (Iowa Falls, Iowa: World Bible Publishers, Inc., 1986). This concordance assigns numbers to words in the Bible text and then renders the roots and definitions in either Hebrew or Greek. For example, the Greek name for Jesus (2424) is derived from the Hebrew *Yhowshuwa* (3091). The title *Christ* is translated from the Greek *Christos* (5547), which is derived from the original Hebrew word *Mashiyach* (4899).

- Galatians 3:14: "In Christ Jesus, the blessings of Abraham might come to the Gentiles." Christians are in Christ Jesus.
- Galatians 3:16: Now the promises were made to Abraham and to his offspring. It does not say "offsprings," referring to many, but "offspring," referring to one: "And to your offspring," who is Christ. Christians are coheirs with Christ.
- Galatians 3:29 NIV: "If you belong to Christ, then you are Abraham's seed, and heirs according to the promise." Christians belong to Christ.
- Romans 11:17–18: "But if some of the branches were broken off, and you, although a wild olive shoot, were grafted in among the others and now share in the nourishing root of the olive tree, do not be arrogant toward the branches. If you are, remember it is not you who support the root, but the root that supports you." This scripture is referring to Israel as the olive tree, yet the analogy between Israel and the olive tree originates from the Psalms, Jeremiah, and Hosea.

Based on the following facts—that the New Testament is frequently referring the reader to the Old Testament, that the Old Testament was originally written in Hebrew, that all of the prophets were Jews, that the Savior is the fulfillment of Jewish prophecies, that God says Israel is the apple of His eye, and that Jesus is returning as a Jew to Jerusalem—it is only logical that a study of the culture and history in which the Bible was written might be educational, and Christians would, in fact, be encouraged to examine their relationship to Israel.

It's not always about us! The following study will be approached like this: all the Bible is *for* the Church, but not all the Bible is *about* the Church.[4] At first glance, this might seem like a

---

[4] I first learned about this revolutionary study approach from Dr. Billye Brim, noted Bible teacher and author from Prayer Mountain in the Ozarks, during one

questionable statement; however, there is a sound scriptural basis for it, and a serious Bible student always wants to authenticate any precept with scripture. By looking at two separate letters from Paul, the explanation can be found. The first part of the statement isn't difficult in the least; of course, *all* the Bible is for the Church! Second Timothy 3:16 is very clear about the fact that every single scripture in the Bible is inspired by God Himself, and these scriptures serve to give instruction, conviction, correction, and training in righteousness. Keep in mind that the scriptures to which Paul was referring were all Old Testament, as they were the only scriptures available at the time this letter to the younger Timothy was written.

To understand the second part of the statement, "not all the Bible is about the Church," one only needs to look at another of Paul's epistles. In a letter to the believers at Corinth Paul plainly differentiates among three separate groups of people. The first of his two messages to this church clarifies that a definite segregation exists among the people of the earth. Paul writes, "Give no offense to Jews or to Greeks or to the church of God" (1 Corinthians 10:32). The divisions fall along these lines: those who have chosen to believe in Jesus are known as the Church, and the others are either Jew or Gentile (some versions translate Greek as Gentile). This makes three groups in total. Once a person believes in Jesus, that person is transferred out of his former group (whether Jew or Gentile) into the Church, and it turns out that after becoming a follower of Jesus, both Jews and Gentiles are automatically and mystically transitioned into becoming part of what Paul refers to as the "one new man."[5] Armed with an awareness of the three different groups, the statement "All the Bible is *for* the Church, but not all of the Bible is *about* the Church" becomes clear and makes

---

of my early trips to Israel, http://www.billyebrim.org.
[5] Galatians 3:28.

perfect sense. Getting hold of this concept will revolutionize one's personal Bible study.

Today's Church is a Gentile Church. The majority of today's Christians do not come from a Jewish heritage or background. Most were Gentiles before becoming part of the eternal Church, and have very little understanding about the Jews or their traditions. This is a direct inversion of the early Church that was composed predominantly of Jewish believers. As converts continued to increase, growing numbers of an emerging and proportionally larger Gentile base lost touch with the original customs and approach to study that Jesus and the disciples would have used. One striking example of the resulting differences is in regard to the name of God. Even among Jews who do not consider themselves to be religious, most have a healthy respect for the actual name of God. Within stricter circles of Judaism, even the spelling for the word *God* is printed out as "G–d." And due to the fact that the precise pronunciation of the sound for God's name is in question, many observant Jews will avoid the accidental offense of mispronunciation by referring to Him as *HaShem*, which is Hebrew for "the Name."[6] Inasmuch as minor differences in vocabulary tend to separate people from each other, a review of the origins of the Jewish story is a good starting point for finding common ground between the two groups of Jews and Gentiles. Because the new covenant begins and ends with Jesus, because Jesus came to earth as the long-awaited Jewish messiah, and because, so far as the Jew

---

[6] God reveals His multi-faceted roles and characteristics through His many names such as *El Shaddai* ("the Almighty") or *Avinu* ("our Father"), for instance. The name most often used in Hebrew scripture, however, is *YHWH*, which comes from the four Hebrew letters *Yod, Hay, Vav, Hay*, and this is how the translated pronunciations of Jehovah and *Yahweh* have come about. By contrast, observant Jews will not attempt to pronounce this name. Why? Since the original Hebrew language was written without vowels, no one knows for certain how this word, *Yod-Hay-Vav-Hay*, should be pronounced. Therefore, out of respect, Jews will often refer to God as *HaShem* or "the Name." To further demonstrate reverence, the word *God* is written as "G–d."

is concerned, Jewish history begins with Abraham, the starting point will begin with Abraham's immediate family.

First things first. Judaism has three patriarchs: Abraham, Isaac, and Jacob, who happen to be father, son, and grandson, respectively. Although his parents had named him "Jacob," God changed his name to "Israel." Look at the name, Israel, as it appears for the first time: Then he said, "Your name shall no longer be called Jacob, but Israel, for you have striven with God and with men, and have prevailed" (Genesis 32:28). Before these words were spoken to him, Jacob was a man who had learned to live by his wits, always planning and conniving to get ahead. He was a twin, but he hadn't been the firstborn. The older twin, by virtue of birth order, automatically held the advantage for inheriting the birthright. But Jacob was ambitious and wanted the position of tribal leader, which a birthright would insure. Furthermore, he hadn't been his father's favorite son. So he learned to scheme and strategize instead.

Reading through Jacob's story as it unfolds, beginning in Genesis 25:29, it can be seen that his cunning finally succeeded in wresting the birthright from his elder brother and twin, Esau. Resorting to outright fraud, Jacob, with help from his mother, carried out a risky family coup. Sinking to the depths of a plot predicated on bold-faced lying, Jacob achieved his goal by tricking his blind and aging father into imparting the blessing to him. This was the very blessing that had originated with God and had been handed down from Abraham to Isaac. And Jacob meant to have it for himself, regardless of the consequences. Once his duplicity was discovered and the facts came to light, an enraged Esau began to plot his brother's murder.[7] Fortunately for Jacob, these plans for revenge were uncovered, but in order to save his life, his parents were forced to send him hundreds of miles to the north. And it was there in Haran (north of the Euphrates River in modern Turkey) that he

---

[7] Genesis 27:41.

would finally meet his match in chicanery. His uncle, Laban, who later became his father-in-law, proved to be even more proficient at deceit than Jacob himself. Chapters 29–31 of Genesis reveal the grueling life Jacob experienced at the hands of this wily older man during the long years spent in Haran. After twenty years of doing hard service, Jacob finally saw an open window of escape from Laban and his jealous brothers-in-law, and he went for it! A covert and very desperate attempt to break away from a web of dead-end servitude was made possible only by the cooperation of his two wives, Leah and Rachel. Seizing the moment, he determined to sneak away, taking his wives, children, servants, and personal livestock. His wealth was tied up in the latter.

Forced to travel many miles over rough terrain with such a large and diverse company meant that Laban and his sons were able to catch up with the fleeing family after only ten days. But God was with Jacob and intervened on his behalf by sending a dream to Laban. In the dream, God warned Laban against doing any harm to his son-in-law. Thus, Jacob was able to depart without bloodshed; encouraged, he continued traveling south to his own father. He also sent a solicitous and carefully worded message on ahead to Esau. The returning courier, however, brought back the alarming report that brother Esau was already on the way to meet him, accompanied by four hundred men. This was certainly not good news for Jacob who understood that his brother would be justified in any vengeance he might be planning to take. Indeed, the Bible records that he was greatly afraid and distressed.

Jacob is renamed by God. That night, while alone and on the brink of a long-dreaded reunion, he paced the ground under the silent stars. This is the panic-stricken Jacob about whom it is recorded that a "man" wrestled with him until daybreak. Up until this time, and even though he'd often had to suffer the consequences—one way or the other—he'd eventually prevailed over other men. Now, from the poignant account recorded in Genesis 32, one hears the heavenly being essentially asking the same question that his father, Isaac, had asked years before: "What is your name?" "Who are you?" This time, however, the one posing the question was not blind. The answer is a painful, stripped-to-the-bone confession, for Jacob had instantaneously come face to face with the shocking realization that his name, "supplanter, schemer, swindler, cheater," was truly an apt one. The man was defined by his name and laid bare before his maker. But God! "Then he said, 'Your name shall no longer be called Jacob, but Israel, for you have striven with God and with men, and have prevailed'" (Genesis 32:28). God had seen the man's desperation and hunger for the blessing, and He loved him for it. God loved him in spite of his many failings.

Renamed and commissioned by God, Jacob became "Israel." He had a new name and a new identity with God now embedded within his very name. For *Sar* is Hebrew for prince, ruler, or commander (*Sar Shalom* is "Prince of Peace," for instance), and *El* is Hebrew for "the Mighty," one of God's own names. Thus, Jacob the cheater became a ruler with the Mighty: God's prince or prince of God. A prince represents the king's realm, and a prince inherits his kingdom from the king. *Selah* (the Hebrew word meaning "to pause and reflect.")

God names the foundation stones. Notice that God personally named each of the three patriarchs. In ancient Israel, a person's name usually indicated that individual's character or something about the parents' relationship to God.[8] For instance, look at the names given to each of Leah's sons in Genesis 29, and then read why each of the boys was given his particular name. In the case of the patriarchs, God took on the role of a parent by giving names to all three of Judaism's founding fathers. The first name change took place after the covenant had been made as God changed the name *Abram* (exalted father) to *Abraham* (father of a multitude). The

---

[8] Abraham, Genesis 17:5; Isaac, Genesis 17:19; and Jacob, Genesis 32:28.

second of the three patriarchs, Isaac, was named before he was even conceived. Proving that He has a sense of humor, God decreed that this unborn male child should be introduced as *Isaac* (laughter). Sure enough, both of his aged parents laughed to themselves upon hearing that they could expect a baby. God seems to have said, "Laugh if you want, my dear children, but remember My promise whenever you call out the name of your little boy; it is "Laughter!" The third of the patriarchs was Jacob, a cheater, but his brand-new name of *Israel* is replete with nobility: "prince of God." These then are the foundation stones of a nation: Abraham, Isaac, and Israel. Each stone was established and personally named by God.

ישראל. This is fascinating. Contained within the name of Israel are the identities of each of the patriarchs and matriarchs. Written from right to left, Israel is spelled: *yod, shin, resh, aleph and lamed.* ישראל

- • **Y**od (י) stands for Isaac and his son, Jacob. In Hebrew, Jacob's name is Yacov (remember, there is no "J" in Hebrew).
- • **S**hin (ש) stands for Sarah.
- • **R**esh (ר) stands for Rebecca and Rachel.
- • **A**leph (א) stands for Abraham.
- • **L**amed (ל) is the largest letter of the Hebrew *alephbet* and stands for Leah, the mother who contributed the most sons. (*Aleph* is Hebrew, whereas *alpha* is Greek; therefore, it is alephbet instead of alphabet.)

The more one examines the original Hebrew, the more these seeming coincidences appear to have rhyme and reason or pattern, if you will.

The Old Testament is the *T'nach*. The following explanation will facilitate a brief overview of terms and organization of Jewish scripture. What Christians know as the Old Testament, a Jew would refer to as the T'nach. The Hebrew letters *Tav, Nun and Kaf* (*T–N–K*)

11

are pronounced "t'-nock" and written as "Tanakh" or "T'nach." The word *T'nach* is an acronym composed from the first letters of each of the three sections that make up the book. The sections are:

1. **𝑇orah (ת)**. *T* stands for "Torah." This first section is known corporately as the *Chumash,* and is composed of the first five books of the Bible. The literal meaning is "instruction." These five books are known as the law of Moses, and they are the law to which Jesus referred in Matthew 5:17–18. Genesis, Exodus, Leviticus, Numbers, and Deuteronomy are the five books in all.

2. **𝑁eviim (נ)**. *N* stands for "Neviim" or "prophets." This section is traditionally divided into two parts. The first part, or the "former prophets," is composed of the books Joshua, Judges, 1 and 2 Samuel, and 1 and 2 Kings. The second part of Neviim, known as the "latter prophets," contains the books of Isaiah, Jeremiah, Ezekiel, and Hosea through Malachi. Hosea through Malachi are recognized by Christians as the twelve minor prophets. Included in this group are Hosea, Joel, Amos, Obadiah, Jonah, Micah, Nahum, Habakkuk, Zephaniah, Haggai, Zechariah, and Malachi.

3. **𝐾etuvim (כ)**. *K* stands for "Ketuvim," and literally means the "writings." This final division of the T'nach contains the Psalms, Proverbs and Job; the "five scrolls" (within this grouping are the books of Ruth, Esther, Song of Songs, Ecclesiastes, and Lamentations); and finally, Daniel, Ezra, Nehemiah, and 1 and 2 Chronicles.

Immediately obvious is the fact that the books are out of order in relation to the Christian Bible. But if one considers that this was the sequence arrived at by Jewish scholars before the later New Testament books were even written, then maybe they're not so out of order after all. In total, the T'nach, or Old Testament, is the written record that details the history of the people of Israel and their relationship to God. It includes their interactions with other nations and God's plan of blessing for them, and then, through them, His blessing to the rest of humanity. It can be summarized as follows:

- Genesis. This is God's personal revelation of the creation process, mankind's fall, and the promise of the one who would crush the serpent's head; it is a recounting of the first ten generations from Adam to Noah, followed by the next ten generations from Noah to Abraham. Also included are the personal histories of the patriarchs, the covenants, and the prophesied exile into Egypt.
- Exodus–Deuteronomy. This is Moses's account of the years spent in Egypt, the subsequent forty years of wandering in the desert, and the giving of the law.
- Joshua. Herein are the details of the conquest of Canaan in a chronological format.
- Judges and 1 Samuel. Herein are the details about life in Israel under the fifteen judges.
- Second Samuel, 1 Kings and 1 and 2 Chronicles. These detail the history of the forty-two kings of Judah (the southern kingdom) and Israel (the ten tribes of the northern kingdom). The histories also include snapshots of personal characteristics and interactions between particular individuals of special interest.
- Second Kings through Esther. Here is the unfolding story of Israel's two captivities as a consequence of disobedience to God. The northern kingdom fell in 722 BC to Assyria. The southern kingdom was conquered by Babylon's King Nebuchadnezzar in 586 BC.

- Ezra and Nehemiah. Here is the detailed account of the prophesied return from Babylon and Israel's restoration to the Promised Land.
- The Prophets. This series of prophetic compilations provides a written record of God's pleas and warnings concerning the consequences of disobedience. It includes His promises of blessing and His "code talk" or prophecies that foreshadow the ultimate blessing of the future Messiah.

The Bible during the time of Jesus. The Old Testament scriptures were the only scriptures available for study in the time of Jesus. They are the written word that Jesus would have learned as a boy. They are the writings the disciples and early Christians would have read or heard. An understanding of these Old Testament scriptures and the subsequent fulfillment of them by Jesus influenced the first generation of believers to such an extent that they chose to dedicate their lives to Him as their Messiah. The first-century believers were Jews and recognized Jesus as the one about whom the Old Testament prophets had spoken. They are the ones who began the evangelistic movement that set the world on fire for the Gospel. Galvanized by their testimony, the Gentiles also subsequently embraced Him as Savior; submitting themselves to their Jewish teachers, they began to learn about the God of Abraham, Isaac and Jacob and His covenant.

The New Testament and how it came to be. When His blood was spilled, God's own Son became the sacrifice for all humanity. From before the foundation of the world, Jesus was anointed to be the sacrificial Lamb of God. His life made possible the *new* covenant between God and man. Within a generation, the four Gospel writers (Matthew, Mark, Luke, and John), along with the Lord's half-brothers (James and Jude), the apostles (Peter and Paul), and the author of Hebrews, began writing letters that detailed the life of Jesus and His teachings.[9] These men explained to their readers how Jesus had perfectly fulfilled all the prophecies concerning the long-awaited Messiah. Out of necessity, they went on to develop and adapt a moral code based on Hebrew law for the new Gentile believers, most of whom were emerging from various backgrounds of pagan worship and practice. Much later, and after having been collected and compiled, these letters are what Christians know today as the New Testament. Simply put, the New Testament is the explanation and revelation of Jesus as the fulfillment of the Old Testament messianic prophecies. It is also the textbook by which the new followers would learn to transform their lives and apply the meaning of the Crucifixion to their former heathen mentality. Thus, early Christian life emerged within a definite context of Jewish morality.

Today. Two thousand years later, an exorbitantly blessed and strategically placed generation has the privilege of living during the times foretold by the ancient Hebrew prophets. The world's current generation is an eyewitness to the re-gathering of Israel from the far corners of the earth.[10] Rising from the ashes of the Holocaust, the Jewish people have returned to the cradle of their existence. This is a reality that previous generations of Jews and Christians could believe only through the eyes of faith. Yet Israel is in the headlines daily. Having become so accustomed to the fact that a literal and modern state of Israel exists, one can simply overlook the miracle that it is.

---

[9] Jesus grew up in a family of at least seven children. The names of His half-brothers are: James, Joses, Judas, and Simon. Two of the Gospels mention more than one half-sister. See Matthew 13:55 and Mark 6:3.

[10] "I will restore the fortunes of my people Israel, and they shall rebuild the ruined cities and inhabit them; they shall plant vineyards and drink their wine, and they shall make gardens and eat their fruit. I will plant them on their land, and they shall never again be uprooted out of the land that I have given them, says the Lord your God" (Amos 9:14–15).

We live in unprecedented times. How is it that one can take for granted so easily the wonderment of an ancient and persecuted people brought back to their land of origin after more than two millennia of dispersal? Israelis are once again speaking Hebrew, a resurrected language previously relegated solely to a liturgical purpose. This is amazing. Military troops are sent to far-off places with exotic names like Baghdad, and the headlines scream of war in Damascus. Both locations, prior to this century, were known mainly from geography class trivia or adventure novels. After the passage of thousands of years, Israel's ancient capital is the center of global controversy. Interestingly, it is in circumstances such as these—and prophesied by the Lord Himself—that He will return to a prearranged location just east of the Temple Mount in Jerusalem. Seen in this light, it is plausible that the present generation stands poised to be living during the time when the Lord will return.

The line drawn in the sand. By the time adulthood is reached, most people are aware of situations that ended tragically and could have been averted if only the individuals involved had followed another course of action. In Hosea 4:6, God has said, "My people are destroyed for lack of knowledge," but one doesn't have to fall into that perishing and lacking category. Everyone recognizes that traveling through uncharted territory blindfolded, without a compass or map, and depending solely upon individual perception and information is perilous. In the same way, proceeding without any idea of God's thoughts and plans concerning Israel is dangerous and foolish. This is especially so since the prophet Joel clearly warned that the nations will eventually be judged on the basis of their relationship to Israel.[11] Becoming familiar with what the Bible

---

[11] "For behold, in those days and at that time when I shall reverse the captivity and fortunes of Judah and Jerusalem, I will gather all nations and will bring them down into the Valley of Jehoshaphat, and there will I execute judgment upon them for [their treatment of] My people and of My heritage Israel, whom they have scattered among the nations and [because] they have divided My land" (Joel 3:1–2 AMP).

records as God's agenda for Israel is knowledge that every believer should have. That information is found in the book of books!

Chapters 2–4 of *this* book will offer very basic overviews of God's covenant with Israel, as well as a biblical and more recent secular history. These chapters will lay the foundation for understanding the circumstances that have evolved into the Middle East's current and perilous situation.

The believer's bottom line. It would seem that a line has been drawn in the sand concerning Israel and that the finger drawing the line just happens to belong to God. At this juncture in history, no one can afford the luxury of remaining ignorant or even noncommittal on this subject. The decisions made regarding the small Jewish nation will not only impact the present generation but also their children, their children's children, and the future nations. So on which side of the line should one take a stand? According to the Bible, the events surrounding the end of the age will be centered on the little Middle Eastern country of Israel, and since this nation has now returned to the world's stage, it is a safe bet that Israel will remain as a flashpoint until the return of the Lord. Clearly, how one approaches the topic of Israel is actually pivotal to one's very destiny, and the next chapter will begin at the beginning, with what the ultimate text—the Bible—has to say on the subject.

Homework for this chapter: read Luke 4:1–13, Genesis 25:19– 34, and Genesis 27–33.

Chapter 1 Study Guide

1. In Hebrew, the name for Jesus is _____.
   This name means (is translated as) _____.
2. Christ is the English translation for this Hebrew word _____.
   This word means (is translated as) _____.
3. People living by _____ are _____ of _____.
   (Galatians 3:7)
4. Through Jesus, the blessing to _____
   is extended to _____.
   (Galatians 3:14)
5. Those who belong to Christ are _____.
   (Galatians 3:29)
6. According to 1 Corinthians 10:32, the world consists of three
   people groups:
   1) _____ 2) _____ 3) _____.
7. T'nach is the Hebrew name for _____.

   1. Torah. This section is known corporately as the Chumash
      and is composed of the first five books of the Bible. The
      literal meaning is "instruction." Torah is the law of Moses.
      Genesis, Exodus, Leviticus, Numbers, and Deuteronomy—
      five books in all.
   2. Neviim or prophets. This section is traditionally divided
      into two parts: former prophets and latter prophets. Former
      prophets are: the books of Joshua, Judges, 1 and 2 Samuel,
      and 1 and 2 Kings. Latter prophets are: the books of Isaiah,
      Jeremiah, Ezekiel, and Hosea through Malachi.
   3. Ketuvim. This term literally means the "writings." This
      division of the T'nach contains the Psalms, Proverbs, and Job;
      the five scrolls is a group composed of Ruth, Esther, Song of
      Songs, Ecclesiastes, and Lamentations; and finally, there are
      the books of Daniel, Ezra, Nehemiah, and 1 and 2 Chronicles.

Chapter 2

The Promises

Chapter 1 Recap: The Bible is a twofold composition of the Old and the New Testaments. The Old Testament is also known as the T'nach and is the entire extent of scripture that was available to Jesus, His disciples, and the first believers. It laid the groundwork for understanding God's interaction within human history and His prophecies concerning the coming Messiah. Later, and within the same time frame of the first generation of believers, some of them recorded revelations, detailed histories, and explanations about the good news that the promised Messiah had indeed come to earth as a fulfillment of prophecy and that He would return to rule as king of kings. Once compiled, these writings came to be known as the New Testament. While both testaments testify about Jesus the Messiah, who is known in Hebrew as Yeshua HaMashiach (המשיח ישוע), it should be kept in mind that although all the Bible is for the Church, not all the Bible is about the Church.

Promises. It is time to examine the promises that were made to one man and his family and to follow the faithfulness and dependability of those same promises to his son, Isaac, and then to his grandson, Jacob. The good news is that by faith, Gentiles also get to be adopted into the part of the blessing that promises rescue to a fallen humanity through the coming Messiah. "For in

Christ Jesus you are all sons of God, through faith ... And if you are Christ's, then you are Abraham's offspring, heirs according to promise" (Galatians 3:26–29). There are, however, certain promises limited to Abraham's physical (DNA) descendants, and these specific promises will be the focus of the following pages.

The land belongs to God; God created the earth. One of the promises to Abraham specifically related to the transference of land. God made the earth, and all of it belongs to Him, but it turns out that there is a particular plot that He has chosen to keep for Himself, for His own heritage. Therefore, before going further into the promises made to Abraham, it will be necessary to establish the facts about His land. The basis for that will come from the Bible. The following scriptures are just a few of many that make it abundantly clear that God considers Himself to have the ultimate ownership over the land outlined in Genesis 15:18–21. Since God created the earth, He also apportions it. Clearly, God has the final and absolute authority to give, take, or divide land as He so chooses.

- "The land shall not be sold into perpetual ownership, for the **land is Mine** [emphasis added]; you are [only] strangers and temporary residents with Me" (Leviticus 25:23 AMP).
- "Therefore, O mountains of Israel, hear the word of the Lord God: Thus says the Lord God to the mountains and hills, to the ravines and valleys, to the desolate wastes and the cities that are forsaken, that have become a prey and derision to the rest of the nations that are round about; Therefore thus says the Lord God: Surely in the fire of My hot jealousy have I spoken against the rest of the nations and against all Edom, who have given to themselves **My land** with wholehearted joy and with uttermost contempt, that they might empty it out and possess it for a prey and a spoil" (Ezekiel 36:4–5 AMP).
- "I will gather all nations and will bring them down into the Valley of Jehoshaphat, and there will I deal with and execute

20

judgment upon them for [their treatment of] My people and of My heritage Israel, whom they have scattered among the nations and [because] they have divided **My land**" (Joel 3:2 AMP).

Adamah **and** *Eretz* **(dirt and land).** The promises made to Abraham included a Messiah for the entire family of man. Additionally, a chunk of real estate was exclusively allotted to Abraham's family *only*. There are two Hebrew words that should be introduced at this point: the first is adamah, and the second is eretz. In Hebrew, the word *adamah* means "ground" or "dirt." This is the stuff that a tree's roots go down deep into, and it must be tilled before seeds are planted in it. It is the earth's covering known and recognized as dirt, and God made the first man from the dirt of the earth. His very body would come from the dust of this adamah, and that's why he is named Adam.

The Hebrew word *eretz* means "land." This is the word used when referring to the measuring and size of land, and it is also the *idea* of that land. As an analogy, imagine a person standing in a golden field of waving wheat. Momentarily inspired by the beauty, he or she bursts out with a fervent song of love and appreciation for a beloved homeland. When using the word *land* in such a case, one is not actually professing love to a particular plot of dirt (adamah). No, the person is thinking about and experiencing a sense of belonging to all that his country represents: the people, its history, and the ideals embodied in that one word, *land* (eretz). God originally intended that Israel would be an example to the world of His laws, His blessing, and His goodness; Eretz Israel, or "the land of God's law." He also intended that Israel would demonstrate these truths while living within specified boundaries of real estate or adamah. [1]

---

[1] James Strong, STD, LD, *Strong's Exhaustive Concordance of the Bible* (Iowa Falls, Iowa: World Bible Publishers, Inc., 1986), 780. (Strong's 127 and 776)

Genealogy in Genesis chapter 5 and chapter 11. Two enlightening, integral genealogies are listed in the early chapters of Genesis. The entire fifth chapter is a chronological roster and commentary of the first ten generations from Adam through Noah. This exact genealogy is beautifully preserved in mosaic tile on the floor of the ancient Beit Knesset (synagogue) at Ein Gedi. The eleventh chapter (Genesis 11:10) again picks up the chronological order with Noah's son, Shem, and continues down through the next ten generations to Abraham. God made sure that the first twenty generations of human history were recorded so that everyone might understand man's origin and God's infinite care for humanity. But starting with Abraham's generation, the Lord begins to intervene in a new way regarding mankind. Just as He gave the original garden of Eden to Adam, He once again bestows a geographical portion of land. This time, however, He gives land to a man by the name of Abraham. Jewish history begins with Abraham, and the Bible becomes quite specific with the details of this transaction so that one can study, learn, and benefit.[2]

Genealogy of Jesus in Luke 3 and Matthew 1. Two more essential genealogies are listed in the New Testament. Luke 3:23–38 traces Jesus's lineage back to Adam, thereby demonstrating that He is the one spoken of when God addressed the serpent saying, "I will put enmity between you and the woman, and between your

---

[2] Adam was the first man to be created in God's image and likeness; as such, he is the human father of all mankind. Humankind, however, perished during the flood, and the only survivors were the eight members of Noah's immediate family. Genesis 10 lists the history of the generations descending from Noah after the flood and provides names of the patriarchs of the original seventy nations. Goyim is the Hebrew word for "nations." One of Noah's sons was Shem, from whom Abraham traced his ancestry. In the covenant with Abraham, God promised in Genesis 12:2 to make him a *goy gadol* (great nation). Over time, the words *goy* (singular) and *goyim* (plural) have come to mean people other than Jews; goyim is the "other" nations. For this reason, and, as far as a Jew is concerned, Jewish history begins with the father, Abraham, instead of the father, Adam.

offspring and hers; he will crush your head, and you will strike his heel"(Genesis 3:15 NIV).[3] All of mankind, from Adam forward, could look toward a future savior—the only one who would be able to defeat the serpent.

Matthew, considered the most Jewish of the Gospels, traces the Lord's genealogy back only to Abraham. In so doing, Matthew is pointing to Jesus as the promised seed of Abraham. Jewish history begins with Abraham. Paul further explained this same concept in chapter 3 of his letter to the Galatians. The Bible explains that the promise of redemption was given through Abraham, that the very promise Himself was born into Abraham's direct line of descent, and that every believer—whether Jew or *goyim* ("Gentile")—is able to gain redemption by faith. "So then, those who are of faith are blessed along with Abraham, the man of faith" (Galatians 3:9).

Promises: Genealogy of transference from generation to generation. The promises made to Abraham have been recorded. Just as any other legal document is filed in a court, God's transactions and covenants are recorded in the Bible. Bible records afford access to all parties so that defined legal rights can be clearly established. The following are the specifics of the eternally binding transactions made between God and Abraham and through him to his posterity, the Jews.

- "And **I will make of you a great nation** [emphasis added], and I will bless you and make your name great, so that you will be a blessing. I will bless those who bless you, and him who dishonors you I will curse, **and in you all the families of the earth shall be blessed**" (Genesis 12:2–3).

---

[3] Genesis 3:15 is the first of the messianic prophecies.

The last part of this promise speaks of the Messiah Jesus.

- "Then the Lord appeared to Abram and said, **'To your offspring I will give this land** [emphasis added].' So he built there an altar to the Lord, who had appeared to him" (Genesis 12:7).

This promise was made in the locality of Shechem, which is shown on some modern maps as Nablus. World media identifies Nablus as being located in the West Bank.

- "The Lord said to Abram, after Lot had separated from him, "Lift up your eyes and look from the place where you are, northward and southward and eastward and westward, for all the land that you see I will give to you and to your offspring forever" (Genesis 13:14–15).

From this location—and within an entire 360 degrees of visibility—God bequeathed a permanent range of territory in perpetuity. In other words, there is no termination date for the lease. Forever means forever.

- "On that day the Lord made a covenant with Abram, saying, **'To your descendants I have given this land** [emphasis added], From the river of Egypt as far as the great river, the river Euphrates: the Kenite and the Kenizzite and the Kadmonite and the Hittite and the Perizzite and the Rephaim and the Amorite and the Canaanite and the Girgashite and the Jebusite'": (Genesis 15:18–21 NASB).

In these verses, God uses the present perfect tense, "have given," which denotes that the action is complete at the time of speaking. Notice that this is a *unilateral* covenant with stipulated boundaries. Note also that the delineated boundary is much larger than the present day area allotted to Israel. Based on the territories listed here, it would seem that God intends for Israel's boundary to eventually extend from the river of Egypt to the Euphrates in Iraq and to include a large portion of Turkey, along with Lebanon, Syria, and Jordan.

- "No longer shall your name be called Abram, but your name shall be Abraham, for **I have made you the father of a multitude of nations** [emphsis added]" (Genesis 17:5),

Although he got a late start, Abraham would go on to be recognized as the patriarch not only of many children but also of many nations.

- "And God said to Abraham, As for you, you shall keep My covenant, you and your off spring after you **throughout their generations** [emphasis added]. This is My covenant, which you shall keep between Me and you and your offspring after you: Every male among you shall be circumcised. You shall be circumcised in the flesh of your foreskins, and it shall be a sign of the covenant between Me and you. He who is eight days old among you shall be circumcised. Every male **throughout your generations**, whether born in your house or bought with your money from any foreigner who is not of your offspring, both he who is born in your house and he who is bought with your money, shall surely be circumcised. So shall my covenant be in your flesh **an everlasting covenant**. Any uncircumcised male who is not circumcised in the flesh of his foreskin shall be cut off from his people; he has broken my covenant" (Genesis 17:9–14).

God required the covenant sign of male circumcision in exchange for His blessing.

- "And God said to Abraham, 'As for Sarai your wife, you shall not call her name Sarai, but Sarah shall be her name. I will bless her, and moreover, I will give you a son by her. I will bless her, and she shall become nations; kings of peoples shall come from her.' Abraham fell facedown; he laughed and said to himself, 'Will a son be born to a man a hundred years old? Will Sarah bear a child at the age of ninety?' And Abraham said to God, 'If only Ishmael might live under your blessing!' God said, 'No, but Sarah your wife shall bear you a son, and you shall call his name Isaac. I will establish my covenant with him as an everlasting covenant for his offspring after him. **As for Ishmael, I have heard you** [emphasis added]; behold, I have blessed him and will make him fruitful and multiply him greatly. He shall father twelve princes, and I will make him into a great nation. **But I will establish my covenant with Isaac,** whom Sarah shall bear to you at this time next year'" (Genesis 17:15–21).

Here, the terms of covenant are implicitly laid out so that Abraham's second born son is to be the recipient of the covenant. There is no primogeniture in this transaction. The covenant will be to Isaac, the son of Abraham's wife, the elderly Sarah.

- "May God Almighty bless you and make you fruitful and increase your numbers until you become a community of peoples. May he give you and your descendants the blessing given to Abraham, so that you may **take possession of the land** [emphasis added] where you now reside as a foreigner, the land God gave to Abraham" (Genesis 28:3–4 NIV).

Unlike the first time Isaac blessed Jacob, this blessing was made with his full knowledge of who the recipient would be. Clearly, Isaac recognized that God's blessing had been transferred already to Jacob. This is a straight line of blessing from Abraham to Isaac to Jacob.

- Joshua 13–21. This entire book recounts in great detail the Jewish conquest of the Promised Land. Beginning with chapters 13 through 21, the parcels of land still remaining to be conquered are allotted among the tribes. This is yet another instance of the clear line of real estate transfer from Abraham to Isaac and then through Jacob to the twelve tribes.

From these scriptures, it can be seen that the Creator of all the earth has made the decision to bequeath some of it to a particular man and his family. After all, it is God's land, and He will do with it as He chooses. And He has, in fact, already done so. God is specific about which land is to be given, and He is equally meticulous about which of Abraham's heirs is entitled to the inheritance. He chooses Isaac instead of Ishmael, and He chooses Jacob instead of Esau. He leaves no loopholes or vague language that might cause confusion concerning the transactions.

God's mandate to the Jews. Similar to a landlord's lease, God placed certain stipulations of behavior on the heirs to His promises. The rules were known as the Ten Commandments. Because the Jews were the chosen stewards of the Promised Land, God's own land, He laid out precise expectations for Abraham's posterity. The following scriptures demonstrate how their stewardship was predicated upon their obedience to God's laws.

> Keep all my decrees and laws and follow them, so
> that the land where I am bringing you to live may

not vomit you out. You must not live according to the customs of the nations I am going to drive out before you. Because they did all these things, I abhorred them. But I said to you, 'You will possess their land; I will give it to you as an inheritance, a land flowing with milk and honey.' I am the Lord your God, who has set you apart from the nations. (Leviticus 20:22–24 NIV).

Therefore, behold, the days are coming, says the Lord, when it shall no more be said, As the Lord lives, Who brought up the children of Israel out of the land of Egypt, But As the Lord lives, Who brought up the children of Israel from the land of the north and from all the countries to which He had driven them. And I will bring them again to their land which I gave to their fathers. Behold, I will send for many fishers, says the Lord, and they will fish them out; and afterward I will send for many hunters, and they will hunt them from every mountain and from every hill and out of the clefts of the rocks. For My eyes are on all their ways; they are not hidden from My face, neither is their iniquity concealed from My eyes. First [before I bring them back to their land] I will doubly recompense and punish them for their iniquity and their sin, because they have polluted **My land** [emphasis added] with the carcasses of their detestable idols and with the abominable things offered to false gods with which they have filled My inheritance. (Jeremiah 16:14–18 AMP)

You shall therefore keep the whole commandment that I command you today, that you may be strong, and go in and take possession of the land that you are going over to possess, and that you may live long in the land that the Lord swore to your fathers to give to them and to their offspring, a land flowing with milk and honey. For the land that you are entering to take possession of it is not like the land of Egypt, from which you have come, where you sowed your seed and irrigated it, like a garden of vegetables. But the land that you are going over to possess is a land of hills and valleys, which drinks water by the rain from heaven, a land that the Lord your God cares for. The eyes of the Lord your God are always upon it, from the beginning of the year to the end of the year." (Deuteronomy 11:8–12)

Diaspora. The Lord gave His land to the Jew along with the command that they should live a holy life within its boundaries. He warned that to disobey would bring the consequence of eviction from the land. The eventual exile of the Jews is known as the Diaspora. As history records, the Jews were eventually driven from their land, but throughout the Bible, a faithful God has provided a record that explains the reason for this punishment to His chosen people. "And I myself will devastate the land, so that your enemies who settle in it shall be appalled at it. And **I will scatter you among the nations** [emphasis added], and I will unsheathe the sword after you, and your land shall be a desolation, and your cities shall be a waste" (Leviticus 26:32–33). The book of Ezekiel adds the following:

The word of the Lord came to me: "Son of man, **when the house of Israel lived in their own land, they defiled it by their ways and their deeds** [emphasis added]. Their ways before me were like the uncleanness of a woman in her menstrual impurity. So I poured out my wrath upon them for the blood that they had shed in the land, for the **idols** with which they had defiled it. I scattered them among the nations, and they were dispersed through the countries. In accordance with their ways and their deeds I judged them. But when they came to the nations, wherever they came, they profaned my holy name, in that people said of them, 'These are the people of the Lord, and yet they had to go out of his land." (Ezekiel 36:16–20)

Once in possession of their Promised Land, and, in spite of the Lord's admonition, God's people went after the gods of the surrounding nations; they spurned the one who had led them by the hand and fed them with manna. Eventually, as a consequence of their repeated and willful sin, they were evicted from the land and scattered among the nations of the world. But if one continues reading from the same chapters of Leviticus and Ezekiel, one discovers that God also promises to forgive them when they finally repent.

It is imperative for every person to see that God always honors His covenant, in spite of humankind's weakness and disobedience. This is especially good news for Christians as salvation depends upon His honoring of the new covenant through Jesus. Just as the Lord will not break His promises to Israel, neither will He break His promises to Christians. Thankfully, He is not a respecter of persons. (Romans 2:11)

In spite of Israel's disobedience, God keeps His promises. Whether or not the other party keeps their end of the bargain, the eternal God always honors His word. God is a promise keeper.

"This is the covenant I will make with the people of Israel after that time," declares the Lord. "I

will put my law in their minds and write it on their hearts. I will be their God, and they will be my people [emphasis added]. No longer will they teach their neighbor, or say to one another, 'Know the Lord,' because they will all know me, from the least of them to the greatest," declares the Lord. "For I will forgive their wickedness and will remember their sins no more." This is what the Lord says, he who appoints the sun to shine by day, who decrees the moon and stars to shine by night, who stirs up the sea so that its waves roar-- the Lord Almighty is his name: "Only if these decrees vanish from my sight," declares the Lord, "will Israel ever cease being a nation before me." declares the Lord. This is what the Lord says: **"Only if the heavens above can be measured and the foundations of the earth below be searched out will I reject all the descendants of Israel because of all they have done."** The days are coming," declares the Lord, "when this city will be rebuilt for me from the Tower of Hananel to the Corner Gate. The measuring line will stretch from there straight to the hill of Gareb and then turn to Goah. The whole valley where dead bodies and ashes are thrown, and all the terraces out to the Kidron Valley on the east as far as the corner of the Horse Gate, will be holy to the Lord. The city will never again be uprooted or demolished." (Jeremiah 31:33–40 NIV)

Any objection to God's steadfast oath to His covenant people is mute here, as there is not yet an existing record of anyone who has been able to accurately measure the heavens or explore the earth's foundation. Obviously then, God does not intend the Jews' banishment from the land to be a permanent situation. More than six hundred years later, the writer of Hebrews would expound on the same words that Jeremiah had earlier written concerning the prophesied Jewish return to the land. Look at the following verses from Hebrews and notice the lines are rewritten verbatim from the prophet Jeremiah.

> But God found fault with the people and said: "The days are coming, declares the Lord, when I will make a new covenant with the people of Israel and with the people of Judah. It will not be like the covenant I made with their ancestors when I took them by the hand to lead them out of Egypt, because they did not remain faithful to my covenant, and I turned away from them, declares the Lord. **This is the covenant I will establish with the people of Israel after that time** [emphasis added], declares the Lord. I will put my laws in their minds and write them on their hearts. I will be their God, and they will be my people. No longer will they teach their neighbor, or say to one another, 'Know the Lord,' because they will all know me, from the least of them to the greatest. **For I will forgive their wickedness and will remember their sins no more.**" (Hebrews 8: 8–12 NIV)

It would seem from this New Testament passage that God is including the Jews, as a nation, in His *new* covenant. And, as a nation of people descended from Abraham, God intends that Israel will come to know Him—from the least exalted to the greatest. God has called this forth, much as He called, "Let there be light!" He has already determined that Israel's past will no longer be remembered.

The Lord also speaks prophetically to the *land* of Israel. These next verses record His words to Israel's mountains, soil, and cities. Here God is speaking promises of life to His beloved real estate of Israel. He encourages the mountains to look forward to the return of His people, to expect the return of bountiful harvests and the sheer joy of being populated by the divinely-ordained heirs. Think of it: God speaking to His land!

In the following verses from Ezekiel, the "mountains of Israel" are specifically addressed. These are the mountains that form a spine from Mt. Hermon, in the north, all the way down through the land into the great Negev Desert. It is upon this spine of mountains that the towns and villages of the Bible are located: Shechem, Shiloh, Bethel, Jerusalem, Bethlehem, and Hebron. It is remarkable that the actual sales transactions for three of the towns mentioned are available for view. The sale of Shechem to Jacob is found in Genesis 33:19. The sale of Hebron to Abraham is recorded in Genesis 23.[4] The sale to King David of the future Temple Mount in Jerusalem on Mt. Moriah is found in two places: 2 Samuel 24:16–25 and 1 Chronicles 21:18–25.

---

[4] Sondra Baras, *News from the Heartland* (Samaria, Israel: Christian Friends of Israeli Communities, November 18, 2011), http://www.cfoic.com. Referring to the weekly Torah reading about the sale of the land for Sarah's grave, Baras writes, "For many years now, a wonderful tradition has developed in Hebron on the Shabbat when we read this Torah portion. Jews from all over Israel converge upon Hebron for this Shabbat. Every home in Kiryat Arba and Jewish Hebron opens its doors to friends and relatives. Teen-agers come from all over the country and sleep on the floors of schools and other public buildings. Shabbat meals are great gatherings and logistical nightmares. No one knows how everyone fits in, but somehow they do. On Shabbat morning, guests and residents alike stream to the Machpela Cave and there, on the very spot where Abraham buried his wife Sarah, the very place which Abraham purchased thousands of years ago, they read this chapter and praise G–d for His bounty. This Shabbat is Shabbat Hebron!"

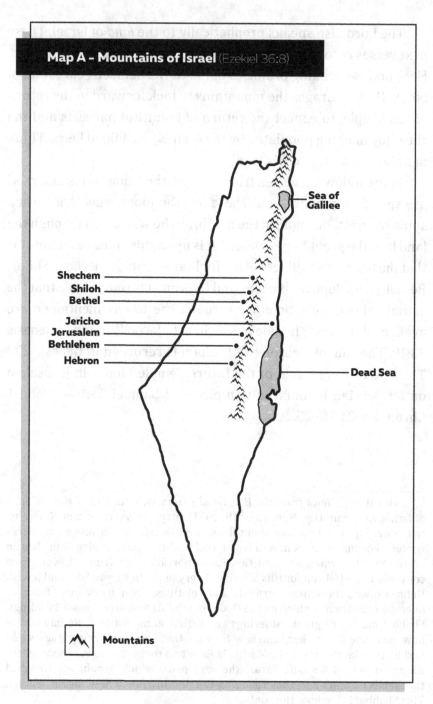

Mountains of Israel

From the following verses in Ezekiel 36, consider how God speaks to the places themselves—not to the people *in* the places.. He promises to bring His people back to these very mountains of Israel.

> But you, **O mountains of Israel** [emphasis added], shall shoot forth your branches and yield your fruit to my people Israel, for they will soon come home. For behold, I am for you, and I will turn to you, and you shall be tilled and sown. And I will multiply people on you, the whole house of Israel, all of it. The cities shall be inhabited and the waste places rebuilt. And I will multiply on you man and beast, and they shall multiply and be fruitful. And **I will cause you to be inhabited as in your former times, and will do more good to you than ever before**. Then you will know that I am the LORD. **I will let people walk on you, even my people Israel. And they shall possess you, and you shall be their inheritance,** and you shall no longer bereave them of children. (Ezekiel 36: 8–12)

Several verses later in this chapter, the Lord turns His words to His people, a people banished from their land because of their disobedience. Yet now, their loving and forgiving Father is speaking to them with words of reconciliation and peace, even offering the promise of a brand-new spirit and heart. All the while, He is reminding them that their original home is waiting for their return. The time for punishment is finished. "Time out" is a thing of the past, and it is now time to come home.

> **I will take you from the nations and gather you from all the countries and bring you into your**

own land. (Emphasis added.) I will sprinkle clean water on you, and you shall be clean from all your uncleannesses, and from all your idols I will cleanse you. **And I will give you a new heart, and a new spirit I will put within you. And I will remove the heart of stone from your flesh and give you a heart of flesh.** And I will put my Spirit within you, and cause you to walk in my statutes and be careful to obey my rules. **You shall dwell in the land that I gave to your fathers**, and you shall be my people, and I will be your God. (Ezekiel 36: 24–28)

Ezekiel 37 tells the story of the prophet Ezekiel who was transported by God to a vast valley piled full of countless dead and dry human bones. After being made to pass through this bizarre landscape and, no doubt, cringing at the crunch of the bleached out bones beneath his feet, God asks the question, "Son of man, can these bones live?" It is obvious from his answer that Ezekiel didn't know how he should reply. Then comes verse 4: "Then he said to me, **"Prophesy over these bones**, and say to them, O dry bones, hear the word of the Lord. Thus says the Lord God to these bones: Behold, I will cause breath to enter you, and you shall live. And I will lay sinews upon you, and will cause flesh to come upon you, and cover you with skin, and put breath in you, and you shall live, and you shall know that I am the Lord" (Ezekiel 36:4–6).

Incredibly, as the following four verses describe what transpired next, one reads that Ezekiel obediently began to speak to the bones as instructed and that as he spoke the bones took on life. The entire valley rattled with the sound of brittle bones beginning to merge into the shape of countless skeletons. Blinking his eyes, the prophet realized that sinews and flesh were also beginning to form around the bones. Next, the Lord commanded Ezekiel, **"Prophesy to the breath** [emphasis added]; prophesy, son of man, and say to the breath, Thus says the Lord God: Come from the four winds, O breath, and breathe on these slain, that they may live." Sure enough, just as before, it happened exactly as God had said. And now an army of living, breathing human beings stood to their feet in the sight of a flabbergasted prophet.

> Then he said to me: "Son of man, **these bones are the people of Israel.** (Emphasis added.) They say, 'Our bones are dried up and our hope is gone; we are cut off.' Therefore prophesy and say to them: 'This is what the Sovereign Lord says: My people, **I am going to open your graves** and bring you up from them; **I will bring you back to the land of Israel.** Then you, my people, will know that I am the Lord, when I open your graves and bring you up from them. **I will put my Spirit in you and you will live, and I will settle you in your own land.** Then you will know that I the Lord have spoken, and I have done it,'" declares the Lord. (Ezekiel 37:11–14)

God provides His own commentary on the meaning of Ezekiel's strange vision. The dry bones are the Jews, and the Gentile nations are the graves where they have been buried. God intends to bring them out of those graves and place them back in the land that He originally gave them. Nearly four thousand years ago, God made a covenant with His friend, Abraham, and although Abraham has long since passed from the face of the earth, his descendants remain.[5] Now God is making good on His promise by returning the heirs to the land of their inheritance. God always keeps His promises!

P.S. Masada. Every tourist who visits Israel is taken to see Masada, King Herod's mountain fortress near the Dead Sea. This

---

[5] In Isaiah 41:8, God referred to Abraham as "My friend."

magnificent fortified palace, rising over one thousand feet from the desert floor below, is famous for an event that took place three years after the destruction of Jerusalem in 70 AD. Here, the last remnants of the Jewish resistance, a small band of nine hundred sixty men, women, and children, were able to hold the mighty Roman Tenth Legion at bay before their ultimate defeat.[6] To modern Israelis, Masada is a poignant symbol of the Jewish spirit. In spite of the overwhelming odds against them, the Jews zealously fought to maintain their freedom. Jews today see themselves as the heirs of this same spirit, and Masada remains as a reminder of that heritage.

In a way, the fact that groups visit the modern state of Israel and then listen to an Israeli tour guide explain Masada's history serves as a postscript to Ezekiel 37. In the 1960s, Israeli archeologists began to excavate the site. Among the artifacts discovered were fragments from the scrolls of two books of scripture: one was from chapter 37 of the book of Ezekiel. Chapter 37 is the story of the Jewish return from the nations to Eretz Israel. Is it only an amazing *coincidence* that after two thousand years the dry bones chapter would be the scripture to emerge at the same time as the Jewish people's return to their homeland? [7]

The Believer's bottom line. If one accepts the Bible as God's final word, it becomes evident that the land of Israel belongs to the Jewish people. It is plain to see that the Creator of all the earth has made the decision to designate this specific parcel of real estate to a particular man and his family. While making the effort to

---

[6] Paul L. Maier, *Josephus: The Essential Works* (Grand Rapids, Michigan: Kregel Publications, 1988), 392.

[7] Dr. Yigael Yadin was the famous archeologist who led the dig at Masada. A fascinating individual, Yadin was part of the *Haganah,* and served as chief of staff of the Israeli Defense Forces during the critical early years after Israel's 1948 War of Independence. He was also prominently involved with other excavations at Megiddo and Tel Gezer. Tour guides in Israel love to tell about this man and his priceless contributions to a constantly unfolding view of the ancient world of the Bible.

research the scriptures, one cannot fail to see that the Lord has left no loophole or vague language that would cause any future confusion about this transaction.

Homework for this lesson: read Romans 9, 10, and 11.

These three chapters explain the mystery of Israel. Because the Jews were driven from their land, some assume that the promises made to them are no longer in effect. God is not finished with Israel, however; these passages make it clear that even though the majority of Jews don't yet recognize Jesus as the Messiah, God has always had a plan for them. It turns out that He is responsible for their *temporary* blindness to the Gospel, and that this blinding was done for the sake of the Gentiles. He will not abandon them to forever remain blind because Romans 11:29 states, "For the gifts and calling of God are irrevocable." God always keeps His promises, and He is perfectly willing and able to keep His promises to Abraham.[8]

---

[8] There is a school of thought, commonly known as "replacement theology," that teaches God is finished with His original "chosen people," the Jews. The reasoning goes like this: since the Jews refused to accept Jesus when He walked the earth, God, in turn, rejected them and subsequently replaced them with the Church. This means that the promises originally recorded in scripture and made first to the Jews have been transferred now to the Church, which *did* accept Jesus. Such errant teaching has been the root of much anti-Semitism throughout the centuries, and Romans 11:25–29 clearly refutes this misguided theology.

Chapter 2 Study Guide

1. **Genesis 12**

   Abraham obeys God and journeys to the Promised Land. He is _____ years old (v. 4). God promises to bless him and give _____ (v. 7).

2. **Genesis 13:14–15**

   God gives _____ to _____ and to his _____. This gift is in effect for _____ years.

3. **Genesis 15:18–21**

   God gives _____to Abraham. The boundaries extend from this river (western border) _____to this river (eastern border) _____.

4. **Genesis 17:19–21**

   The covenant is extended to Abraham's son, _____.

5. **Genesis 28:1–4**

   The covenant is extended to Abraham's grandson, _____.

6. **Joshua 13–21**

   These chapters record the allocation of _____ to the tribes of Israel.

7. **Jeremiah 31:35–37**

   The Lord will wash His hands of Israel when what things take place? _____.

8. **Romans 11:28–29**

   God's gifts are _____.

9. **Genesis 15:18–21**

   God's token gift in the Genesis 15 covenant with Abraham is _____.

Chapter 3

The Trees

Chapter 2 Recap: The Bible references from the previous lesson make it apparent that the Creator of all the earth has made the decision to bestow a small part of it upon a particular man and his descendants. The man, of course, is Abraham, and his descendants are the Jews. After all, the earth is God's property, and He can do with it as He chooses. Clearly, the Scriptures show that He has done that very thing. God is specific about which land is to be given, and He is equally meticulous about which of Abraham's heirs is entitled to the inheritance. He chose Isaac instead of Ishmael, and He chose Jacob instead of Esau. His intention is neither crafted in vague language nor has the Bible account left any loophole that might cause one iota of confusion concerning this transaction.

The Olivet Discourse. Other than the Sermon on the Mount, Jesus's most famous single teaching probably would be what theologians have labeled the "Olivet Discourse," and it is recorded in three of the Gospels: Luke 21, Matthew 24, and Mark 13. The Lord's teaching that day came about like this: Jesus and His disciples had been present on the Temple Mount, observing and talking about the numerous activities taking place in the temple court. After commenting on various people who had given their alms, the Lord left the area, strolled down through the Kidron Valley, and then led the group up to the olive groves of the mountain directly east of Jerusalem, a summit known as the Mount of Olives. The disciples, following along and engaged in animated conversation about the beauty and greatness of the temple itself, were stunned to hear Jesus tell them that the mighty edifice would soon be destroyed—dismantled to the very last stone! They asked, "When will this take place, and what will be the sign of Your coming, and what about the end of the age?" Upon reaching His chosen vantage point that looked out over the temple platform, Jesus sat down and began to answer their questions.[1] The full content of His explanation constitutes the famous Olivet Discourse that is considered to be the ultimate exposition of events leading up to the Second Coming.

The renowned Bible teacher, Derek Prince, often explained that understanding prophecy is much like taking a jumbled collection of bones and then attempting to construct some sort of recognizable skeleton from them. If a photograph of the animal in question is unavailable, the logical first step of the construction process is to start with the spine. After the spine is in place and after fitting the rest of the bones together in relation to that starting point, a body eventually takes shape. Once the bones are reconstructed so as to fit into their correct location, the shape of the animal seems totally obvious. In this instance, the jigsaw placement of bones is used as an analogy to end-time Bible prophecy.[2] Given the fact that the spine is the key or starting point to the creation of a skeleton, many have pointed to Jesus's Mount of Olives prophecy as just such a spine. In other words, The Lord's lesson on that day is the key to understanding future events. Since the

---

[1] The disciples asked three separate questions and Jesus answered each one. They wanted to know when the Temple would be destroyed, when Jesus would be returning as the conquering king, and when the present age would come to an end. To understand His answers, one must read and compare the three separate accounts as recorded in Matthew 24, Mark 13, and Luke 21.

[2] Derek Prince, *Prophecy: God's Time Map* (Archival Classics Series, Charlotte, North Carolina: Derek Prince Ministries, 1971). Derek's analogy can be seen in this vintage DVD that also provides an excellent, detailed explanation of the Olivet Discourse (see Note 1), http://www.DerekPrince.org.

topic of the end of the age is an extremely broad subject, this chapter will narrow its focus to the few verses within the Olivet Discourse that are commonly known as the parable of the fig tree.

The parable of the fig tree. "And he told them a parable: 'Look at the fig tree, and all the trees. As soon as they come out in leaf, you see for yourselves and know that the summer is already near. So also, when you see these things taking place, you know that the kingdom of God is near. Truly, I say to you, this generation will not pass away until all has taken place'" (Luke 21:29–32).

The prophets Hosea, Joel, and Jeremiah, compared Israel to the fig tree, and Jesus appears to be continuing in that vein with this teaching. While looking at Israel (the fig tree) and the nations surrounding Israel (the other trees), it is a stunning realization to recognize that each one made its debut as a modern nation during the twentieth century. These ancient lands, governed for centuries by numerous and long-departed conquerors, have "come out in leaf" as they've joined the existing members of the present global community. Two thousand years after Jesus spoke these words, the fig tree and the surrounding trees are in bud and in leaf, poised to continue their roles at center stage.

Background information for the Middle East nations. There are many who believe that the problems in the Middle East have been primarily fomented by the relatively recent invasion of the area by Jews. This flawed explanation of the region's dilemma usually blames the European Jews, displaced after Hitler's final solution and supported by a wealthy worldwide diaspora, for stirring up the native Arab population. The story goes that as the "new kid on the block," Israel upset the formerly peaceful coexistence of a long-standing neighborhood. A cursory look at the historical facts, however, shows that this is simply not the case.

Between the years 1517 to 1917, the area known as the Middle East was part of the Ottoman Empire. Its center of power was located in what is known today as Turkey. Because the Ottomans developed numerous ongoing social and economic problems, as well as a steady loss of territory, the history books of the 1900s began to refer to the empire as the "Sick Man of Europe." Remaining true to that very apt description, the Ottoman Turks allied themselves with Kaiser Wilhelm of Germany during World War I, and after having been soundly defeated, they lost the remainder of their territories to European victors who then divided the spoils of war among themselves.

When considering the aftermath of the war, as it relates to Israel (fig tree) and the surrounding nations (other trees), the focus can be directed primarily at two of the victorious nations: Great Britain and France. As the great conflict wore on, it became apparent that Germany would be defeated. During this time, representatives of France and Great Britain secretly met and signed the Sykes–Picot Agreement. And it was at this clandestine meeting in 1916 (which did not include their other allies) that the British diplomat, Mark Sykes, and his French counterpart, Francois Georges-Picot, agreed to terms for carving up and dividing a post-war Ottoman Empire between their two governments. Sanctioned by the League of Nations, the two resulting zones of influence came to be referred to as mandates: a British Mandate and a French Mandate. The areas of Lebanon and Syria were assigned to France. Mesopotamia (later to be known as Iraq) and Palestine (originally designated as a Jewish homeland and later divided to create Jordan) were the areas granted to Britain. Before this time, the entire Middle East region had been part of the vast Ottoman Caliphate.[3] In fact, the modern, independent states of Israel, Jordan, Lebanon, Syria, Iraq, and Saudi Arabia did not exist until after World War I. It is against this post-war backdrop that one begins to understand how *all the trees* came to be the specific nations of Lebanon, Syria, Saudi Arabia, Iraq, Jordan, and Egypt. These are the nations immediately surrounding Israel, and these are the other trees mentioned in the Olivet Discourse.

---

[3] *Caliphate* is the term used for an Islamic governmental system or area of jurisdiction. It is presided over by a civil and political leader who is known as the caliph or *kalif*.

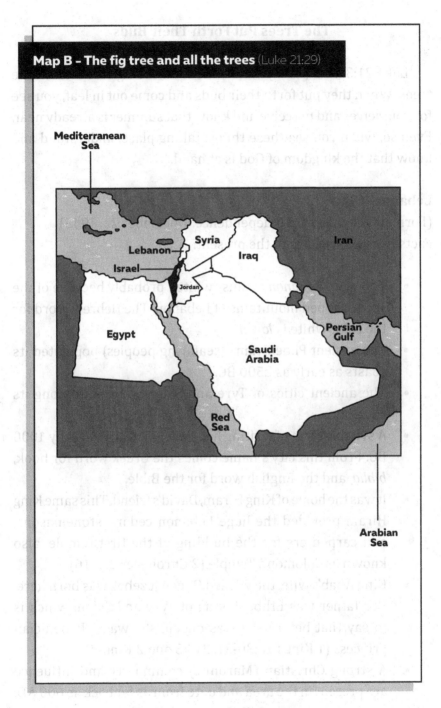

The fig tree and all the trees.

The Trees Put Forth Their Buds

Luke 21:30–31 (AMP) states, "Look at the fig tree and all the trees; When they put forth their buds and come out in leaf, you see for yourselves and perceive and know that summer is already near. Even so, when you see these things taking place, understand and know that the kingdom of God is at hand."

Lebanon, 1943
(Formal recognition of independence: November 22, 1943)
Facts from Bible times to the present:

- The word *Lebanon* means "white," probably because of the snow-capped mountains of Lebanon. The Hebrew word for the color white is *lavan*.
- The ancient Phoenicians (seafaring peoples) populated its coasts as early as 2500 BC.
- The ancient cities of Tyre and Sidon were built along its coastline.
- A syllabic form of writing had developed at Byblos by 1000 BC. From this city's name comes the Greek word for book, *biblia*, and the English word for the Bible.
- It was the home of King Hiram, David's friend. This same King Hiram provided the huge Lebanon cedars, stonemasons, and carpenters for the building of the first temple, also known as Solomon's Temple (2 Chronicles 2:3–16).
- King Ahab's wife, the wicked Queen Jezebel, was born here. Her father was Ethbaal, king of Tyre and Sidon, which is to say that before she was queen, she was a Phoenician princess (1 Kings 16:30-31, 21:25 and 2 Kings 9).
- A strong Christian (Maronite) community and influence are present in the area and date from as far back as 600 AD.

In 1918, France took responsibility for the area as part of the French Mandate. Today, the original five provinces from that mandate make up modern Lebanon. This mountainous area would eventually become known as the Republic of Lebanon, and a unique republican form of government was established for the diverse population, which is composed of approximately 54 percent Muslim (Sunni and Shia), 40.5 percent Christian (Maronite, Greek Orthodox, Greek Catholic, Armenian, and various Protestant denominations), and 5.6 percent Druze. Accordingly, the constitution stipulates that the president must be Maronite Christian; the prime minister must be Sunni Muslim; the speaker of the Parliament must be a Shi'ia Muslim; and the deputy prime minister must come from the Greek Orthodox Church. After twenty-five years, the French Mandate was formally abolished, and the modern nation of Lebanon was recognized on November 22, 1943.[4]

Syria, 1946
(Formal recognition of independence: April 17, 1946)
Facts from Bible times to the present:

- This area was the home of the ancient Ammonites, Arameans, and Assyrians.
- Damascus, the capital, is believed to be the oldest continuously occupied city in the world.
- The area was included as part of that vast territory ruled by Sargon the Great, western history's first great warlord, over four thousand years ago (2300 BC).[5]

---

[4] Central Intelligence Agency. (2014). Lebanon, *The World Factbook*. *www.cia.gov/library/publications/the-world-factbook/geos/le.html* Retrieved 10-29-2014.
[5] Mortimer Chambers, Barbara Hanawalt, Theodore K.Rabb, Isser Woloch, and Lisa Tiersten, *The Western Experience* (New York, NY: McGraw–Hill Companies, Inc., 2010), 10. In spite of constant revisions in regard to early history concerning

- Modern Syria was situated along the King's Highway (the ancient trade route linking Egypt to Mesopotamia, Syria, and Anatolia).
- Naaman, the Syrian military commander healed by Elisha, was from this area (2 Kings 5:1–19).
- The story of Paul's (formerly known as Saul) encounter with the risen Lord took place southwest of Damascus. For a considerable time afterward, he sojourned in that city and taught in the synagogues there about Jesus as the Messiah (Acts 9:1–25).
- This area has been overrun by numerous conquerors—Persians, Greeks, Romans, Moslems, and Turks—throughout the centuries.
- Known officially as the Syrian Arab Republic, the country is over 90 percent Arab and 87 percent Muslim.

In 1918, France took responsibility for the area that came to be known as Syria. As a result of Sykes–Picot, Syria, as well as Lebanon, fell within the zone of influence known as the French Mandate. The country was originally organized as a parliamentary republic, and formal recognition of independence was given on April 17, 1946, when French troops left the country. Since then, its tumultuous and violent history has included numerous military coups. The Ba'ath Party emerged as the strongest political force in 1971 and was led by an air force general, Hafez Assad. Upon his death, his son, Bashar Assad (originally trained in England as an ophthalmologist), took over the country's leadership.[6]

---

the region (due to archeological discoveries, etc.), it is believed that Sargon the Great ruled his Akkadian kingdom from 2371–2316 BCE.

[6] Information and statistics about the countries highlighted in this chapter may be found in numerous, easily-accessed locations including the Bible, any good encyclopedia, and *The CIA World Factbook.* www.cia.gov.

Instead of being assigned to either the French or British Mandates, former Ottoman possessions within the Arabian peninsula were apportioned among various Arab groups. Two of the largest were the Kingdom of Hejaz and the Sultanate of Nejd, and, collectively, they would eventually come to be known as Saudi Arabia.

Saudi Arabia, 1932

(Formal recognition of independence: September 23, 1932)

Facts from Bible times to the present:

- From ancient times, the area was always known as Arabia. The name *Saudi Arabia* did not exist until 1932.
- The Arabian peninsula is approximately the size of the eastern continental United States when measured from the Mississippi River to the Atlantic Ocean.
- This area is the ancient home of Ishmaelite traders, Midianites, and Bedouin tribes.
- Moses married a woman from Midian, a region located in the northwestern section of the Arabian peninsula.
- After his time spent in Damascus, Paul sojourned in Arabia, according to Galatians 1:17.
- It is the birthplace of Mohammed ca. 570–571 AD.
- The peninsula is bordered on the west by the Red Sea, on the south by the Arabian Sea, and on the east by the Persian Gulf. Modern Saudi Arabia shares borders with Yemen and Oman and with the smaller countries of Kuwait, Qatar, and the United Arab Emirates.
- Both the west coast along the Red Sea, as well as the east coast on the Persian Gulf, fell to Ottoman rule during the sixteenth century. The Bedouin tribes populating the center of the peninsula, however, always remained fairly independent, migrating from area to area in a fashion

similar to the transient Laplanders *(Sami)* of Russia and Scandinavia.

• Bibles are not allowed in Saudi Arabia.

Bearing in mind that the first rulers for both modern Iraq and Jordan came from the Arabian peninsula, a brief historical sketch of the region proves to be of special interest.

The ancient trade route connecting the riches of Yemen to the King's Highway ran along the western coastline of the Arabian peninsula, that area bordering the Red Sea and the Gulf of Aqaba. Both Mecca and Medina, two major population centers, grew up along this route. This region, also known as the *Hejaz*, includes the seaport of Jeddah. After the seventh century AD, both Mecca and Medina took on a religious significance to Mohammed's followers, and the two towns, as well as Jeddah, came under Muslim rule. Later, during World War I, Sharif Hussein Ibn Ali, directly descended from Mohammed and heir to the title of Protector of Mecca and Medina, fought alongside the victorious Allies against the Ottoman Turks. In return for his service, Britain gave promises of land and future influence. In fact, he was led to believe that his family would be granted rule over the entire southern part of the Ottoman Empire known as Mesopotamia.[7]

During this same time period, Great Britain was making alliances also with another Arab leader, Abdul Aziz al Saud (Ibn Saud), of the Nejd. Nejd is the name given to the vast central plateau region of the Arabian peninsula, and it is the location of Riyadh, today's capital of Saudi Arabia. Ibn Saud is the Bedouin chieftain who conquered Riyadh in 1902 after years of tribal warring. He

---

[7] Christopher Catherwood, *Churchill's Folly* (New York, NY: Carroll & Graf Publishers, An Imprint of Avalon Publishing Group Inc., 2004). This book—especially chapter 4—shares details from diplomatic correspondence regarding the British difficulty in following through on promises to the Hashemite family. The accounts illustrate the numerous dilemmas encountered by Great Britain in dealing with the different Arab groups.

then proceeded to consolidate both the Hejaz and the Nejd under his leadership. Ultimately, Great Britain found itself in the unenviable position of protecting and negotiating with both groups that were themselves at war with each other. And this is where the study of the trees takes a fascinating turn.

Great Britain needed to make good on wartime promises, but was also interested in forging favorable alliances with strong leaders from among the newly-emerging political bases in the region. The tribal chieftain, Ibn Saud, after having been successful in bringing about a military and political unification of the peninsula's tribes, was eventually rewarded and recognized as king. By the end of the mandate period, a brand-new country was introduced into the modern family of nations as the Kingdom of *Saudi* Arabia. Saudi Arabia's formal date for independence is September 22, 1932.[8]

But what of the earlier promises made to the Sharif of Mecca, Hussein Ibn Ali? The British, aware of the Sharif's position of leadership and influence over the religious faithful, were eager to placate him. As promising oil reserves were being discovered in numerous locations throughout Mesopotamia (the name used by the Turks for present-day Iraq), a solution to the dilemma of rewarding multiple Arab allies was found. The answer lay in the strategic placement of the Sharif's several sons. The British government installed one son as ruler in the former Ottoman Mesopotamia. Another son was provided for when a chunk of land was carved out of mandated Palestine. The first of these new nations would be the country known today as Iraq.

---

[8] It cannot be ignored that the negotiations between these two Arab factions and Great Britain were taking place around the same period of time as vast petroleum reserves were being discovered throughout the region. Saudi Arabia became a nation in 1932, and Standard Oil of California (SOCAL) was granted the concession for oil exploration in 1933.

Iraq, 1932
(Formal recognition of independence: October 3, 1932)
Facts from Bible times to the present:

- During the Ottoman period, the area was known by its ancient name, *Mesopotamia,* which means the "land between the rivers."
- The region of ancient Mesopotamia was specifically defined by two rivers: the Tigris and Euphrates.
- During antiquity, this area was home to the empires of Sumer, Assyria, Babylon, and Chaldea.
- The Tower of Babel was built in this region.
- Abraham came from Ur of the Chaldees; ancient Ur was located north of the Persian Gulf on the Euphrates River.
- The famous city of Nineveh was located on the eastern bank of the Tigris River. God directed Jonah to go to the city and warn the inhabitants of impending destruction.
- As one of the Seven Wonders of the Ancient World, the fabulous Hanging Gardens of Babylon existed in this locale.
- Stories from the Book of Daniel took place here: the lions' den, the fiery furnace, and the writing on the wall.
- The word *Iraq* means "origin" in Arabic; during the mandate period, this name began to replace "Mesopotamia."

Under the British Mandate, Faisal bin Hussein bin Ali al-Hashemi, third son of Sharif Hussein of Mecca, was installed as King Faisal I in 1921. Six years later, oil was discovered in the northeastern part of Iraq at Baba Gurgur.[9] The British Mandate ended on October 3,

---

[9] Numerous information sites concerning Baba Gurgur provide fascinating reading. Due to the escape of gases from fissures in the rock, steadily burning fires have been spotted throughout the surrounding area for thousands of years. There is even some speculation that Baba Gurgur could be linked to the fiery furnace mentioned in the book of Daniel. Because the oil industry was in its

1932, when Iraq was formally recognized as an independent nation. Because King Faisal I was originally from the Arabian area known as the Hejaz, his kingdom was known as a Hashemite kingdom. This Arabian prince and his family, however, were not able to maintain their hold on power. In 1958, the monarchy was deposed by a military coup, with the Baath Party eventually taking over the national leadership; that party's leader was Saddam Hussein. Today, Iraq is a republic.

Jordan, 1946
(Formal recognition of independence: May 25, 1946)
Facts from Bible times to the present:

- This area was the home of the ancient Moabites, Ammonites, and Edomites.
- After the destruction of Sodom and Gomorrah, Lot and his two daughters eventually settled in the area (Genesis 19:24–38).
- Mt. Seir was located here; Esau made his home in Mt. Seir (Genesis 36).
- Home of the infamous King Balak during the time of Moses; he hired Balaam to curse the Israelites as they fled from the pharaoh (Numbers 22).
- This is the area of the Promised Land, where Gad, Reuben, and half of the tribe of Manasseh settled after the Exodus from Egypt.
- It is the original homeland of Naomi's daughter-in-law, Ruth, the Moabite ancestor of both King David and Jesus.
- The renowned red, rock city of Petra is located here. Recognized as a world heritage site, it was built originally by the ancient Nabateans.

---

infant stage and lacked sophistication in the ways of environmental protection, an ecological crisis resulted after the 1927 oil discovery.

- Amman, capital of modern Jordan, was known by its earlier name, *Philadelphia,* during the time that John wrote the book of Revelation.

The area occupied by Jordan today was originally part of the Balfour Declaration of 1917 and had been expressly set aside for the establishment of a Jewish nation.[10] However, circumstances including various wartime alliances and agreements, as well as Britain's own best interests, eventually resulted in a major change to the earlier geographical boundaries of the Balfour Declaration. This divergence from the original map would bring about the creation of yet another new state, introduced to the world as Transjordan. During the First World War, the Sharif of Mecca's second son, Abdulla, helped the British to accomplish a successful Arab revolt against Ottoman rule. Working with T.E. Lawrence (also known as Lawrence of Arabia), he successfully used guerrilla

---

[10] The Balfour Declaration originated as a letter. Dated November 2, 1917, it was written by British Foreign Secretary Arthur James Balfour to a leader in the British Jewish community, Lord Rothschild. The original letter is now kept in the British Library.

Foreign Office
November 2nd, 1917

Dear Lord Rothschild,

I have much pleasure in conveying to you on behalf of His Majesty's Government, the following declaration of sympathy with Jewish Zionist aspirations which has been submitted to, and approved by, the Cabinet:

His Majesty's Government view with favour the establishment in Palestine of a national home for the Jewish people, and will use their best endeavours to facilitate the achievement of this object, it being clearly understood that nothing shall be done which may prejudice the civil and religious rights of existing non-Jewish communities in Palestine, or the rights and political status enjoyed by Jews in any other country.

I should be grateful if you would bring this declaration to the knowledge of the Zionist Federation.

Yours,
Arthur James Balfour

tactics to raid and plunder Turkish garrisons. The end of World War I found Abdullah at the head of a British-trained and British-armed military force. It also found him fully expecting a reward for his part in the recent action. Thus, as the anticipated division of spoils began to be parceled out among the victors, this son of Sharif Hussein Ibn Ali, Protector of Mecca and Medina, was primed and waiting for the English to fulfill their part of the bargain.

Operating within the authority of its mandate, Britain found a way to create a kingdom for the younger son of the Sharif. Jordan was established first as an emirate,[11] and Abdullah was installed as the emir of Transjordan, "trans" being understood to mean "across the Jordan." The name for the new territory indicated its location within the original Balfour Declaration of 1917. In other words, it was to be the land segment *across* the Jordan River from the rest of Balfour's designated territory. Thus, Abdullah's territory came from the land originally set aside for a Jewish homeland. As it turns out, approximately 77 percent of the originally designated Jewish homeland became Transjordan.[12] The land division came about during 1921–22 as a result of the various agreements made between the Allies and their Arab war partnerships.

Eventually, Britain granted independence to this protectorate on May 25, 1946. Three years later, in 1949, Prince Abdullah, now King Abdullah, changed his country's name so that it became the Hashemite Kingdom of Jordan. By including Hashemite in its title, he was able to identify and pay homage to his roots in the Arabian Hejaz. After his assassination in 1951, his son, Talil, attempted to

---

[11] In Arabic, a prince, leader, or one in command is known as an emir. Consequently, the political territory, country, or province ruled by an emir is known as an emirate.

[12] The exact percentage of land allotted to Transjordan is difficult to pin down. Figures vary from 75 to 80 percent, depending on the source. This is due in part to the original wording of the documents crafted by career diplomats trained in the jargon of international law. It is safe to say, however, that Israel ended up with about a quarter of the land originally designated as a Jewish homeland by Balfour.

rule, but after a short time, a grandson was placed on the throne. This grandson, King Hussein I, ruled his country between the years 1952–1999. His son, and the first Abdullah's great-grandson, currently sits on the throne of Jordan as King Abdullah II.[13] Jordan is a constitutional monarchy.

Egypt, 1922
(Formal recognition of independence: February 28, 1928)
Facts from Bible times to the present:

- It is the land of the pharaohs, the Nile, and the pyramids.
- Joseph was sold into slavery and brought down to Egypt (Genesis 39).
- It is the birthplace of Moses (Exodus 2).
- It is the land of the Exodus (Exodus 12).
- To escape Herod's infanticide, Joseph took the infant Jesus and His mother down to Egypt (Matthew 2).
- Mizraim is the ancient Hebrew name for Egypt. Egyptians themselves referred to Egypt as *Kemet.*
- It is home to the Coptic Christians. According to tradition, the sect was founded by the apostle Mark and is also known as the Coptic Orthodox Church of Alexandria.
- It is the site of the Suez Canal, completed in 1869; the canal is 120 miles long and connects the Mediterranean Sea to the Red Sea.
- Egypt is the land of the famous Queen Cleopatra.
- Egyptian cotton is known to be the finest, most luxurious, and most expensive cotton in the world.

---

[13] The Oscar-winning *Lawrence of Arabia* (1962), filmed partially in Jordan, might be of special interest now that it's been seen where individual personalities fit into the context of recent Middle East history. The movie was primarily based on T.E. Lawrence's personal account, although the typical Hollywood changes were made with respect to certain characters and events.

Egypt, as a united kingdom (Upper Egypt and Lower Egypt), has a proud history dating back more than three thousand years before Christ. As with most of the ancient lands in this part of the world, Egypt has ruled and has been ruled by numerous other great civilizations. It was conquered by Persia, Greece, and Rome. These three were followed by successive waves of Muslim groups such as the Fatimids, who originated in Tunisia; the Ayyubids, a Kurdish people originating in Armenia; the Mamluks; and finally, the Ottoman Turks. Civil war broke out in the 1500s, and an Albanian, Mohammed Ali Pasha, emerged as the major military dominance. Most historians point to this man's rule as the beginning of modern Egypt. The country remained an autonomous vassal state within the Ottoman Empire during the time of European colonization elsewhere in the region.

Although a French company built the Suez Canal, Egypt's territory lay within what was known as the British sphere of influence by 1882. After war was declared against the Ottoman Turks in 1914, Egypt became a British protectorate, with the handpicked Sultan Hussein Kamel installed as ruler. Great Britain unilaterally granted independence to the Kingdom of Egypt on February 28, 1922. That government was of short duration, however, and following a series of revolutions, the country is known today as the Arab Republic of Egypt. In 1956, President Gamal Abdel Nasser oversaw the nationalization of the Suez Canal and the exit of British military presence from the country. Anwar Sadat succeeded Nasser as the next leader, became a peace partner to Israel, and later received the Nobel Peace Prize for his efforts.[14] Upon his assassination, Hosni Mubarak replaced him as

---

[14] Anwar Sadat's negotiations with Israel were extremely unpopular with radical Muslim elements throughout the Middle East. He was assassinated in 1981 as he sat in a Cairo grandstand reviewing a military parade. Although Iran is not immediately adjacent to Israel, it is another of the ancient Biblical nations that has reappeared prominently on the world's stage; hence, the following facts, along with a very brief overview, are included.

president. Mubarak, in turn, was overthrown as a result of the 2011 "Arab Spring."

Time marches on. God promised Abraham that his descendants would be as numerous as the stars and as the sands of the sea. He also warned that they would go into a foreign land to become slaves through four generations. True to His word and at some point toward the end of that fourth generation of captivity, a preordained moment arrived when the completion of the prophesied time period was realized. Both the Egyptians (draped in their linen sheaths) and the shackled Hebrews were unaware of the precise hour of that momentous time shift; nevertheless, it did not pass unnoticed in the courts of heaven. At the decisive juncture, the king of the universe began to perform His oath on behalf of His covenant man, Abraham. As He spoke from a burning bush deep in the Midian desert, the plan was being set into motion. Promises that had seemed forgotten, like seed lying dormant for over four hundred years, began to come

---

IRAN
(Modern Iran recognized at the beginning of the Pahlavi dynasty: December 12, 1925)
Facts from Bible times to the present:

- As early as 3,000 BC, the area was home to the Elam civilization.
- In Bible times, Iran was known as Persia.
- Iran is an Arabic word that is translated "land of the Aryans."
- Ahasuerus (Xerxes I), Cyrus the Great, the evil Haman in Queen Esther's story, and Darius originated from this ancient nation.
- Iranians speak Farsi, another name for the Persian language.

Under Cyrus the Great, who was known for showing respect and consideration to the nations he conquered, Persia amassed power over most of the known world. Persia was a major world power during the sixth century BC. Iranians are not Arabs; they are Indo-Europeans. Historically, various Muslim armies began moving into the area in the late seventh century after Christ, and this is the reason the ancient home of Zoroaster became a Muslim country. During the following centuries, numerous Islamic dynasties ruled the area, with the Pahlavi dynasty coming to power in the 1920s. On April 1, 1979, after Shah Mohammad Reza Pahlavi was forced into exile, the Ayatollah Ruhollah Khomeini took control of Iran. Today's Iran is a theocratic republic and is known formally as the Islamic Republic of Iran.

alive as the Israelites began a journey that has come to be known as the Exodus. To the exact day as promised, God led His people back to the very land He'd earlier given to their ancestor, Abraham. "At the end of 430 years, on that very day, all the hosts of the Lord went out from the land of Egypt" (Exodus 12:41).

Over the centuries, many civilizations have risen to conquer and then be conquered in this region known as the Middle East. The mighty names of antiquity—Sargon, Nebuchadnezzar, and Titus, among others—marched through the land as conquerors, subjugating and scattering the Jewish people to the far corners of the globe. Today, and as foretold in Ezekiel 37, Abraham's descendants are coming up out of their foreign graves and once again returning to their homeland. Simultaneously, the surrounding nations are also awakening to reassert their ancient personalities.

The believer's bottom line. The end of the age is speedily coming to its close, and only God is able to pinpoint its precise location along the timeline of history. Scripture has given clues as to when this might happen, and Jesus Himself disclosed a monumental marker during the Olivet Discourse. As promised, in accordance with the Lord's parable, leaves and buds have come forth from the trees that surround the fig tree. "Look at the fig tree and all the trees; when they put forth their buds and come out in leaf, you see for yourselves and perceive and know that summer is already near. Even so, **when you see these things taking place, understand and know that the kingdom of God is at hand** [emphasis added]. Truly I tell you, this generation (those living at that definite period of time) will not perish and pass away until all has taken place" (Luke 21:29–33 AMP).

Scripture admonishes the believer to stay alert and watch. The previous pages have been an opportunity to "watch" the nations surrounding Israel. The next chapter will focus specifically on the fig tree - Israel.

Chapter 3 Study Guide

Israel and the Surrounding "Trees"
Chapter 3 - Study Guide

Name these countries:

A. _____

B. _____

C. _____

D. _____

E. _____

Name these bodies of water:

F. _____

G. _____

H. _____

Name this area:

I. _____

Media's name for:

J. _____

Bible's name for:

J. _____

Fill in the blank:

Modern State of Israel established May 14, _____

What is the meaning of the word *Israel?* _____

_____

Israel and the Surrounding "Trees"

Chapter 4

The Secular History of Israel: 63BC to the Present

Chapter 3 Recap: Immediately following World War I, the world's geopolitical landscape was given a decided facelift. The victorious European powers set about reorganizing diverse ethnic groups from out of the old Ottoman Empire and forging them into newly-created states. It was hoped then that the young nations would mature safely under the guidance of British and French spheres of influence. According to plan, the areas, known as mandates, came of age and were welcomed formally into the twentieth century's family of nations. Israel, as well as the surrounding nations, was among those making their debut at this time. If one compares Christ's parable about the trees to the emerging, post-war nations, the allegorical language suggests that the ancient nations of the Bible—the modern Middle East—have returned to the current world stage. A global audience looks on as the players assume their roles and step into their places.

The "lost" two thousand years. For the average Christian, once the chronicling of the Church ended with the close of the New Testament, the story of Israel also faded from view. And though the little Jewish nation did not cease to exist, interest in the people of that land simply began to pale as world events generally moved in a westerly direction. At present, most believers have a rather hazy notion that the Jewish people obviously continued to flourish *somewhere* after the time of Jesus; they know this because of the shockingly irrefutable fact that Hitler's reign of terror resulted in the murder of six million of them. But being able to trace facts about what actually happened to Abraham's descendants during the past two thousand years—from the cross to recent history—is a bit blurry to the average Gentile. Most are aware that the survivors of the Holocaust were given their own country—Israel—after World War II. And those who have seen *Fiddler on the Roof* might be able to connect the events portrayed in that musical to the years of imperialist Russia. But for the majority of non-Jews, the realization that the fiddler's experience was the rule instead of the exception and that the 1800s were a particularly difficult and dangerous time for Russian Jews is brand-new information.

For the most part, unless one lives in New York City or Miami, the average American Gentile has minimal interaction with the Jewish community. Reference points are most commonly limited to the famous Jews: Jerry Seinfeld, Karl Marx, Albert Einstein, or Steven Spielberg. And while it's true that songs include nostalgic lyrics about the little town of Bethlehem during the Christmas season, few realize that an ongoing Jewish life has continued in the Judean Hills up to the present. In fact, today's headlines increasingly make mention of other Jewish towns such as Jerusalem and Hebron; these are names right out of a Sunday school book.

This chapter will review approximately two hundred decades that have passed since the days when Caesar Augustus ruled and will look at how those intervening years affected the Jews and their relationship to Christians. The majority of believers are profoundly unaware of repeated abuse and wrongdoing to the Jewish community that has occurred throughout these centuries. Tragically, the fact that many of the transgressions were carried out in the name of Christ by those who called themselves "Christians" has cast an evil aura (from the Jewish perspective) over the whole of Christianity. The true Gospel has been tainted, and the average Christian has been left clueless that these crimes ever happened. But the Jews have not forgotten the source of such bitter persecution. Meanwhile, the Lord's followers are often at a loss to understand why Jewish friends seem to be so adamantly closed off to the idea of Jesus, and the intensity of their revulsion to the Gospel remains a baffling phenomenon.

In order to understand the Jewish attitude toward Christ, one must acknowledge what the previous generations have perpetrated against those whom Jesus identified as "My brethren." Although the following thumbnail sketch of Jewish history is far from complete, it is hoped that even this cursory overview will be an eye-opener. In an effort to confront a past that many of today's Christians never knew existed, one must look at Israel's history from the time of Roman occupation to the present.

63 BC. Under Pompey's rule, Rome annexes the land of Israel. Israel becomes a province of the Roman Empire and is subjected to forced taxation and the presence of an occupational military force.

37 BC. Rome appoints Herod to rule as king. Although he will eventually be known as Herod the Great, he is never fully accepted by the Jewish population as their true king because he does not come from the line of David. He does, however, renovate the existing temple to such an extent that its white marble, Corinthian-style columns are lauded throughout the world for their outstanding aesthetic grandeur.[1]

---

[1] Nathan Ausubel, *The Book of Jewish Knowledge* (New York, New York: Crown Publishers, Inc., 1964). A contemporary description of the second temple can be found on page 462, offering such evidence of Herod's obvious abilities that even such a sophisticated visitor from Alexandria would be impressed. I have found that just about anything written about Herod always includes an acknowledgment of the numerous and colossal building projects he accomplished throughout his kingdom. In spite of his madly cruel, butcher-like tendencies, it cannot be denied that the man possessed a type of visionary genius.

Life of Jesus. From previous study of New Testament writings, this part of Jewish history is familiar, and it is unnecessary to reiterate it here. It is important, however, to keep in mind that Jesus was Himself a Jew, as were his original twelve disciples. The fact that many translations identify both the Jewish leaders and the Jews who followed Jesus as "the Jews" is confusing. It can be misleading also. This unfortunate mistranslation from the original Greek opens the door for anti-Semitism to creep into the Church, especially if one begins to subconsciously characterize "the Jew" as an enemy to the Lord.[2]

66 AD. Unhappy with their Roman overlords, the small vassal state of Israel revolts against the mighty Roman Empire. The insurrection ushers in a seven-year period of war; not surprisingly, the Roman war machine ultimately triumphs.[3]

69 AD. Rome dispatches its great general, Vespasian, to quell the rioting that has spread from the Mediterranean coastal area of Caesarea to rebel pockets in the hills throughout the land. Meanwhile, the Roman armies find themselves locked into fighting wars on several fronts; this is in addition to dealing with civil unrest in Rome itself. Sizing up the situation, Vespasian takes advantage of the political disorder in the capital and returns to Rome. Once on

---

[2] A good example of this can be found in John 7:1: "After this Jesus went about in Galilee. He would not go about in Judea, because the Jews were seeking to kill him." In this case, the Greek *hoi Ioudaioi* was translated as "the Jews" when it should have read "Judean leaders." Rabbi Neil Lash points out that it was the translator's option when translating these two Greek words to use *Jews, Judeans,* or *Judean leaders.* Further, the fact that they chose to use "the Jews" is a "classic example of mistranslation." If one does not read Greek, this choice of words makes "the Jews" always appear to be the enemy and is yet another element that has contributed to anti-Semitism over the years. Thankfully, recent versions of the Bible such as *Tree of Life Bible* (TLV) and the *Complete Jewish Bible* (CJB) take care to accurately translate hoi Ioudaioi according to the context of the situation. Neil and Jamie Lash, *Jewish Jewels* (Fort Lauderdale, FL, September 2010), 3–4.

[3] For a clear and very readable account of the Jewish War, I recommend chapter 9 of the following book: Adrian Wolff, *A Chronology of Israel* (Israel: Second Edition 2010), 97–106. aewolff@inter.net.il.

the scene, he is soon recognized as the new emperor. His son, Titus, is sent to deal with the Jewish rebels.

70 AD. Jerusalem is finally defeated, and the beautiful temple destroyed after months of siege and warfare. By an astonishing coincidence, this takes place on Tisha B'Av (Ninth of Av according to the Hebrew calendar). This is the same date that the first temple fell to the Babylonians in 586 BC. Although the inhabitants of Jerusalem are brutally slaughtered, the campaign has taken an extended and concerted effort on the part of four formidable Roman legions to accomplish victory. It is estimated that the Jewish population was between five to seven million at the time. According to the historian, Josephus, 97,000 were taken captive from the city alone, and an astounding 1.1 million were killed or starved during the siege of Jerusalem.[4]

132 AD. A little over sixty years later, Jews begin another revolt against the Romans. This rebellion will end up lasting three years before it can be put down. Led by Shimon Bar Kochba, many of his followers believe that he is the Messiah, and his people fight with religious fervor. Even the leading Jewish sage of the day, Rabbi Akiva, believes the long-awaited savior has finally arrived. Along with mass civilian casualties, Bar Kochba and his forces are finally defeated at their fortress of Betar; the date is Tisha B'Av.[5]

135 AD. Eventually, the insurgents are defeated and Jerusalem is once again devastated. The Emperor Hadrian sets about erecting shrines to the Roman gods upon the Temple Mount. A

---

[4] Paul L. Maier, *Josephus: The Essential Works* (Grand Rapids, Michigan: Kregel Publications,1988), 376. Although Jerusalem was certainly of substantive size, the attack befell a city with a population swollen with Passover visitors who were also trapped by the Romans. Thus the city's population was larger than it would have normally been.

[5] The *Mishnah,* which is the compilation of Jewish oral tradition, mentions this date, Tisha B' Av, in relation to many tragedies befalling Israel. In addition to the destruction of both temples, as well as the Bar Kochba defeat, Tisha B'Av is also associated with the return of the twelve spies mentioned in Numbers 13–14.

special temple dedicated to the Roman god, Jupiter, is built over the location where the second temple had stood. Lamentably, with the exception of a daily pass issued for Tisha B'Av, Jews are banned from entering the city. And in an effort to further crush the defeated population's morale, Jerusalem's very name is changed to *Aelia Capitolina*. With another excruciating blow, the Romans attempt to erase completely Jewish history from the region; by decree, Israel's name is changed to Palaestina. Deliberately adding insult to injury, the name is carefully selected because it flaunts the memory of Israel's ancient enemy, the Philistines. This particular name change will have lasting consequences; for it turns out that the Anglican version of Palaestina is *Palestine*. Within a relatively short time, Jerusalem's artificial title of Aelia Capitolina fades from history; tragically, however, Rome's newly-assigned name for the land of Israel continues to hang on in the common person's vocabulary. In one sense, the Jews have been effectively separated from their heritage as Israel becomes Palestine.

313 AD. Christianity is no longer a persecuted sect but recognized as the official religion at the court of Emperor Constantine. After his conversion, Constantine convenes a council of leaders to sort out and establish official statements for his new religion. Rulings from these subsequent councils will eventually separate Christians from Jews, even those Jews who are followers of Jesus.

325 AD. The first of these meetings is held just south of the Sea of Marmara and is known as the First Council of Nicea. Among other things, it brings about the first separation between the celebration of Christ's resurrection (Easter) and the Jewish Passover. This is accomplished by discontinuing the use of the Hebrew calendar. Constantine is credited with having said that Christians should not continue emulating the Jewish custom and that the Passover of the "odious" Jews should no longer be followed.

Such is the spirit of the council laying down future doctrine for the Christian Church.[6]

360 AD. Leaders from the churches in Asia Minor meet at the Council of Laodocia. Out of this synod gathering will come the beginnings of differences in observing the weekly Sabbath. According to Canon 29, Christians are instructed to *not* rest on the traditional Sabbath (Saturday), as this is the custom of the Judaizers. The name *Judaizers* is the one assigned to Jewish believers who continue to follow certain Jewish customs. Instead, Christians are instructed to honor the Lord's Day (Sunday) as their only day of rest. It is understood that to do otherwise is nothing less than anathema to Christ. [7]

506 AD. Presiding over the Council of Agde, in France, is the Bishop of Arles. He sees to it that the council forbids socialization between Christians and Jews. Christians are expressly forbidden from attending religious or social gatherings where Jews are present. But there is yet another divisive ruling issued from this council, and it is the required *additional* instruction now mandated for Jewish believers before they are allowed the sacrament of baptism.[8]

Sixth century AD. During these years, Jerusalem changes hands several times. This century will see the beginnings of the Muslim invasions. After being conquered by the Persians, the city is next seized in 637 by Omar, also known as Umar ibn al-Khattab. While he goes about the business of establishing an Arab territorial government (caliphate), the Jews prosper as they are allowed freedom of religion and free access to Jerusalem and the

---

[6] Heinrich Graetz, *History of the Jews*, vol. 2 (Philadelphia: The Jewish Publication Society of America, 1893), 563–564.

[7] http://ecclesia.org/truth/sabbath-history.html, Accessed 9/8/2015.

[8] For eye-opening and extensive details about the church councils, further information can be found in *The Cambridge History of Judaism*, vol. 4, ed. Steven T. Katz (New York: Cambridge University Press, 2006).

surrounding area. The Umayyids, another Muslim army, are the next to rule over Jerusalem.

691 AD. The Dome of the Rock is completed and erected on the Temple Mount, over the site of the former temple. Intended to be a shrine for Muslim pilgrims, it is built by Caliph Abd al-Malik.[9]

Throughout the tenth and eleventh centuries (900–1099 AD), various Muslim factions fight for control of Jerusalem. In 1065, for instance, one of these Muslim armies successfully conquers the city but then proceeds to massacre three thousand Christians. Jerusalem will now become the trophy in a battle waged for control of the Holy Land.

1096. Pope Urban II launches the first of seven major wars known as the Crusades. From this date until 1291, Europe is involved intermittently in an ongoing military effort to conquer and administer Jerusalem as a safe haven for visiting Christian pilgrims. As the army moves forward, thousands of Jews are butchered in Bohemia, France, and Germany. Although the Muslims are the official enemy, many of the crusading knights are eager to punish the "killers of Christ" as they journey eastward toward the main confrontation at Jerusalem. After three years of traveling across the continent, the Crusaders finally reach Jerusalem in 1099. As far as the Christian community back in Europe is concerned, the First Crusade to recapture Jerusalem from the infidels is a military success. However, this is what the Jews remember: while in Jerusalem, and, in addition to fighting the Muslims, the Christian Crusaders round up the city's Jewish population, herd them into the

---

[9] The ornate mosaic tile facade that is familiar today was added much later. In the sixteenth century, Suleiman the Magnificent ordered the colorful Iznik tile exterior. During the twentieth century, the dome was overlaid with an aluminum, bronze, and gold covering. It is said that Jordan's King Hussein sold one of his homes to pay for the $8 million renovation. It should also be noted that the edifice is a shrine instead of a mosque, as some mistakenly believe. Therefore, Muslim prayers are said in the Al-Aqsa Mosque, another building located to the south, on the Temple Mount.

synagogue, and set fire to the building, burning alive men, women, and children. [10]

1184. The institution of the Inquisition takes place in France. Soon, this latest effort to root out heretics from among the Roman Catholic faithful spreads throughout central and western Europe; the most infamous trials, the Spanish and Portuguese Inquisitions of the fifteen and sixteenth centuries, are yet to come. During the 1180s, many Jews are tortured and executed; others choose to convert to Christianity in an effort to save their lives. Among the latter, there are those who convert outwardly but continue to practice their Judaism in secret.

1190. The Jewish community of York, England, is massacred by a mob at York Castle. Afterward, the debt records of funds owed to these Jews are destroyed. King Richard the Lionheart demands punishment for the crime; the historical record shows that the perpetrators are issued a fine.

1215. At the Fourth Lateran Council, Pope Innocent III rules that Jews are to remain confined inside their homes during Easter week. The council also requires Jews to identify themselves by wearing clothing that displays an oval badge denoting its wearer as a Jew. With Jews now clearly marked out from the general population, they are becoming social pariahs. Christians are discouraged from forming business partnerships with Jews. Because they are not allowed to own land, Jews turn to vocations such as money lending and rent collection. These are unpopular occupations and will be the beginning of the "money-loving Jew" image so often used in derisive jokes and cartoons.

1290. Jews are expelled from England. King Edward I imposes the Edict of Expulsion on July 18, 1290. After suffering through centuries of "blood libel" persecution, the Jews are ordered to leave

---

[10] Rabbi Benjamin Blech, *The Complete Idiot's Guide to Jewish History and Culture* (New York, NY: Alpha books, A Division of Macmillan General Reference, 1999), 153.

the country. With very few exceptions, they depart with only what can be carried in their arms. According to the Hebrew calendar, July eighteenth falls on the ninth of Av, Tisha B'Av.[11]

1306, France's Phillip IV (Phillip the Fair) realizes that his treasury is in trouble. Looking around his kingdom, he decides on a short fix; he simply imprisons the Jewish population, thereby "inheriting" their property and possessions. While still incarcerated, the French Jews learn that their belongings have been confiscated and that upon their release from prison, they must leave the country within the month. Driven from their homes, with only the clothes on their backs, this eviction comes to be known as the Great Exile of 1306.

1348-49. The Black Plague decimates Europe, and in many communities throughout the continent, the Jews are blamed. Not knowing the origin of the plague, a terrified populace accuses the Jews of instigating the outbreak by somehow poisoning the well water. Persecution follows.

1391. By this time, Jewish communities in Spain are openly segregated from the rest of the country's Roman Catholic population. Following decades of rabid preaching that Jews must either be baptized or killed, violence breaks out in early June. Seville, whose Jewish population numbered seven thousand families at the time, witnesses the mob-led murders of four thousand Jews. All of the Jewish areas are burned, and two thousand Jewish lives are lost in Cordoba. Violence continues to spread to the entire region. Throughout the summer, Christian mobs rape, murder, and seize property, all in the name of Christ. In a desperate effort to save

---

[11] Blood libel is a spurious myth that seems to have begun in twelfth century England with the death of a young boy. Soon, the lie spread that local Jews had ritually murdered the child for his blood, which was then used for making the Passover *matzah*. Throughout the decades in Europe, a new outbreak of mob violence toward the Jewish community could be sparked by the reemergence of the infamous "blood libel." Easter and Passover came to be a particularly dangerous time for Jews within all of Europe because of this ridiculous accusation.

their lives, many Jews "convert" and are baptized. They are known today as "Marranos."[12]

1492. In the same year Columbus is commissioned to sail the ocean blue into the New World, Ferdinand and Isabella sign the Alhambra Decree. This document gives the Jews of Spain exactly four months to liquidate their holdings before being banished from the country. Within a short span of time, many thousands of Spanish Jews become refugees, and many are murdered and robbed as they make their way out of the country. They are forbidden from taking gold or silver currency during this exodus and given a deadline departure date of July 31, 1492. The date corresponds to Tisha B'Av, according to the Hebrew calendar.

1517. Ottoman Turks take control of Cairo after the military defeat of the Mamluk Sultanate. Prior to this loss, the Mamluks had also ruled Egypt and Syria. This means that as part of Greater Syria, Israel (known as Palestine since 135 AD) also comes under Ottoman control.

Now, Jews living in Egypt and Greater Syria are subject to the laws of the Ottoman Empire. As non-converts to Islam, they are given a sub-status known as *dhimmi*, allowing them a certain measure of religious freedom, providing certain guidelines are followed. Among these duties is the dhimmi's obligation to pay extra taxes, to get permission before making repairs to a synagogue, and to always demonstrate proper respect to any Muslim. This relationship between Arab conquerors and their subjected peoples is modeled on the original treaty between Mohammed and the Jews of Khaybar (628 AD).[13]

---

[12] *Marrano* is the name given to any Spanish or Portuguese Jew who was forced to convert to Christianity during the time of the Inquisition. The Marranos would eventually migrate to all parts of the globe, with some continuing to practice Catholicism, while others return to their original Jewish faith.

[13] Bat Ye'or, *The Dhimmi: Jews and Christians Under Islam.* 1980. English Ed. Reprint (London: Fairleigh Dickinson University Press/Associated University Presses, 1996), 44–45.

1648. Having been driven earlier from areas in western Europe, many Jews have settled in Poland. By the mid–1600s, Poland and Lithuania are exerting an expanding influence in the region north of the Black Sea, and Jews are serving as court physicians and tax collectors. When ultimately the Ukrainians begin to rise up against their hated Polish overlords, Jews become easy scapegoats. Incited and led by the anti-Semite, Bohdan Chmielnicki, Ukrainian Cossacks proceed to slaughter thousands of Polish Jews. Some sources give a number as high as one hundred thousand, thereby earning the infamous Chmielnicki massacre a very dark place in history.[14]

1867. Mark Twain writes about his visit to the Holy Land in the travel memoir, *Innocents Abroad.* He describes the area as bleak and sparsely populated.[15]

1881. Although anti-Semitism is nothing new to Jews in Russia, the assassination of Czar Alexander II in 1881 ignites waves of violence that will continue for decades. The attacks on Jewish lives and property are known as pogroms and are often carried out with tacit approval from the authorities. The word *pogram* comes from the Russian word for "destruction," and the mob terrorism of the pogroms is the reason that many Russian Jews begin fleeing to Ottoman Palestine.

---

[14] Mitchell G. Bard, "CHMIELNICKI (Khmelnitski), BOGDAN." 1998. March 2, 2014, http://www.jewishvirtuallibrary.org/jsource/judaica/ejud_0002_0004_0_04259.html.
See *The Jewish Virtual Library* to learn more about the massacre's background and the gruesome atrocities perpetrated against Jews in Poland and Ukraine during this Cossack-led reign of terror. In fact, to learn more about anything having to do with the Jewish people, the Jewish Virtual Library is a superb source of history, maps, and current events. The site is a truly comprehensive online encyclopedia.

[15] Mark Twain's observations of Ottoman-controlled Palestine are one of the most popular contemporary sources cited when describing the Holy Land of the nineteenth century. Twain's descriptions of a sparsely populated backwater certainly add to the contention that there was little Arab presence before the early Zionists began to stoke a nonexistent local economy with opportunities for jobs and money.

1894. The Dreyfus Affair. In this sensational trial that attracts the attention of the entire western world, a Jewish French military officer, Alfred Dreyfus, is accused of spying for and sharing military secrets with Germany. One of the news correspondents covering the Paris trial is Theodor Herzl, an Austrian journalist and lawyer. After Dreyfus is found guilty, Herzl writes about hearing the mobs in the street cry out, "Death to the Jew!" And he ponders the fact that they do not cry out instead, "Death to the *traitor!*" It is Herzl who will spearhead the Zionist dream of a Jewish homeland, believing that the Jew will never be allowed to assimilate and that, no matter what country he calls home, he is destined to always be the outsider. The Dreyfus Affair, as the trial and subsequent military cover-up are known, is a blatant example of the anti-Semitism running rampant in Europe toward the turn of the century.[16]

1896. Theodor Herzl publishes *Der Judenstaat (The Jewish State).* For the first time, a concept for the practical implementation of a Jewish state is brought forward. The idea that the Jews of the world are to return to Zion now evokes both spiritual and political elements.

1897. The First Zionist Conference meets in Basel, Switzerland during the last three days of August. Attended by two hundred delegates from the Jewish Diaspora, The World Zionist Organization is established as a political entity, and *Hatikvah* (The Hope) is chosen as its anthem. Most importantly, the delegates agree that the Zionist movement should set about the business of securing a legal home in Palestine for the Jews. After this conference, Herzl

---

[16] In spite of an ongoing military cover-up, an editorial published by the famous novelist, Emile Zola, brought about a widespread public outcry for justice, and the president of France eventually pardoned Dreyfus in 1899. After being released from his Devil's Island prison, Dreyfus still had to wait until 1906 to be publically exonerated. Reinstated to the artillery branch of the military, he served France during World War I, was made a Knight of the Legion of Honor, and retired with the rank of lieutenant colonel. Incidentally, later evidence ultimately pointed to a certain Major Esterhazy as the spy.

writes in his diary, "Were I to sum up the Basle Congress in a word - which I shall guard against pronouncing publicly - it would be this: 'At Basle, I founded the Jewish State. If I said this out loud today, I would be answered by universal laughter. If not in 5 years, certainly in 50, everyone will know it.'"[17]

His words prove to be prophetic. The vote for partition of the British Mandate and statehood is taken in the UN General Assembly on November 29, 1947—fifty years after the words in Herzl's diary are penned.

1914–1918: World War I, infamous for trench warfare and for supposedly being the war to end all wars, is ultimately the theatre for the deaths of nine million combatants on the battlefield. Its aftermath changes everything for the Middle East. During the negotiations and treaties that finalize the conclusion of war, a secret meeting is held between two of the Allies. Beginning in late 1915, two mid-level diplomats, Sir Mark Sykes and Francois Georges Picot, conclude negotiations concerning the eventual division of the Ottoman Empire. Britain and France map out their proposed division of lands held by the soon-to-be defunct Ottoman Empire, and, assuming victory, the two nations negotiate their spheres of influence. Known as the Sykes–Picot Agreement (Asia Minor Agreement) and signed on May 16, 1916, it effectively redraws the map of the Middle East.[18] One of the territories within the British Mandate (Britain's sphere of influence) known as Palestine is referenced as the designated Jewish homeland. The Zionists' dream is becoming a reality.

---

[17] Theodor Herzl, *Der Judenstaat,* tr. Sylvie D'Avigdor, 1896 (American Zionist Emergency Council Edition, 1946). PDF e-book compiled by MidEastWeb at http://www.mideastweb.org.
[18] Inherent problems with Sykes–Picot immediately surfaced, namely, the other allies had been cut out of the decision making process. Additionally, both nations had made promises to other countries that were in direct conflict with Sykes–Picot.

1917. The British government announces to the world that Great Britain endorses the establishment of a Jewish homeland in mandated Palestine. This foreign policy statement is introduced in a letter written by Foreign Secretary Arthur James Balfour to Baron Rothschild, a prominent member of the British Jewish community. Its contents are transmitted to the public, and become known as The Balfour Declaration.

... ...

Foreign Office

November 2nd, 1917

Dear Lord Rothschild,

I have much pleasure in conveying to you, on behalf of His Majesty's Government, the following declaration of sympathy with Jewish Zionist aspirations which has been submitted to, and approved by, the Cabinet.

"His Majesty's Government view with favour the establishment in Palestine of a national home for the Jewish people, and will use their best endeavours to facilitate the achievement of this object, it being clearly understood that nothing shall be done which may prejudice the civil and religious rights of existing non-Jewish communities in Palestine, or the rights and political status enjoyed by Jews in any other country."

I should be grateful if you would bring this declaration to the knowledge of the Zionist Federation.

Yours sincerely,

Arthur James Balfour

... ...

Post-war years 1920–1939. Negotiations formally ending World War I are finally concluded in Paris by late 1919. The League of Nations ratifies the Balfour Declaration and appoints Great

Britain to administer the mandate for Palestine. Between 1921 and 1922, the British secretary of state for the colonies, Winston Churchill, proceeds to create two brand-new areas within the mandate. The first area, Mesopotamia, is to be known henceforth as the Kingdom of Iraq and ruled by T. E. Lawrence's ally, Faisal. The second area divides Palestine into two sections; after this separation, everything east of the Jordan River is to be known as Transjordan and ruled by Faisal's brother, Abdullah. Both men are sons of the Protector of Mecca, Sharif Hussein. Although this "stroke of the pen" by Sir Winston appears to appease Arab interests, the area originally allocated for a Jewish homeland is now reduced by nearly four-fifths.

Since the 1880s, Jewish pioneers have been investing in what was, at the time, Ottoman Palestine. By the mid-1920s, the number of new immigrants reaches one hundred fifty thousand, and the Arab population is none too happy with the Jewish influx, also known as *aliyah*.[19] Violence breaks out in numerous areas as Jews are murdered, and even the traditionally peaceful hamlet of Hebron falls victim in 1929. By 1936, The Black Hand, an Arab terrorist group, is targeting immigrants and their property in the northern Galilee region. The British are forced to intervene and this further incites Arab resentment. Soon the caretakers of the British Mandate find themselves caught in the middle between Arab and Jewish interests as an increasing number of attacks and reprisals now come from both sides. Accusing the British of favoring the Arabs, the Irgun, a Jewish underground militia, begins carrying out acts of

[19] *Aliyah* is from the Hebrew word that means "to go up." When a Jew immigrates to Israel, it is said that he or she has made aliyah. During temple times, pilgrims traveling to Jerusalem for the celebration of the three major festivals were considered to be "going up," both spiritually and literally, as Jerusalem, the spiritual apex, is located at a higher elevation than the surrounding terrain. The joyous throngs sang specific songs as they traveled along the roads toward Jerusalem. The songs are Psalms 120–134 and are identified in the Bible as the "Songs of Ascent" or "Songs of Aliyah."

violence and sabotage, the most infamous of which is the disastrous 1946 bombing of the King David Hotel, site of British headquarters.

Faced at home with a British public tired of war, the Peel Commission of 1936–37 is convened in an effort to find a solution to the tensions.[20] It recommends that plans for the remaining one-fifth of the original Palestine area should be abolished and replaced by a two-state solution upon British departure from the region. In spite of the drastic reduction of the originally anticipated area for a homeland, Jewish opinion is divided. Many hold the view that a little of something is better than nothing at all. Arabs, however, are adamantly opposed to giving up any territory or sovereignty to the Zionists. Meanwhile, as German Jews desperately try to escape new laws of the Nazis Reich, surrounding European countries begin to set limits on the number of people allowed to emigrate. Many Jews now turn their sights to Palestine as an alternate place of safety. As a potential Jewish avalanche threatens to descend upon British Palestine, the authorities bow to Arab pressure and implement the infamous "White Papers." severely restricting the Jewish quota for entrance to their anticipated homeland.

In Germany, Adolph Hitler is poised to activate the beginnings of his carefully planned "ultimate solution." The Fuhrer's true colors exploded upon an unsuspecting world during a cold night in November.

November 9, 1938. This night is forever known to history as *Kristallnacht* or crystal night and more accurately as "Night of Broken Glass."[21] On this date, German citizens are officially urged

---

[20] The Peel Commission takes its name from Lord Robert Peel who was appointed to head up a fact-finding investigation into the recent eruptions of violence in the Mandate. The commission ultimately recommended another division of the land between Arabs and Jews and that the mandate be abolished. Although the commission's originally proposed land divisions were shelved, it established the idea of land partition as the solution to the problem between the two peoples in Palestine.

[21] Much has been written about the infamous Kristallnacht, but a picture is worth a thousand words. Old black and white photographs of the destruction

to raid the businesses and synagogues of their Jewish neighbors. While the destruction of property is encouraged, clear guidelines are issued that there is to be no looting. The result is that the windows of all Jewish-owned businesses are smashed, contents are destroyed, and the streets are littered with shards of glass, like crystal. Afterward, Jewish men are rounded up and jailed until they can be relocated into a properly designated concentration camp. This night is a turning point for Germans because now the handwriting is on the wall concerning treatment of Jews.

May 1939. After Kristallnacht, conditions continue to deteriorate for German Jews. As the immigration quotas in nearby countries are activated, every possible effort is made to immigrate to America. On May 13, 1939, the *S.S. St. Louis* sets sail from Germany. The ship, which is carrying approximately nine hundred refugees who have purchased inordinately expensive tickets for this passage, heads west across the Atlantic. The passengers' goal is to travel to Cuba; once there, and, after having obtained a visa, they plan to wait their turn for quota admittance to the United States. It is understood that the United States requires visas in addition to strictly adhering to an immigration quota. A fact that is not known to the passengers, however, is that due to a recently instituted Cuban law, the *S.S. St. Louis* is not to be allowed dockage once the destination is reached. Worldwide media coverage follows the plight of the ship's human cargo, but despite frantic, behind-the-scenes negotiations, the ship is not allowed into port. Next, the *S.S. St. Louis* heads to Miami but is refused dockage there also. Although cables are urgently sent to Washington, President Roosevelt, who could have issued an executive order for an exception, makes no comment. By the middle of June, the ship is forced to return to Europe and is allowed to dock in Antwerp. Although many on board

---

can be viewed at the Jewish Virtual Library, http://www.jewishvirtuallibrary. org/jsource/Holocaust/kristalpics.html.

are able to eventually make their way through Belgium and on to freedom, over two hundred end up in concentration camps.[22]

December 12, 1941. The Greek ship, *S.S. Struma*, flying under the flag of Panama, sets sail on December twelfth from the Black Sea port of Constanta (Romania) with 769 passengers.[23] The fleeing Romanian Jews have paid an exorbitant price for their passage to Istanbul, where they believe they will be processed with immigration papers allowing their admittance into British Palestine. As it turns out, the ship is not seaworthy and ends up having to be towed into port at Istanbul. Not allowed to come ashore by the Turkish authorities, the pitifully overcrowded ship sits in the harbor as conditions for its passengers continue to deteriorate. During an onboard outbreak of dysentery, the local Jewish community supplies the refugees with food and water. International negotiations fail to reach any agreement whereby the Jews can proceed to Palestine, either by sea or overland. As the British continue to refuse to budge from their stringent quota system, no country opens its doors to the men, women, and children on board the *S.S. Struma*. Tragically, after months of diplomatic stalemate, a Turkish force is dispatched to tow the vessel out of Turkey's maritime jurisdiction. After a passage through the Bosphorus Strait, and upon reaching the international waters of the Black Sea, the crippled ship is cut loose and set adrift, its engine still inoperable. The next day, February 24, 1942, the *S.S. Struma* is torpedoed and sunk by a Russian submarine. With only one survivor, 768 souls are lost, many of whom are children.

---

[22] For photographs and eyewitness accounts, see an article by Mike Lanchin for the BBC World Service.
May13, 2014. *"SS St Louis: The ship of Jewish refugees nobody wanted."* http://www.bbc.com/news/magazine-27373131. Accessed 5/14/2015.
[23] Mitchell G. Bard, "Immigration to Israel: 'Struma' Illegal Immigration Ship." 1998. Accessed July, 2014, http://www.jewishvirtuallibrary.org/jsource/History/struma.html.

July 1945. Even in the aftermath of World War II, with its resulting loss of six million Jewish lives, devastation of European cities and infrastructure, and the displacement of millions more, Great Britain continues to maintain the unreasonably low quota of eighteen thousand Jews per year allowed to immigrate into Palestine. Disoriented, often starving and still reeling from the horrors of the Holocaust, Jewish survivors doggedly set their faces toward the promised homeland.

In an effort to head off any potentially illegal immigration, the British navy sets up a blockade in the eastern Mediterranean. Many boats make it through, but many do not; one such ship, the *S.S. Exodus,* is part of that latter group.[24] Having originated in France, the *S.S. Exodus* is intercepted off the coast near Gaza. A scuffle erupts as the refugees—mostly survivors of Nazis concentration camps—refuse to get into the prison ships provided by the Royal Navy. Three Jews are killed. Great Britain becomes the scourge of world opinion as the *S.S. Exodus* is towed under escort into Haifa Bay. A horrified international community watches as the British Empire refuses admittance to the refugees and enforces the return of forty-five hundred Holocaust survivors to Europe. Incredulously, they are ultimately relegated to displaced persons camps in Germany. American sympathy for the Jewish cause is ignited by the movie based on Leon Uris's bestselling book *Exodus.* Although the ill-fated ship never reaches its intended destination, the *S.S. Exodus* becomes the symbol of a determination to realize the Zionist dream of a Jewish homeland. Furthermore, the publicity generated by the actions of the defiant forty-five hundred refugees is a spark that galvanizes the drive towards establishment of a Jewish nation.

---

[24] For more information concerning the Exodus Ship, see video by Rabbi Berel Wein and Destiny Films at www.jewishhistory.org and http://www.aish.com/jl/h/dv/The_Exodus_Ship_Miracle_of_Israel_10.html. May 30, 2012.

November 29, 1947: UN Resolution 181. Essentially, this resolution is a new and improved version of the Peel Commission's report. Based on population dispersal (demographics), the mandate area west of the Jordan River is now to be carved up into Jewish and Arab sections. From a cartographer's point of view, the area looks like an indefensible patchwork quilt; nevertheless, the Jews agree to accept the recommendations. The prevailing attitude is that a little of something is better than a lot of nothing. With regard to the proposed Arab sections, the Arabs say no.

After months of fruitless negotiations with Arab interests, on November twenty-ninth, the General Assembly of the United Nations meets to vote on the partition of Palestine. By a vote of thirty-three yea votes to thirteen nay votes, with ten abstentions, Resolution 181 is accepted, and Palestine is formally divided into two states: one Jewish and one Arab. Reaction is varied; the Jews in Palestine are jubilant, whereas Arab leadership is united in demanding total jurisdiction over all of Palestine while also threatening to drive the Jews into the sea.

Eager to recall their troops from duty, Britain announces that the mandate over Palestine will expire at midnight on the fourteenth of May. Six months later, on May 14, 1948, the Jewish People's Council gathers in Tel Aviv and formally announces the establishment of a Jewish state. It is to be known as the State of Israel.[25] Celebrations and dancing in the street break out across the new nation, but, the next day, May fifteenth, the fledgling Jewish state is faced with the first of many wars from her surrounding neighbors. Invading what is now recognized internationally as Israeli territory, the Arab states of Egypt, Lebanon, Syria, Iraq, and Transjordan are joined by forces from Saudi Arabia, Yemen, and the Muslim Brotherhood. The war is known by several names:

---

[25] The name for the Jewish state was not a foregone conclusion during the years 1947–48, and various choices were put forth as the time came closer to statehood. Other possibilities included Zion and Eretz Israel.

the War of Independence and the 1948 Arab–Israeli War. In Arabic, it is known as *al-Nakba*, the "catastrophe."

The believer's bottom line. The Jewish people have shared a unique history of persecution throughout the centuries, with the violence often perpetrated by those who have called themselves Christians. The mistrust that exists between the Jewish and Christian communities is better understood once the magnifying glass of history is applied. The summary of events listed on previous pages is certainly not exhaustive. It is hoped, however, that even a cursory overview of Israel's experience, since the days of Jesus, might offer a better understanding of the Jewish mindset concerning the Gentile world and, in particular, Christians.

Already introduced in an earlier chapter, it is an intriguing afterthought that the nation emerging onto the world stage in May 1948 chose to be known as the State of Israel. This fact is fascinating for many reasons. It should be noted here, however, that it was God who originally named this family; amazingly, that very same name endures into the present. Additionally, it is a touching memorial to the patriarchs and matriarchs that each one is remembered in the five Hebrew letters that compose Israel: ישראל. Hebrew is read from right to left, and the letters are *yod, shin, resh, alef,* and *lamed.*

י (yod) represents Isaac and Jacob.
ש (shin) represents Sarah.
ר (resh) represents Rebecca and Rachel.
א (alef) represents Abraham.
ל (lamed) represents Leah.

Chapter 4 Study Guide

1. 586 BC: The first temple (Solomon's Temple) is destroyed by this nation: _____.

2. 70 AD: The second temple was destroyed by this nation: _____.

3. 135 AD: As a result of the Bar Kochba Revolt, _____ was renamed Aelia Capitolina. _____ was renamed Palestina.

4. Events affecting the Jews during the following years: 1090s1200s (series of eight "holy wars").

   _____

5. 1215: _____

6. 1290: _____

7. 1306: _____

8. 1492: _____

9. 1880s: _____

10. 1897 (Basel, Switzerland): _____

11. 1917: _____

12. 1948: _____

Chapter 5

Ishmael and Islam

Chapter 4 Recap: Once the Gospel caught fire with the Gentiles, the Jewish roots of Christianity began to fall by the wayside. Within time, the Gentile majority was consistently traveling along a fissured path that would eventually see Jewish believers separated within the Church, and Jews, in general, alienated from the Church. For nearly two thousand years, a series of incidents bringing death and untold misery to the ones Jesus called "My brethren," have resulted in a general distrust of Christians. Because the majority of Christ's followers remain ignorant to the extent of crimes perpetrated by so-called Christians, the previous chapter focused on a chronological short-list that is general knowledge among most in the Jewish community. In the retelling, a very general history of Jewish life from the time of Jesus until today was included.

    Abraham to Muhammad. Six hundred years after the time of Christ, a new religion burst forth from the desert sands of Arabia. Its armies were given a directive to bring the rest of humanity into the fold of absolute submission to a god known as Allah. Today, more than one and a half billion souls are followers of Islam. Islam is a religion that is the antithesis of Christianity in that it denies the trinity of the godhead and declares that God has no Son. That very Son, Jesus, came to live on planet earth because God so loved the whole world. His Father's heart is still longing for His precious people, including the one and a half billion who are deceived by Islam. The seeds for the hijacking of this large community can be found in the Bible, and the saga begins with Abraham.[1]

The story of Abraham is one of the Bible's most fascinating accounts of an individual's faith walk. His is a larger-than-life story, for he becomes the patriarch of a tribe from whom the Lord chooses to provide the earthly DNA for His Son, Jesus. As a citizen from Ur, he comes on to the scene at the very end of the eleventh chapter of Genesis and passes from the stage during chapter twenty-five. Within these fifteen chapters, the reader is privy to a fairly detailed, behind-the-scenes account of Abraham's life, and some of these episodes are not only difficult to understand but painful to read. The chapters that include his son, Ishmael, are among these.

It is complicated. This is one father–son relationship that had seeds for complication right from the outset. Abram (he is not known as Abraham until later) was the unquestioned patriarch of a very large company of people. He was extremely rich, with livestock, silver, and gold, and he had many servants. At least 318 of his servants were specifically trained in warfare and defense, and it is reasonable to assume that these men would also have had wives and families.[2] Thus, as the years went by and the families continued to multiply, the large and assorted company traveling with Abram was a formidable force as it followed the grazing flocks. Having authority over hundreds, he was accustomed to handling immense responsibility and dealing with the daily business of governing all aspects of his nomadic people. And after many decades, he was

---

[1] According to figures released from the Pew Forum, 23 percent of the world's population (1,618,143,000) was Muslim in 2010. By 2020, it is estimated that 24.9 percent of the world's population (1,912,254,000) will be Muslim. Statistics provided by The Pew Forum on Religion and Public Life, A Project of the Pew Research Center. http://www.pewforum.org, October 25, 2012.
[2] Genesis 14:14.

reaping the reward of honor and respect because he had sought and then followed the one true God.

Yet in Abram's heart of hearts, there remained the one chief desire that had always eluded him—a son. In spite of remaining childless throughout the years, he tenaciously clung to the promises that his God had given him, in particular, the promise concerning an heir. A full ten years after God had first promised a heritage of descendants to Abram, the much-longed-for child had still not been born. After this lengthy passage of time, Abrams's wife, Sarai (she is not known as Sarah until later), suggested that they follow the custom of the day; this tradition acknowledged Sarai's right to take the child of a servant as her own. Believing that God's promise was true, perhaps Sarai reasoned that since the birth of the baby was taking such a long time to come about, possibly this was the strategy that God had meant to use all along. Whatever Sarai's reasoning and motives, her maid, Hagar, was pushed forward as a surrogate mother to carry and deliver a baby for the elderly couple. The end result was that "Hagar bore Abram a son and Abram called the name of his son whom Hagar bore Ishmael" (Genesis 16:15).

Sarah and Hagar were not fond of each other. It would have been unusual if an owner and her slave property were best friends. Even if they'd appreciated qualities in each other before the baby situation, once Hagar became pregnant, it's recorded that she also became contemptuous of Sarai. This is hardly the attitude that Sarai would have expected or accepted from a servant. Already deeply disappointed that she was not able to bear children, Sarai must have been hurt and indignant to see that Hagar despised her. While Sarai may not have been able to conceive a child, she definitely had the wherewithal to inflict retribution on Hagar, and she dealt severely with her. The Bible gives the account of how Hagar ran away to escape, but the angel of the Lord met her, counseled her to return "to her mistress," and verified that the baby would be a boy; she was told he should be named Ishmael. The chronicle continues as Hagar returned to the camp, gave birth to a son, and Abram named him Ishmael.[3]

Abram hears from God for the fifth time in twenty-four years. The record is silent on the intervening years of Ishmael's life until he is thirteen, a teenager. At that time, God appeared to Abram once again. The most obvious outcome of this meeting was the institution of circumcision as a requirement on Abram's part in the covenant between himself and God. Always quick to obey, Abram took his thirteen-year-old son, Ishmael, all the males who were born in his house, *and* those bought with his money to be circumcised that very same day. From this account, one sees that Abraham's commands carried immense weight and authority. Abraham himself was ninety-nine years old when he was circumcised.[4]

During the same visitation that resulted in the circumcisions, the Lord also conferred upon Abram a new name. Abram, which means "highly exalted father," was renamed. Henceforth, he would be addressed as Abraham, "father of a multitude." In addition, Sarai's name was also changed; her new name, Sarah, means "princess" or "queen."[5] That she would be renamed as a co-ruler is not to be overlooked, for although she was responsible for having engineered the plan for Ishmael's birth, it is evident that God still considered her to be worthy of honor and authority. Next, the Lord announced that the birth of a son was imminent. Astoundingly, God clarified that His covenant would only be established and perpetuated through this yet-to-be-born child and that the child's mother would be none other than Abraham's wife, Sarah.

The covenant is established with Isaac. To read through Genesis 17 is to witness a man of faith come to grips with seemingly

---

[3] The entire account of Sarah's attempt to "help" God and Ishmael's birth is found in Genesis 16.

[4] Genesis 17:10–14 and Genesis 17:23–27.

[5] Strong, James. *Strong's Exhaustive Concordance of the Bible* (Iowa Falls, Iowa: World Bible Publishers, Inc., 1986),,160. (Strong's 8282)

incredible promises that he learns are to be his. The book of Romans states that Abraham *seriously* considered the promises against the physical limitations of his and Sarah's bodies, and then he *chose* to believe. Even so, one sees Abraham answering God with the words he thinks he *should* be saying, while he's actually feeling another way in his heart. God ignores the words from Abraham's mouth and goes straight to the core of the matter. For God answered the question in Abraham's heart of hearts.

> And God said to Abraham, As for Sarai your wife, you shall not call her name Sarai; but Sarah [Princess] her name shall be. And I will bless her and give you a son also by her. Yes, I will bless her, and she shall be a mother of nations; kings of peoples shall come from her. Then Abraham fell on his face and laughed and said in his heart, Shall a child be born to a man who is a hundred years old? And shall Sarah, who is ninety years old, bear a son? And [he] said to God, Oh, that Ishmael might live before You! But God said, Sarah your wife shall bear you a son indeed, and you shall call his name Isaac [laughter]; and I will establish My covenant with him for an everlasting covenant and with his posterity after him. And as for Ishmael, I have heard and heeded you; behold, I will bless him and will make him fruitful and will multiply him exceedingly; He will be the father of twelve princes, and I will make him a great nation. But My covenant, My promise and pledge, I will establish with Isaac, whom Sarah will bear to you at this season next year.[6]

---

[6] Genesis 17:15–21 AMP.

Sure enough, about a year later, the elderly Sarah gave birth to Isaac, just as the Lord had promised. Abraham was one hundred years old and Sarah was ninety.

A party for Ishmael's little half-brother. For fourteen years, Ishmael had been the heir apparent. It is certain that Abraham doted on this son of his old age; no doubt, he exulted in his every milestone: Ishmael's first steps, his prowess with a bow, his efforts to please his father. Abraham was training him up to become the next leader, for that is the way of patriarchs and their heirs. And although the boy was being brought up as Sarah's son, everyone within the compound knew that Hagar was his mother. Living in close proximity to all parties, Ishmael most likely was put in the awkward and difficult position of being caught in the middle between the two women. Perhaps he felt trapped in an inevitable contest of maternal competition. One thing is for sure; in the past, he'd been the focal point of his father's hopes for the future, but everything in Ishmael's world changed when little Isaac was born.

When the time came for Isaac to be weaned, it was celebrated with the customary festivities. Apparently, much was made of this event, for it is written that Abraham provided a spectacular feast. It is easy to imagine the great man personally checking the progress of the meal, inspecting the meats as they roasted on numerous cooking spits, happily greeting his guests, and obviously reveling in the joy of having two healthy sons. But this party became the setting for a fissure in Abraham's family that has lasted until today. As is the way with younger brothers, it is fairly certain that little Isaac would have adoringly looked up to his older brother. The best estimates are that Isaac was between the age of two and three at the time, which would make Ishmael somewhere between sixteen and eighteen. It is easy to envision the toddler hero-worshipping his teenaged brother and the latter alternately indulging the little guy or else enduring the antics of a younger sibling.[7]

Although the exact circumstances are not detailed, it is recorded that at some point during the celebrations, Ishmael mocked Isaac. To mock another person is to make that person feel ridiculed; it is to treat a person with contempt or to make derisive sport of them with mimicry. The details of the mocking aren't disclosed in the record, and it isn't known to what extent Isaac was even aware of what was going on. However, there was one person who was acutely alert to what had transpired, and it so happened that this person was in a position to put a stop to it. "But Sarah saw that the son whom Hagar the Egyptian had borne to Abraham was mocking" (Genesis 21:9 NIV). Notice that neither boy is named; only the mothers are mentioned. The wording of this verse indicates the influence both women had with their sons. Maternal fury rose up in Sarah; she went to her husband to demand Ishmael's removal from the premises.

These next verses in the story are hard to read, but the Lord was clear with His instruction. "And she said to Abraham, 'Get rid of that slave woman and her son, for that woman's son will never share in the inheritance with my son Isaac.' The matter distressed Abraham greatly because it concerned his son. But God said to him, 'Do not be so distressed about the boy and your slave woman. Listen to whatever Sarah tells you, because it is through Isaac that your offspring will be reckoned.'" (Genesis 21:10–12 NIV). The time had come for Abraham to make the separation between these two beloved sons, for only one of them was the son of covenant.

God had clearly shown this truth to Abraham before Isaac was born; Isaac would be the child of covenant, but now Abraham

---

[7] According to the Companion Bible, Isaac was five years old when he was weaned. Should this be the case, Ishmael would have been about nineteen. *The Companion Bible* (Grand Rapids, Michigan: Kregel Publications, 1922), Appendix 50, viii, 71.

was face to face with the weight of what that would mean to him personally. Perhaps over time, the distinction had blurred as Abraham enjoyed the company of both his boys. Although the nature of the covenant was one of blessing, it also brought about separation as God began to set His people apart from others to become a holy company before Him. The bottom line was that Ishmael had to go. Perfectly empathizing with the heart of a parent and longing to encourage His friend, the heavenly Father assured Abraham that his son, Ishmael, would not die. God promised that a great nation would eventually come from the boy. Even as this soul-wrenching task was laid upon him, Abraham was quick to obey. Accordingly, it was early the next morning when Abraham sent Hagar and Ishmael away. Mother and son eventually lost their bearings in the wilderness south of Beersheba, but the Lord rescued them and proved that He would take care of them.[8]

Arab history begins with Ishmael. Ishmael grew to manhood in the rugged Paran wilderness, which is the area located northwest of the Gulf of Aqaba. The scriptures record that his Egyptian mother arranged a marriage for him with an Egyptian wife; therefore, the children born from this union were three-quarters Egyptian. Many years later, Esau, Abraham's oldest grandson by Isaac, would marry one of Ishmael's daughters.[9]

We already know something of Ishmael's character because the angel of the Lord prophesied to Hagar that her son would be "as a wild ass among men; his hand will be against every man and every man's hand against him, and he will live to the east and on the borders of all his kinsmen" (Genesis 16:12 AMP). This description translates to a life that is solitary, independent, and quick to defend

---

[8] Genesis 21;14–21
[9] Genesis 28:8–9. Earlier, Esau had married two Hittite women, Judith and Basemath; therefore, Uncle Ishmael's daughter, Mahalath, became Esau's third wife. The record does not indicate that Esau consulted with the Lord or with his parents concerning the choice of any of his three wives.

with vicious kicks and bites; it means living on the fringe or border of filial relationship.[10] Abraham's oldest son grew up to become an archer, and it is written that his children eventually settled broadly in the area of the Arabian peninsula. Some years later, the men in the caravan that purchased and eventually carried Joseph down into Egypt would be composed of Ishmaelite traders.

Over time, a deep root of bitterness was allowed to grow up in this branch of Abraham's family line. As a matter of fact, it is easy to see how this might have happened. With the passing of time, both Ishmael and his mother would have had ample opportunity to nurture resentment and jealousy. For these two, recalling the years spent in Abraham's camp always brought back numerous memories that caused offence. Add to this Esau's own unique set of personality traits, along with an understandable dose of hurt and anger, and it doesn't take much imagination to surmise the particular topic of conversation that routinely recurred around the evening campfires. This son of Hagar might easily have assumed a victim's mentality. Fast-forward across the centuries to the present, and one arrives at the current state of affairs in the Middle East. Keep in mind that the covenant included real estate. Today, Isaac's descendants are residing in their God-given home, and Ishmael's descendants are crying, "Unfair!"

Jews in Arabia. After the Roman destruction of Jerusalem in 70 AD, those who survived being killed or taken captive were temporarily dispersed throughout the region. Among them were large groups that migrated south into Arabia. Putting their roots down into the sands of the Arabian desert, these Jews participated in various pursuits of agriculture, business, tent making, and the production of sought-after knives and swords. They raised their families, built many synagogues, and continued their contribution

---

[10] The entire conversation between the angel of the Lord and Hagar is recorded in Genesis 16:8–12.

to the area for five hundred years.[11] The largest concentration of Jewish population centered in the town of Yathrib. Today, however, Yathrib is known as Medina.

Arabs in Arabia. Further south from Yathrib lay the oasis of Mecca, located along a busy caravan route. This extensive, ancient roadway connected Yemen at the southern tip of the Arabian peninsula to both Mesopotamia and Egypt. During the sixth century AD, the primary groups living in the region were the Arabs, the Abionites (a group that had originated in Christianity but didn't accept either atonement or the Trinity), Nestorians, Christians, and Jews. Although relatively small in number by comparison to the other groups, the Jews had amicable relations with their Arab neighbors and were firmly established in the area.[12]

Mecca is the home of *Al Kaaba (Ka'ba)*, the cube-shaped shrine built around the Black Stone, a fallen meteorite. Several Arab traditions describe the famous stone. One teaches that Abraham and Ishmael traveled to Mecca, where they erected a building around the stone that eventually came to be known as the Kaaba. This Kaaba stone, draped in black cloth, is the focus of every Muslim's pilgrimage to Mecca. In pre-Islamic Arabia, many different ethnic groups lived together, worshiping their own gods. Consequently, many deities were worshiped throughout the peninsula, and over time, al Kaaba became the central repository for hundreds of idols within this polytheistic society. Allah was the name used by Muhammad's tribe for the moon god.[13] Perhaps this is the reason the shape of the crescent moon has come to be associated with Allah worship.

Possibly it was because of its location as a trade center that Mecca eventually became the hub of idol worship to such

---

[11] Mark A. Gabriel, PhD, *Islam and the Jews* (Lake Mary, Florida: Charisma House, 2003), 66.
[12] Ibid., 67–68.
[13] Gene Little, ThD, *The Mystery of Islam* (Jasper, Arkansas: 2003), 315.

divergent groups of people. Idol production proved to be an extremely lucrative business, and by the mid-sixth century AD, local entrepreneurs had come to rely on a flourishing idol trade. It was into this atmosphere of multiple religions and ethnic groups that Muhammad was born.

Muhammad bin Abdullah.[14] It is believed that Muhammad was born around 570 AD. He was born into the Quraysh tribe, the ruling tribe in the important trade center of Mecca. His father was Abdullah (Abd'allah). The name means "slave of Allah" in Arabic, indicating "that Allah was already one of the many deities worshipped at the Ka'ba" before ever Muhammad was born.[15] Abdullah died several months before his son's birth, and Muhammad's mother died when he was only six years old. Left without either parent, he was sent then to live with his paternal grandfather. After the death of his grandfather, an uncle took over the responsibility of the small boy. Uncle Abu Talib was a caravan trader, and Muhammad accompanied him on his many travels. Muslim tradition tells the story that once, while traveling in Syria with one of his uncle's caravans, a Nestorian priest noticed a birthmark on Muhammad's shoulder and prophesied that the young man was marked to be the world's last prophet.[16]

When he was twenty-five years old, Muhammad began working for a rich widow by the name of Khadija who owned a caravan company and belonged to the Abionite faith. They married, and the union produced two sons and four daughters, but only one child lived into adulthood. That child, a daughter, was named

---

[14] Mohammed or Muhammad are both correct forms.
[15] Avner Boskey, *A Perspective on Islam* (Nashville, Tennessee: Final Frontier Ministries, 2001), 7.
http://www.davidstent.org.
[16] Gabriel, op. cit., 66–67.

Fatima, and she was eventually married to her cousin, Ali, the son of Uncle Abu Talib.[17]

When Muhammad was forty years old, he began going up into the mountains surrounding Mecca. There, in the Sirat Mountains, he would pray and meditate. According to Islamic historians, in the year 610 AD, Muhammad had a dream or vision (the account is not clear) in which an angel appeared to him. Muhammad believed the angel to be the angel Gabriel of the Bible. After numerous appearances from this same spirit, Muhammad became convinced that the visitations were a revelation of truth. The angel declared that there is only one true god and that his name is Allah. Furthermore, Muhammad had been chosen to serve as his final prophet. This meant that the other 359 idols within the Kaaba's collection at Mecca were to be done away with, and only Allah was to be be worshipped.[18] The orphan with the tragic childhood had become a man with a great commission. As the prophet of Allah, Muhammad was charged with spreading the message that all mankind must submit to Islam.

The first follower of Islam was Muhammad's wife, Khadija. A rich merchant by the name of Abu Bakr became his second disciple. Following in the footsteps of these two converts was a man named Omar, a local leader in Mecca. Because he was not able to read or write, Muhammad dictated the angel's messages to Khadija. After the messages had been transcribed and recorded, they were collected into *surah* (chapters). The compilation of the surah became known as the Koran, which is the Arabic word for "recitation." It comes as no surprise that Muhammad's monotheistic preaching about Allah was not well received by the local merchants who made a living by producing and selling a variety of idols. As a result, he was persecuted in Mecca, and after the deaths of Khadija and Abu

---

[17] *The World Book Encyclopedia*, vol. M (Chicago, London, Sydney, Toronto: World Book Inc., 1988 edition), 914.

[18] al-Waqidi. "as cited by Boskey," op. cit., 7

Talib, Muhammad was forced to escape to the city of Yathrib, about two hundred miles to the north. This flight, known as the Hegira, took place in 622 AD and is the beginning date for the Muslim calendar.[19]

Muhammad had expected the Christians and Jews of Yathrib to join him and embrace his message. He even referred to them as "the people of the book" because he mistakenly supposed that the new revelations that he'd embraced were in accord with the Bible. Muhammad believed that his revelations were, in fact, the true religion that Adam had originally followed in Eden. Muhammad intended to reintroduce the commands of his god, known as Allah, while simultaneously unveiling his position as the last in a long line of prophets. Muhammad taught that the first prophet had been Adam.[20] Adam was the first, and he himself was to be the last prophet. He preached that between Adam's time and his own there had been other prophets; these included Abraham, Ishmael, Lot, Moses, and Jesus. Upon seeing that his teachings were rejected, and after a Jewish woman conspired with his enemies by attempting to poison him, he turned on the Jews with a vengeance. Steadily, his forces were able to gain strength, and he finally conquered Yathrib in 628 AD. In the final battle for the city, between eight to nine hundred Jews who refused to convert were slaughtered in a trench at Khaybar, a settlement just over ninety miles north of Yathrib.[21] At the head of his army of jihad, Muhammad returned to Mecca, and conquered it in 630 AD. He lived for two more years before dying in Yathrib, which later became known as Medina, the "Prophet's city."

The Spread of Islam. The religion that Muhammad taught came to be called Islam and its followers known as Muslims.[22] Within

---

[19] *The World Book Encyclopedia,* op. cit., 914–915.

[20] http://www.islamicbulletin.org/newsletters/issue_1/adam.aspx. Accessed 9/5/2015

[21] Gabriel, op. cit., 112.

[22] "Moslem" and "Muslim" are both correct forms, although the latter is becoming more prevalent.

a century of Muhammad's death, Muslim conquests had brought the whole of Egypt, along with the Maghreb (the North African countries of Libya, Algeria, Morocco, and Tunisia), under the banner of Islam. After crossing the narrow Strait of Gibraltar and pushing into the Iberian Peninsula, Islam became a major ruling presence in Spain from the early 700s until the late 1200s. The rest of Europe may well have gone the way of the countries mentioned if it had not been for two strategic battles fought centuries apart. After establishing themselves in Spain, the Moors crossed the Pyrenees into France.[23] In a desperate bid to cut off further incursions into western Europe, Charles Martel's French army was victorious after the hard-fought Battle of Tours in 732 AD. Christian Europe was once again saved from Islam in 1683. In that year, it took the combined forces of the Holy Roman Empire, Poland, and Lithuania to defeat the Ottoman armies at the Battle of Vienna.

Ishmael's children are caught in the web of Islam. Today, a little more than 90 percent of all Arabs are Muslim, and God loves each one. In fact, He has made a way for them to become His children. God yearned over His creation to the extent that He was willing to send His only Son into the world so that *anyone* who would believe in Him would never have to perish, but could have eternal life. This good news includes the billion and a half souls who have been blinded by Islam. In his earlier life as Saul, Paul set himself squarely in opposition to God by hunting down the Christian believers, and today's radical Muslim is doing the same thing. And just as Paul didn't realize that Jesus was taking his actions personally, Muslims are ignorant of their great trespass against the Lord. So what was the Lord's response to Paul? He appeared to him on the road to Damascus in order to save him from himself. Being thus confronted and blinded wasn't pleasant for Paul, but it saved him!

---

[23] *Moor* is the name given to those Muslims who invaded and conquered Spain.

Psalm 83. In Asaph's prophetic psalm, Psalm 83, it appears that the Lord intends to initiate a confrontation with His Arab people in order to save them. Reading through the verses, it can be seen that certain nations have aligned themselves with one motivation, and that motivation is an unrelenting intention to destroy Israel. By looking a little more closely, one also recognizes a shared family history in many of the nations mentioned. Amazingly, most of the clans and tribes trace their roots back to Ishmael; here, the DNA markers are obvious. It would appear that the roots of bitterness and jealousy, cultivated by centuries of conversation around Arab campfires, have finally produced a fully mature and war-weathered hatred. Going even a little further, it can be seen that *all* the nations are tied by an allegiance and fidelity to Islam.

Read through the entire psalm, and notice that the goal of these nations is to do away with the very people God has sworn to guard and defend, a nation He protects as the "apple of His eye."[24] The nations scheme and conspire toward their avowed purpose, all the while unaware that the one who protects Israel is listening to every word. By forming their confederation, they have unwittingly set themselves on a collision course with Israel's covenant partner, God Himself. He takes each of the "crafty schemes" against His people personally. "They devise crafty schemes against your people; they conspire against your precious ones. 'Come,' they say, 'let us wipe out Israel as a nation. We will destroy the very memory of its existence.' Yes, this was their unanimous decision. They signed a treaty as allies against you" (Psalm 83: 3–5 NLT).

Ancient enemies, modern enemies. Examine the individual members of this confederation that seek to do away with the name and even the memory of Israel. The groups mentioned in Psalm 83 are, in fact, a coalition in operation today.

---

[24] God references Israel as the "apple of His eye" in Deuteronomy 32:10 and Zechariah 2:8. The apple of one's eye is the pupil of the eye and, purportedly, the most sensitive part of the human body.

5

- **Tents of Edom** (v. 6). Edom was the home of Esau, who lived south of the Dead Sea into Mount Seir. Though not a descendant, he married into Ishmael's family (modern Jordan and northwest Arabia).
- **Ishmaelites** (v. 6). Ishmael lived east and south of Israel in the Arabian peninsula (Saudi Arabia).
- **Moab** (v. 6). Descendants of Lot and his older daughter (Jordan).
- **Hagrites** (v. 6). Descendants of the Ishmaelites, they are the Bedouin of Arabia. Some say the name comes from Hagar (Arabian and Sinai peninsulas, Israel, Jordan, Libya, and the Sudan).
- **Gebal** (v. 7). Ancient name for Lebanon, which was populated by the Phoenicians, a non-Arab people (Lebanon).
- **Ammon** (v. 7). Descendants of Lot and his younger daughter (Jordan).
- **Amalek** (v. 7). Descendants either of Esau's grandson or descendants of the treacherous Amelekites (Sinai peninsula and Negev).
- **Philistines** (v. 7). Descendants of the ancient Phoenicians who originated in Crete and Asia Minor, they inhabited Israel's southern coast (Gaza Strip).
- **Tyre** (v. 7). According to Amos 1:9, the people of Tyre worked as middlemen to deliver Jews to the Edomites (Lebanon).
- **Assyria** (v. 8). Descendants of the Sumerians, the Assyrians conquered the ten northern tribes of Israel in 722 BC (northern Iraq, eastern Syria, and southeastern Turkey).
- **Sisera** (v. 9). Chief military commander under King Jaban, he harassed Israel for twenty years, but he died at the hand of Jael, who drove a stake through his head (northern Israel).
- **Jaban** (v. 9). Canaanite king who ruled from Hazor. He was soundly defeated by the troops of Barak and Deborah (upper Galilee, south of Lebanon and west of Syria).

- **Oreb and Zeeb** (v. 11). Both men were princes of Midian (northwestern Arabia).
- **Zebah and Zalmunna** (v. 11). Both men were kings of Midian (northwestern Arabia). The ESV, NAS, ERV, and AMP mention that these kings decorated their camels with crescent-shaped ornaments (Judges 8:21).

Egypt, Lebanon, Syria, Iraq, Jordan, Arabia—these ancient names are today in the throes of a frenzied submission to Allah. Traditionally, they are people who respect strength, and this psalm suggests a future confrontation in which the false god of Islam will be exposed. Perhaps the confrontation will be similar to that of Dagon, the Baals, and the many gods of Egypt. True to God's nature, the purpose for such a cataclysmic defeat is found in the last verse: "That they may know that you alone, whose name is the Lord, are the Most High over all the earth" (Psalm 83:18).

It is God's will for Ishmael's children to be set free of the Islamic snare, and He will insure that they have the opportunity to see for themselves that He alone is the "Most High" over all the earth.

Understanding the essence of Islam. The word *Islam* means "submission" in Arabic, and it is a religion based on total submission to Allah, as revealed by the writings in the Koran. The *Hadith* is the second important work in Islam. It grew out of the Koran and relates stories from Muhammad's life and sayings, as recorded by his wives and intimate followers. The *Sira* is Muhammad's biography, written by Ibn Ishaq, about one hundred fifty years after his death. According to Islam, Muhammad, the last prophet, is the greatest of all other messengers sent by God, and earlier religions have no validity unless he approved them. To openly defy the prophet's rulings and the laws, as set forth by the Koran, is to challenge the community of Allah. "Therefore, the establishment of the State of Israel in which the Jews not only are not under Muslim patronage but even rule over Muslims, has created a situation which is in contravention of the laws of nature ... the establishment of a Jewish State on Islamic land is an open rebellion against Islamic law, insolence toward its prophet, and impudence towards Allah."[25]

The Koran. *Koran* is Arabic for "recitation," and an equally accepted alternate spelling is *Quran* or *Qur'an.* It is composed of 114 chapters known as *surah,* and it is a book that can be divided into two parts. The reason for the division is that Islam is a religion of *Nasikh*; this means it is a religion of progressive revelation.[26] In other words, the latest ruling or revelation negates anything previous to that specific subject. Therefore, the earlier peaceful surah have become annulled, abolished, or abrogated by the later ones, as the new always trumps the old. Consequently, the Koran is catalogued according to Muhammad's earlier "tolerant years" and his later "aggressive years."[27]

1. "Tolerant years." Muhammad was living in Mecca during this time. He was trying to influence a dubious audience; he didn't have many followers, and he was vulnerable. During this period, Islam was presented as a peaceful religion, with basic tolerance of those with other belief systems.

2. "Aggressive years." These are the years after Muhammad was driven from Mecca and took up residence in Medina, the town formerly known as Yathrib. As he gained followers, he was no longer limited to merely preaching, and he quickly learned the benefit of implementing the tactics of coercion. Now his armies aggressively carried the message of Allah, demanding that the people of Medina submit or suffer the sword.

---

[25] Moshe Sharon, PhD, professor of early Islamic History at Hebrew University and advisor on Arab Affairs. The quoted excerpt is from his seminar collection entitled *Islamic Jihad-Israel and the West* (Jerusalem, Israel: 2006), 6.

[26] "Whatever a verse do we abrogate or cause to be forgotten, we bring a better one or similar to it. Know ye not that Allah is able to do all things?" Surah 2:106

[27] John Hagee, *Jerusalem Countdown* (Lake Mary, Florida: FrontLine, A Strang Company, First Edition, 2006), 33.

According to the adherents of Islam, it is the earth's destiny to have Allah's will imposed on it. The world must be made to be in a state of submission to Allah. Only those who will agree to submit will find themselves at peace with Allah. Therefore, the Muslim views the world as divided into two spheres:[28]

1. *Dar al-Islam:* the "House of Islam." This is that part of the world's population that is "at peace" because they have submitted to Islam. This is the Islamic world and includes all Muslims.
2. *Dar al-harb:* the "House of War." These are the countries and territories where Islam does not yet prevail. Inhabitants of all nations outside of Islamic law find themselves in this house.

The Five Pillars. There are five basic tenants of Islam, and each Muslim is taught the five major principles of the religion. Collectively, they are known as the Five Pillars.

1. *Shahada.* This declaration is Islam's creed. To become a Muslim, one must testify, "There is no god but Allah, and Muhammad is his messenger."
2. *Salah.* Prayer must be made five times daily, and Muslims pray while facing Mecca.
3. *Zakat.* The giving of alms is important to Muslims, and they are instructed to give a portion of their income to charity. The amount is usually 2.5 percent of the annual income and is called zakat.
4. *Sawm.* During the entire month of Ramadan, Muslims are required to fast from sunrise until sunset. The fast includes abstinence from food, water, nicotine, and sexual activity.

---

[28] Little, op. cit., 317.

5. *Haj (Hajj)*. Each Muslim must make every effort to travel to Mecca at least once in his or her lifetime in order to take part in the Haj. The most popular time to make the trip is in the third month after Ramadan, when up to three million Muslims travel to Mecca.

Terminology is important. It is important to be aware that certain words are not interchangeable. For instance, an Arab is not necessarily a Muslim and vice versa.

- **Arab**. An Arab is a descendant of Ishmael. The first Arabs, Ishmael's children, were one fourth Aramean (Abraham) and three-fourths Egyptian. The modern interpretation of this term generally denotes an Arab as being any person who speaks Arabic and originates from the Arabian peninsula. The word *Arab* is an ethnic term, which means that an Arab may be a Christian Arab, a Muslim Arab, an Agnostic Arab, and so forth. Christian Arabs are numbered into the millions within the Arab world.[29]
- **Arab World**. This geographic group is composed of the Arabic-speaking peoples who populate the twenty-two countries in the Middle East and North Africa, in which Muslims are the majority. The Arab World's population is four hundred twenty-two million.[30]
- **Muslim or Moslem**. This word comes from the Arabic word for peace: *salaam*. It speaks of a person who, through submission, is "at peace" with Allah. An adherent of Islam is known as a Muslim.

---

[29] Different sources provide figures ranging from eleven to fourteen million.
[30] http://www.unesco.org/new/en/unesco/events/prizes-and-celebrations/celebrations/international-days/world-arabic-language-day/, as cited by en.wikipedia.org/wiki/Arab_world. Accessed 9/5/2015.

- **Islamic World**. Currently counted in excess of one and a half billion souls, the Islamic World includes the fifty or so countries worldwide with a Muslim majority. Indonesia has the world's largest Muslim population, followed by Pakistan and India.

Branches of Islam. Just as Christianity has many sects so does Islam. Although there are other definite divisions, the following groups (along with a brief explanation) provide a snapshot of the major branches of Islam.

1. *Sunni.* The greatest majority of Muslims are Sunni. Following Muhammad's death, differences arose as to who should lead the Islamic community. The group favoring his faithful companions over a hereditary leadership came to be called Sunni. They chose Abu-Bakr as Islam's first caliph. Egypt, Syria, Saudi Arabia, Jordan, and the Gulf States are primarily composed of Sunni Muslims.
2. *Shia.* This branch traces its beginnings back to the prophet's followers who advocated leadership to Mohammed's son-in-law, Ali. Ali was both Fatima's husband and the son of Muhammad's uncle, Abu Talib. *Shia* is the noun and *Shiite* is the adjective, although the latter is also sometimes used as a noun. Only 15 percent of Muslims are Shia.[31] Iran, Iraq, and Bahrain are primarily composed of Shiite Muslims.
3. *Wahhabi.* The Wahhabi sect is known as the puritanical or fundamentalist branch of Sunni Islam. The Saudi royal family is an advocate of this rigid and strict movement that wants to purify Islam by following the seventh-century practices of the prophet. Saudi Arabia is primarily Wahhabi.

---

[31] Shira Sorko-Ram, *Maoz-Israel Report* (Tel Aviv, Israel: Maoz-Israel, April 2015). Accessed 5/20/2015, http://www.maozisrael.org/site/News2?abbr=maoz_&page=NewsArticle&id=10536&news_iv_ctrl=-1.

4. *Bahai*. This sect grew out of Islam but is not considered part of Islam by Muslims because it embraces all the nine major religions. Ironically, its headquarters are located in Haifa, Israel.

Islamic Terms:

1. *Midrash*. A school where Islam is preached and taught.
2. *Mullah*. A person who has graduated from a midrash.
3. *Iman*. A pious man who is knowledgeable in the faith, and the spiritual leader who leads prayer in the mosque.
4. *Caliph*. This term actually refers to the deputy who, following Muhammad's death, served as leader. He was responsible for providing spiritual and political leadership. The last caliph passed from history with the dissolution of the Ottoman Empire.
5. *Mosque*. This is the Muslim house of worship and literally means a "place of kneeling."
6. *Jihad*. The Arabic word for "struggle." The term has evolved to mean a Muslim's willingness to kill or be killed for the sake of his or her religion. In reality, Jihad is the command to holy war issued by Allah for the purpose of imposing Islam upon Dar al-harb.
7. *Sharif*. An Arabic word, its literal meaning is "noble." Sharif is one who can trace his lineage back through Fatima, Mohammed's daughter, to the Prophet himself.

The believer's bottom line. History reveals that the Middle East's conflict can be traced to a family schism that has resulted in periodic outbreaks of violence since Abraham's time. His sons inhabit separate camps, and the tension between them casts a dark cloud over the entire region. The original Father's heart for reconciliation belongs to God, and He has great and loving compassion for all of His children in each of the nations. Psalm 83 illustrates His willingness to confront a nation's waywardness so that the truth can be seen, namely, "That they may know that you alone, whose name is the Lord, are the Most High over all the earth." At present, the majority of Ishmael's family branch lives behind the veil of Islam, inadvertently placing itself at cross-purpose with Israel's covenant partner, God. Longing to see their eyes opened, the heavenly Father has determined to bring about circumstances that will leave no doubt about the identity of the one true God and that He alone is Lord and "the Most High" forever. Truth brings freedom.

Chapter 5 Study Guide

1. Descendants of Abraham through _____ are known as Arabs.

2. The religion of _____ acknowledges Allah as the only god and teaches that Muhammad is his prophet.

3. Muhammad bin Abdullah was born an _____ and became a _____ when he submitted to Allah as his god.

4. According to the religion of Islam, the world is divided into two parts:
   A) Dar al Islam _____.
   B) Dar al harb _____.

5. Muslims are divided into two main groups. The majority is _____. They trace their line of authority back through Muhammad's tribe (caliph leadership).

6. _____ is the other major group. Their leadership is traced back to Hussein, the son of Fatima (daughter of Muhammad) and Ali (son of Abu Talib).

7. The Koran is a book of Nasikh, also known as _____.

Psalm 83

Fill in the blanks with the modern countries/nations.

Tents of Edom _____   Amalek _____

Ishmaelites _____   Philistines _____

Moab _____   Tyre _____

Hagrites _____   Assyria _____

Gebal _____   Midianites _____

Ammon _____   Oreb and Zeeb _____

                              Zebah and Zalmunna _____

"Fill their faces with shame, **that they may seek, inquire for, and insistently require Your name, O Lord** ... That they may know that **You, Whose name alone is the Lord, are the Most High over all the earth** [emphasis added] " (Psalm 83: 16 and 18 AMP).

Chapter 6

Who Are the Palestinians?

Chapter 5 Recap: Some six hundred years after Christ, a new religion emerged from the sands of Arabia. Today, more than 1.5 billion souls are submitted to it. Islam demands complete obedience to the teachings of its god, Allah, as preached by Muhammad, who is known as the Prophet to his followers. Although divided into sects, the followers of Islam are united in their hatred of Israel and in the belief that God has no son. Although this places them on a collision course with the Creator, the Lord intends that they should have the chance to recognize Him alone as "the Most High" over the earth. To this end, the God of Abraham, Isaac, and Jacob has great love for each and every Muslim and has made provision for their eternal salvation through the atoning, sacrificial death of His Son, Jesus.

In the news. Hardly a week goes by without the report of a problem coming out of the Middle East. The present generation has come to expect violence and strife from this part of the world, with the latest report often being broadcast from Jerusalem. It is ironic that the pulse of current global events most frequently erupts from an area that for centuries was either dismissed or ignored. Yet, the past fifty years have witnessed the re-emergence of antiquated cities such as Gaza, Jerusalem, and Damascus. Previously, the majority of news from the region (perhaps with the exception of oil price fluctuations) was left to collect dust on obscure shelves in the history section of a college library. Today, however, these archaic names share headlines with Washington, DC, Brussels, Moscow, and Beijing. Obviously, a major shift in the global geopolitical paradigm has taken place. Is it merely happenchance or could the hand of God have something to do with it? One thing *is* for certain, since the Middle East also includes the State of Israel, Christians must seriously review the march of current events within the context of scripture, particularly when military and political involvement affects that nation.

Israel is a flash point for world opinion. In this region, a major flash point that periodically erupts in conflict frequently involves a smallish parcel of land about the size of New Jersey. Located at the eastern end of the Mediterranean, it is the nation of Israel. Without going into a detailed litany of wars, treaties, or United Nations' resolutions—about which many thousands of books and articles have been written—it must first be acknowledged that the Bible has much to say about Israel. Although this chapter will address some of the facts concerning the area and its resident peoples, for the Christian, scripture must always be the recognized authority in any final analysis. In order to understand the intense scramble for land ownership, one must also recognize that two very different groups of people are contending for rights to the same parcel of real estate. Two different peoples claim both legal and historical legitimacy to the sovereignty of the land itself: the Jews and the Palestinians.

To further complicate international debate concerning this topic, many in the worldwide Christian community have weighed in to take sides, as it were, between the divergent viewpoints. Groups within Christendom generally fall into three camps: pro-Palestinian, pro-Israel, and surprisingly, there are also those for whom the matter holds very little significance either way. Within the first two groups, however, emotions run high whenever discussion of the Palestinian–Israeli conflict is introduced. Although there are seemingly innumerable complications to this deepening quagmire, as a general rule of thumb, the pro-Israel lobby argues that the land in question belongs to Israel based on the following reasons.

They are the ancient deed recorded in the biblical account, legitimate and recognized international treaties, and last, but not least, the hard-fought wars of self-defense. On the other hand, the pro-Palestinian contingency shares the opinion that the Jews unfairly usurped land from its rightful owners and are illegally occupying Palestinian territory. It is within this latter context— and with an eye to adding the weapon of economic clout to their convictions—that some church denominations have even issued formal boycotts on the purchasing of products from the "occupied territories."[1]

Where is Palestine? Before tackling the question of the Palestinian identity, one needs to look at the land in question. Keep in mind that the present states in the Middle East (Israel, as well as the surrounding nations) were created relatively recently, and their international boundaries were established only as a direct result of World War I. Aside from learning what the Bible has to say about this disputed area, it is beneficial to have basic background knowledge of recent archeological discoveries, as well as information as to what these digs have uncovered about the groups of people that were living in the region during ancient times.

The contested area was originally known as Canaan. At some point during the years 2000 to 1800 BC, Genesis 11:31 states,

---

[1] In July 2013, the largest Protestant church in Canada, The United Church of Canada, approved a campaign to boycott goods manufactured in settlements from the West Bank and East Jerusalem. The products include brands such as Ahava, SodaStream, and Keter Plastic, http://forward.com/articles/177623/canadas-largest-protestant-church-to-boycott--isr/#ixzz2ZVq8SPpa. May 29, 2013. A year earlier at their annual 2012 General Assembly, the Presbyterian Church (USA) also voted to boycott goods from the same area, http://www.haaretz.com/news/diplomacy-defense/presbyterian-church-in-u-s-votes-to-boycott-israeli-settlement-goods-1.449329. July 6, 2012.

"Terah took Abram his son and Lot the son of Haran, his grandson, and Sarai his daughter-in-law, his son Abram's wife, and they went forth together from Ur of the Chaldeans to go into the land of Canaan, but when they came to Haran, they settled there."

Some years later, after Terah had died, scripture says, "And Abram took Sarai his wife, and Lot his brother's son, and all their possessions that they had gathered, and the people that they had acquired in Haran, and they set out to go to the land of Canaan. When they came to the land of Canaan, Abram passed through the land to the place at Shechem, to the oak of Moreh. At that time the Canaanites were in the land" (Genesis 12:5–6).

The ancient Egyptian Amarna Letters also refer to the land of Canaan.[2] Nevertheless, and as a result of God's promise, the area is always referred to as Israel after Joshua's conquest of Canaan (1400–1375 BC). This recognition continues through the historical record up until the time of Herod.

Israel is renamed *Palestine* in 135 AD. The land making up the modern state of Israel was known as Israel from the times of the judges forward because the name was originally derived from the people group also known as Israel.[3] From approximately 1400 BC until 135 AD, (a period of over fifteen hundred years), the area was *always* identified as Israel, Judea, or Samaria.[4] Many centuries after the judges, and on the heels of a revolt that had lasted for three years, the mighty Roman Empire was finally able to quell a Jewish insurrection known to history as the Bar Kochba Revolt

---

[2] During the fourteenth century BC, Akhenaton moved his capital from Thebes to Amarna. Ancient clay tablets, known as the Amarna Letters that were written in cuneiform, record the diplomatic relationships between Egypt and her neighbors, including Canaan.

[3] In those days, there was no king in Israel. Everyone did what was right in his own eyes. (Judges 21:25)

[4] Henry H. Halley, *Halley's Bible Handbook* (Grand Rapids, Michigan: Zondervan Publishing House, 1965), 168. The exact years for the period known as "the Judges" is not certain but can be broadly identified as the three hundred years falling between 1400–1100 BC.

(132–135 AD). Rome, furious as a result of a series of uprisings from this subjugated yet stubborn people, decided to head off any future attempts at another insurrection. To that end, Emperor Hadrian not only exiled the remaining defeated Jewish population but he also banned them, on pain of death, from reentering the gates of their capital, Jerusalem. Next, Hadrian added insult to injury by renaming Jerusalem in honor of his own family and the god, Jupiter Capitolinus. Thus, Jerusalem became Aelia Capitolina.

At the same time these post-war policies were being implemented, the emperor also sought to completely erase Jewish history from the land itself, and he proposed to do this by changing the name of the country. It is at this juncture that Hadrian determined to remove every memory of the original land; he renamed Judea *Palaestina*. His selection of this name was deliberately chosen in an effort to further humiliate the Jews, for it was intended to be a galling reminder of Israel's ancient foe—the Philistines.[5] The Philistines! Remember that Goliath, the menacing giant who threatened a young David, was a Philistine. At another time, the Philistines had succeeded in capturing the Ark of the Covenant. And who could ever forget that Samson, Israel's mighty judge of renown, was double-crossed by the Philistine temptress, Delilah? The evidence is clear that the name was chosen with careful deliberation.

This then is the historical origin of how Israel, Judea, and Samaria came to be known collectively as Palaestina or *Palestine*. And although this largely forgotten event took place in 135BC, the unlikely result has been that the word *Palestine* was not also forgotten and laid aside. With the passage of time, Aelia Capitolina faded from the vernacular as people began to speak of Jerusalem once again, but a strange thing happened regarding Israel; the name *Palestine* continued to be used. This historical anomaly is

---

[5] Simon Sebag Montefiore, *Jerusalem* (New York, NY: Alfred A. Knopf, 2011), 143.

an example of how original names for peoples and places become substituted over the centuries and are then passed down to later generations through a common, Latin-based vocabulary. Taking into consideration that Spanish, Portuguese, French, and Italian are among the twenty-three Romance languages that originally descended from Latin, one can readily see how Palestine came to be the accepted (yet wholly mistaken) terminology for the land that, previous to 135 AD, had been known as Israel. In the long run, it seems that Hadrian's decree had surprisingly far-reaching consequences, inasmuch as many people today have not the slightest inkling that the area commonly referred to as Palestine is actually historical and biblical Israel.

The Holy Land (known as Palestine) becomes a battleground.[6] Nine hundred years after Hadrian, the same area became the site of a tug-of-war between Christianity and Islam. The Crusades, as the extended military conflict came to be known, were composed of a series of intermittent wars that occupied medieval Europe for nearly two hundred years (1099–1291). United under the banner of the Latin Church, European Crusaders marched to Palestine to liberate Jerusalem from the Muslims. Muslims had moved into the area during the mid-seventh century AD. Following the Christian Crusades, and for many years afterward, the region continued to be a battleground for various invading groups, including the Mongols, as well as successive and competing waves of Muslim armies.

By the early sixteenth century, a Sunni Muslim group—the Ottoman Turks—finally emerged as the recognized power in the region. Ever seeking to expand, the Ottoman Empire ultimately came to rule a vast territory that would eventually include the

---

[6] "And the Lord will inherit Judah as His portion in the holy land and shall again choose Jerusalem"(Zechariah 2:12). This scripture is the only time the Bible refers to Israel as the Holy Land. The term *Holy Land* was not even used in common conversation until the Middle Ages.

modern states of Israel, Lebanon, Syria, Iraq, Jordan, parts of Saudi Arabia, and Egypt.[7] The Ottomans would maintain their rule over the lands then known as Mesopotamia and Palestine throughout the following four centuries. During these years, Palestine was sometimes also referred to as Southern Syria. In time, this immense Turkish caliphate came to an inglorious end as a result of having joined forces with Germany during World War I. The empire's former land holdings were confiscated and carved up by the victorious Allies at the end of that war. Such is the penalty for participants on the losing side of battle. It was, therefore, at the end of World War I—a war that had been so hopefully styled as the "war to end all wars"—that France and Britain created a family of brand-new nations out of their Ottoman portion of the spoils. Planning to oversee their respective fledglings nations achieve eventual independence, France and Britain now assumed a quasi-parental, supervisory role within their separate "spheres of influence."

Palestine is a geographical term. Palestine is merely the post-Roman terminology for the nation of Israel. Throughout the two thousand year period from 135 AD to the present, no nation of Palestine has ever existed. No language known as Palestinian has ever emerged, and no distinct Palestinian culture is to be found. The reason for this non-existence is that Palestine is no more than the Roman designation for the area of ancient Israel, an area historically occupied and populated by the Jewish people. In actuality, Palestine is an aberrant term for historical Israel that has mistakenly remained in use from the times of the Roman legions. Throughout the intervening centuries, the area has been subjected to the rule of various invading powers and most frequently governed in absentia. For example, the area was administered during the Ottoman period from the Turkish capital, Constantinople (modern

---

[7] *The World Book Encyclopedia*, vol. N–O (Chicago, London, Sydney, Toronto: World Book, Inc., 1988), 884.

Istanbul). At the end of World War I, and throughout the entire mandate period, management for the area of Palestine came from Whitehall in London. It was not until David Ben-Gurion announced the formation of the State of Israel that the true name for the land finally reemerged.

But what about the people who are known as Palestinians? Since the very name *Palestinian* presupposes a connection with the area designated as the land of the Philistines (Palaestina), it is a common assumption that the Arab residents of the mandated area trace their ancestry to the ancient Philistines. If this were the case, as many believe it to be, then the Philistine descendants would have a viable claim to the land, along with the Jews, right? Wrong. It turns out that the Philistines are not the ancestors of today's Palestinians, and there is no relationship between them ethnically, linguistically, culturally, or historically. In fact, in large part, the Arab connection to the land came about around 150 years ago.

Modern Palestinians did not descend from the ancient Philistines. Who were the Philistines? Looking to the Bible, one finds that Genesis 10:14 places this people group in Casluhim and Caphtorim, or, in other words, as descending from Mizraim, a son of Noah's grandson, Ham. Another reference in Ezekiel 25:16 describes the Philistines as a group, along with the Cherethites, as originating in Crete. First Samuel 30:14 refers to Cherethites living in what was Philistine territory, and this also suggests that they were part of the same family.

Other non-biblical sources trace the Philistines to the "sea peoples" from the Aegean Sea region.[8] Based upon archeological excavations and ancient writings, additional sources identify Crete as the Philistine point of origin.[9] Since Caphtor is the

---

[8] Ibid., vol. P, 382.
[9] Bard, op. cit. "Ancient Jewish History: The Philistines." 1998. December, 2012. http://www.jewishvirtuallibrary.org/jsource/History/Philistines.html.

ancient name for Crete, an Indo-European origin would be strongly indicated. At any rate, Egyptian writings mention that the sea peoples began arriving in waves along the Mediterranean coast during the twelfth century BC, and they were defeated by Ramses III after a series of naval battles.[10] In all probability, they were among the groups that relocated along the southeastern end of the Mediterranean Sea sometime between the years 1200–600 BC.

Because the Philistines faded from history without leaving any written record, detailed information is left to conjecture, and any knowledge about them is incomplete. Unless further archeological discoveries are made, the available database remains wholly dependent upon the Bible and other contemporary sources, none of which are of Philistine origin. What *is* known is that the Philistines were an ancient people occupying lands in the region of the Mediterranean Sea. Evidence shows that the Philistines were either descended from Japheth (in Asia Minor) or possibly from Ham (in Egypt), but in either case, they were definitely not Ishmaelites. This means of course that the Philistines did not descend from Shem, who was the ancestor of both the Jews and Arabs. As sketchy as the existing information on this ancient people group is, the following are interesting facts that emerge concerning the Philistines:

- Assyrians called them "Pilisti"; Hebrews called them "Pelishti."
- Abimelech was a Philistine. Scholars differ in their opinions about whether or not Abimelech is the name of an individual person or a title (such as "king"). It is known, however, that

---

[10] Rameses III had the details of his military victory over the sea peoples recorded in stone relief upon the walls of his mortuary temple, Medinet Habuin, located at Luxor.

Abimelech ruled the Philistine area of Gerar during the Patriarchs' lifetimes.

- Five city states. Philistines evidently lived by groups or clans in City States, and five are known by name: Ashkelon, Ashdod, Ekron, Gath, and Gaza. (The present-day Gaza City is located in the northern most region of the area known as Gaza.)

- They were finally conquered by King David and forced to pay tribute to Israel by the time of Jehoshaphat (848–783 BC).

- Assyria conquered the Philistines, and the Assyrians required tribute from their vassal Philistine subjects.

- They left no written record. Thus far, no archeological dig has uncovered any record or history written by the sea peoples themselves.

- They adopted the various Canaanite gods and worshiped Dagon, Ashteroth, and Baal-Zebub. See 2 Kings 1:2–3, 6, 16; 1 Samuel 31:10; and Judges 16:23–24.

- Archeological evidence shows that the Philistines were influenced by Greek, Egyptian, and Canaanite styles. It would seem that the Philistines enjoyed a cultural and religious smorgasbord.

- The pottery remains of beer mugs demonstrate their preference for the colors red and black.

- Philistine men wore short tunics, carried round shields, and were clean-shaven.

- Philistines entered the Iron Age before their Israelite neighbors, and they zealously guarded the secrets of their advanced iron metallurgy from the Hebrews (1 Samuel 13:19–22).

- The land of the Philistines—Philistia—was a coastal strip approximately twenty-five miles in length, located at the southeastern corner of the Mediterranean Sea. The area was strategically situated along a major trade route between Egypt and Syria.

- After Nebuchadnezzar carried the Jews away to Babylon (597–586 BC), the Philistines seem to have held on to their territory for a time because Zechariah mentions them (Zechariah 9). In spite of their efforts to save themselves, they, along with others in the region, were ultimately dispersed or assimilated by mighty Babylon and Persia. At this point the Philistines fade from the pages of history.

Who are today's Palestinians? So if Palestinians cannot trace their roots to the Philistines, who then are the people living within the confines of the refugee camps? And if not from the ancient yet mythical country of Palestine, then where did this people originate? It turns out that today's Palestinians are simply the descendants of an Arab population living within the mandated territory at the time of Israel's statehood in 1948.

As of 2013, according to statistics from the United Nations, there are approximately five million Palestinian refugees.[11] This number is up from the 3.7 million who were listed in mid–2000. At that time, it was estimated that approximately one-third of the registered refugees lived within the camps. The remaining two-thirds were living either in or within close proximity to towns inside those countries that host the camps.[12] Today, this disenfranchised people, numbering in the millions, are the ones known as Palestinians. Surprisingly, however, they have not always been identified as Palestinians. In fact, it was not until the

---

[11] http://www.unrwa.org, October 2013 (United Nations Relief and Works Agency).

[12] Mitchell G. Bard, *Myths and Facts A Guide to the Arab-Israeli Conflict* (Chevy Chase, MD: American Israeli Cooperative Enterprise, 2001), 185. The official camps are located in the West Bank, Gaza Strip, Lebanon, Syria, and Jordan.

mid–1960s that the name *Palestinian* became synonymous with the Arab refugees.

Prior to 1967 and the Six-Day War, Jews were the people group referred to as Palestinians, but most people living outside of the Middle East today have either forgotten or never knew this to be the fact. Before the mid-sixties, Jews living in the mandated territory even called themselves Palestinians. Conversely, an Arab would have considered the same identification an insult. At the time, the Arab communities continued to refer to themselves by their former origins: Syrian, Aramean, etc., and it was the Jews who were known as the Palestinians. The famed *Jerusalem Post* was originally established as the *Palestine Post,* and it wasn't until a few years after statehood that the name was changed. The announcement about the birth of the new state of Israel was printed on the front page of the May 16, 1948 edition of the *Palestine Post.* Israel's largest bank, Bank Leumi, was set up initially by members of the Zionist movement and known as the Anglo-Palestine Bank. Similarly, the world-acclaimed Israel Philharmonic Orchestra was founded first as the Palestine Symphony Orchestra. As it happens, the latter was actually a recognized refuge for many of the tyrannized Jewish musicians fortunate enough to escape Nazi Europe.

From the days of the British Mandate, it was clearly understood that Palestine was the area designated, per Balfour, as a Jewish homeland. Many Arabs actually considered Palestine to be a Zionist invention. During the mandate, and in the years preceding the birth of Israel, Arabs in the area *never* considered themselves Palestinians and did not hesitate to vocalize their objection to such an association with Palestine. Consider the following from a resolution adopted at the First Congress of Muslim–Christian Associations during the process of choosing a Palestinian representative to the Paris Peace Conference (Jerusalem, 1919): "We consider Palestine as part of Arab-Syria, as it has never been separated from it at any time. We are connected to it by national, religious, linguistic, natural, economic, and geographical bonds."[13] Clearly, Arab leaders saw themselves as part of the Arab–Syrian culture, as opposed to a Zionist Palestine. Also consider these words: "There is no such country [as Palestine]! 'Palestine' is a term the Zionists invented!" declared Auni Bey Abdul-Hadi, local Arab leader addressing the Peel Commission in 1937.[14] Mr. Hadi was merely voicing his fellow Arabs' assessment of the artificial creation of a country called Palestine. Recognized Islamic scholars were vocal about putting distance between themselves and the entity known as Palestine. Professor Philip Hitti said in 1946, "There is no such thing as 'Palestine' in history, absolutely not."[15] Prior to 1967 then, Arabs did not consider themselves to be Palestinians.

Palestine would never have won a beauty contest. Before World War I, Arabs and Jews alike recognized Palestine (also known as Greater Syria) as the area located south of the Ottoman province of Mesopotamia. The region was poverty plagued and neglected. Palestine was an area within the Ottoman realm managed and heavily taxed by mostly absentee landlords who preferred life in Cairo, Damascus, or Beirut. The local peasant population, periodically plundered by Bedouin raiders on the one hand or threatened with prison by unscrupulous tax collectors on the other, was a transitory one; they often packed up and moved on to another area in the hope of finding better conditions. Mark Twain, the famous American wit, wrote about his travels to visit Palestine at the end of an extended European tour in 1867. Included in his

---

[13] Mitchell G. Bard, "Pre-State Israel: Jewish Claim to the Land of Israel." 1998. January, 2015.

[14] Ibid.,https://www.jewishvirtuallibrary.org/jsource/History/The_Jewish_Claim_To_The_Land_Of_Israel.html.

[15] David Bar-Illan. Article published November 1998 in *The Los Angeles Times*, as cited by "Israel My Beloved," http://israelmybeloved.com/was-there-ever-a-state-of-palestine/. As an added note: Professor Hitti, known to Americans as the father of Arabic Studies and certainly no fan of the creation of a Zionist state, was a distinguished professor of Semitic Literature and Languages in several colleges. At different times, he taught at both Princeton and Harvard.

humorous and insightful comments are the repeated observations of an empty and broken land. When describing the Jezreel Valley, for instance, he writes, "There is not a solitary village throughout its whole extent -- not for thirty miles in either direction. There are two or three small clusters of Bedouin tents, but not a single permanent habitation. One may ride ten miles hereabouts and not see ten human beings." Filling the pages for a full ten chapters, Twain laments his disillusionment with the Holy Land: "There is no timber of any consequence in Palestine."[16] He notes that the multi-ethnic population of Jerusalem, at a mere fourteen thousand souls, is "composed of Muslims, Jews, Greeks, Latins, Armenians, Syrians, Copts, Abyssinians, Greek Catholics, and a handful of Protestants." He goes on to conclude with the comment, "Jerusalem is mournful and dreary and lifeless. I would not desire to live here." He reported on crumbling, crooked, filthy streets, and on his shattered imaginative dreams of the land where the Savior walked, now forever vanished and "inhabited only by birds of prey and skulking foxes. Palestine is desolate and unlovely."[17]

It was to this undeveloped and lackluster land that the Jews of the Diaspora began to return in the mid-to-late nineteenth century.[18] In their ancient homeland, they hoped to find a safe haven from persecution and pogroms. Not surprisingly, absentee landlords were only too happy to unload property considered to be much less valuable than prime real estate. The new immigrants were idealistic and energetic, brimming with plans and new technologies for reviving the rocky soil. And it was not long before Arabs from

---

[16] Mark Twain, *The Innocents Abroad* (New York and Scarborough, Ontario: Signet Classic, 1966), 349.

[17] Ibid., 362–442.

[18] Mark Twain was not the only well-known personality to record firsthand accounts of a lackluster Palestine during this same time period. A decade earlier than Twain, Herman Melville, of *Moby Dick* celebrity, wrote of his agitation and profound disappointment relating to the conditions of the people and places in his *Clarel: A Poem and Pilgrimage in the Holy Land.*

the surrounding areas began to flock into a newly-generated job market, incidentally arriving with no sentimental or familial ties to the land itself. On the other hand, the Jewish connection could be traced back to Abraham.

Having lived under harsh and monotonous conditions in the practically feudal Ottoman Caliphate for centuries, Arab peasants eyed the first waves of the European *aliyah* with mixed emotions.[19] On one hand, jobs created as a result of Jewish agrarian and technical industry were cause for rejoicing; however, suspicion of modern European ways, coupled with a history of familial animosity that could be traced back to the Patriarchs, was bound to fuel tension. The first major modern wave of Jewish immigration took place throughout the last two decades of the 1800s. It was followed by a relatively small but steady influx of mostly eastern Europeans who put down their roots in collective agricultural communities known as *kibbutzim*.

Just as Abraham had scrupulously insured that the purchase of Sarah's gravesite was legally and publically recorded (Genesis 23), Jews who bought plots from the Arab landholders did the same. In early efforts meant to appeal to the existing residents by not uprooting them, Zionist leaders originally bought only the uncultivated land that was lying fallow and lacked existing tenants.[20] Swampland was frequently the most available and affordable, but Jews paid top price for the privilege of ownership. For the sake of comparison, at the same time as rich, black Iowa farmland was going for $110 per acre, the price of a similar acre of arid or semi-arid land in Palestine cost $1,000 to $1,100.[21]

---

[19] *Aliyah* (ah-lee-AH) is the Hebrew word used when referring to Jewish immigration to the land of Israel (Eretz Israel). When a Jew relocates to Israel, that person is said to have "made aliyah." The word literally means "to go up" and thus symbolizes spiritual elevation from out of the Diaspora.
[20] Bard, op. cit., 44.
[21] Ibid.. http://www.jewishvirtuallibrary.org/jsource/History/Arabs_in_Palestine.html.

Land purchases were transacted with prominent citizens, including the mayors of Gaza, Jerusalem, and Jaffa. Even King Abdullah of Transjordan was among the Arab leaders who leased land to the Jews. In the years between 1880 and 1948, studies show that "73 percent of Jewish plots were purchased from large landowners, not poor fellahin."[22] Far from being a wrenching of emotions, the transfer of Palestinian land to Jewish ownership was seen in Arab eyes as nothing more than a business deal— clear and simple.

Jews have had a continuous presence in the land since Abraham's sojourn. Although there were villages where Arabs and Jews had lived peacefully beside each other for centuries, there is no question that there were other Arabs who resented the Jews. It is a common misconception that the Jewish population was forced to completely abandon their homeland after the destruction of the second temple in 70 AD and their subsequent defeat by Hadrian in 135 AD. This is not the reality, however, as there had always remained a Jewish remnant in the land. In spite of the massacres of the Crusades inflicted upon the *resident* Jews, a steady migration back to their homeland had resulted in a Jewish population that was in excess of ten thousand by the early 1800s.[23]

By the mid–1800s, that number was continuing to increase. America's own Secretary of State William Seward visited the area in 1871. Traveling throughout Ottoman Palestine, he estimated a total population of two hundred thousand and kept a journal of his activities and impressions. After a visit to Jerusalem, he observed, "The Mohammedans are four thousand, and occupy the northeast quarter, including the whole area of the Mosque of Omar. The Jews

---

[22] Bard, Ibid.http://www.jewishvirtuallibrary.org/jsource/History/Arabs_in_ Palestine.html.
[23] Bard, *Myths and Facts*, 24. From the late Middle Ages, respected and well-known rabbis, along with their followers, were establishing flourishing communities throughout the Galilee, as well as in towns such as Safed and Jerusalem.

are eight thousand, and have the southeast quarter." Long before any "invasion" of European Jews, and prior to the first aliyahs, the Jewish population in Jerusalem was double that of the Muslim presence.[24]

With the dissolution of the League of Nations at the end of World War II, the area within the British Mandate became the legacy of the newly-formed United Nations. The years between the two world wars had seen the question of Palestine put before various committees and commissions, with the most notable being the Peel Commission of 1937. Without exception, the main debate in those meetings always concerned the unwillingness of the local Arab population to accept the establishment of a sovereign Jewish state. Although an Arab population might be willing to tolerate Jewish existence *within* the greater Arab world, the emergence of an autonomous Jewish state was proving to be another matter altogether.

The original Mandate for the Jewish homeland is divided into two areas: a homeland for Jews and a homeland for Arabs. In 1920, the World War I Allied powers met at San Remo to finalize agreements concerning former Ottoman territories. They were specifically focused on Syria, Mesopotamia, and Palestine. Along with other decisions, the delegates confirmed and incorporated Britain's 1917 Balfour Declaration, which had pledged the establishment in Palestine of a Jewish homeland. The mandate system allowed for a continued European administration of the territories until such time as they were judged capable of assuming authority for themselves. Once the Arab leadership realized that full and immediate Arab self-determination was not to be forthcoming in Syria and Mesopotamia (as had been the expected reward for their part in the late war), the idea of a Jewish state was always met with anger and rising instances of violence.

---

[24] Lenny Ben-David, *Lincoln's Secretary of State's Jerusalem Visit,* December 3, 2012. Israeldailypicture.com.
http://www.israeldailypicture.com/search?q=william+seward.

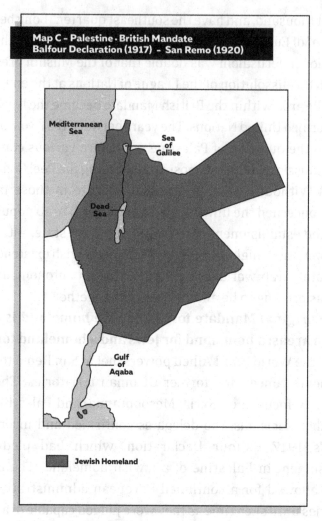

Palestine: British Mandate
Balfour Declaration (1917) at San Remo (1920)

During this same time, the British government was feverishly working behind the scenes to establish and maintain good working relationships with the various Muslim tribes in Arabia, Palestine, and Mesopotamia. Walking a diplomatic tightrope, as well as facing a war-weary public at home, His Majesty's government was dealing also with the potential for new wars against several nations at once:

the Soviets, the Turks, and the Irish. In short, Great Britain was in a desperate political and diplomatic situation, with something needing to be done and done quickly.

During a meeting in Cairo in March 1921, a large chunk was taken out of the area known as Palestine. Present at this meeting was the colonial secretary, Winston Churchill. Churchill's aim of course was to reduce Britain's problems as cheaply and as quickly as possible.[25] With British national considerations in mind, and in an effort to appease the different Arab factions, the original plot of land appropriated for a Jewish homeland was now partitioned between the Jews *and* the Arabs. This division altered the original mandate by giving the larger, carved-out section to Abdullah, a member of the ruling dynasty from Mecca. He was soon installed on the throne as 77 percent of Palestine became the new Arab emirate of Transjordan. The mandated area of Mesopotamia was presented to Abdullah's younger brother, Faisal. The distribution of land between the rival Hashemite and Saudi tribes had required the greatest of diplomatic finesse.

---

[25] Christopher Catherwood, *Churchill's Folly* (New York: Carroll & Graf Publishers, 2004), 102.

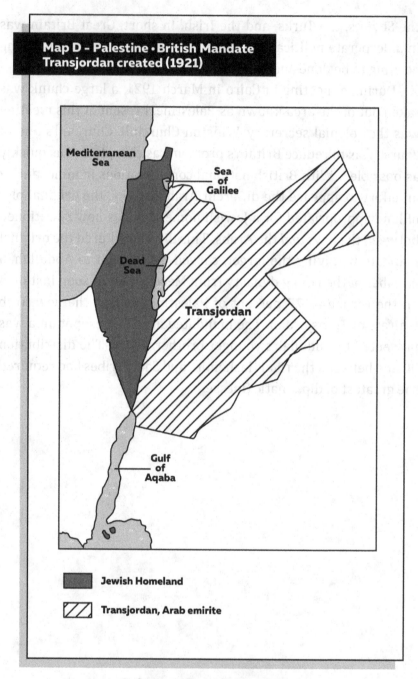

Palestine: British Mandate
Transjordan Created (1921)

Within four years of issuing the Balfour Declaration in 1917, the British government found itself presiding over the division of the proposed Jewish homeland. As a result, the Arab emirate of Transjordan occupied 77 percent of the original mandate, leaving the Jews with 23 percent of the initially earmarked territory. The Jewish homeland had been reduced by nearly four-fifths. Further, it was ruled that Jews would no longer be allowed to settle in areas of mandated Palestine located east of the Jordan River. For the Arab population, however, continued settlement anywhere in mandated Palestine remained legal, including areas both east and west of the Jordan River. The net result of this British policy meant that Arab Palestine (Transjordan) was open to Arabs only, whereas Jewish Palestine remained open to both Jews *and* Arabs.[26] In spite of these accommodations, Arab leaders persistently protested the possibility of a Zionist state, and riots erupted. As a result, the festering hostilities culminated in what came to be known as the 1936 Arab Revolt and perpetuated a three-year period of continued violence from 1936 to1939.

Palestine is divided *again* into two areas: a Jewish state and another Arab state. By the 1930s, Great Britain was finding the political and military responsibility for the area to be untenable, especially as war with Germany loomed on the horizon. It was this impending war cloud that made Middle Eastern oil a particularly vital commodity. Britain was caught on the horns of an awkward dilemma as Arab goodwill easily became more important than the previous government's commitment to the Zionist dream of a Jewish homeland. The 1937 Peel Commission began an inquiry and investigation into the situation. As might have been expected, this Royal Commission on Palestine eventually established that Britain was no longer able to maintain fully its commitments to either Arabs or Jews and that the situation between the latter

[26] Norma Parrish Archbold, *The Mountains of Israel* (Israel and USA: Phoebe's Song), 70.

two was irreconcilable. Its recommendation was that Palestine be partitioned yet once again into two states—one for Jews and one for Arabs. In 1939, the infamous British White Paper was issued, which, among other things, attempted to appease the Arab community by severely limiting Jewish immigration into Palestine. Despite the fact that both British efforts (in 1937 and 1939) called for the establishment of a Jewish *and* Arab state within Palestine, Arab leadership consistently refused to negotiate.[27]

November 29, 1947. As the world drew a collective sigh of relief that the Second World War had come to an end, situations that previously had been put on the international back burner were finally able to be addressed. One such matter was the Palestine problem. The economically sapped, battle-weary British were eager to turn their administrative woes in Palestine over to the newly formed United Nations. Following a subsequent study by the United Nations Special Commission on Palestine, it came as no surprise that the recommendation was for Palestine to be divided once again. The remaining 23 percent of the Balfour Declaration would be split into two separate states: one for Arabs and one for Jews. Accordingly, the question for this partition was brought to a vote before the UN General Assembly on November 29, 1947. In spite of most predictions, the assembled delegates voted to approve a partition plan that is known today as UN Resolution 181.[28] The plan would allow Palestine to be divided again between Jews and Arabs.

Neither of the two parties directly affected by the vote was satisfied with the conditions of the land division. The Jews were worried about being able to maintain a Jewish population majority within their territory allotment. They were also nervous about the realization that Jewish areas were essentially cut off from

---

[27] Bard, *Myths and Facts,* 57.
[28] For the resolution to pass, a two-thirds majority was required. The UN's fifty-six member states (as of November 1947) voted 33 to 13 in favor of partition. There were ten abstentions.

each other, according to the Partition's crazy quilt map. Another challenge was that the majority of Jewish land was located in the Negev Desert. Tremendous concern was especially centered on the hundred thousand Jewish residents of Jerusalem. The map had left Jerusalem's Jewish residents essentially isolated and surrounded by an Arab controlled jurisdiction and consigned to administration under an international trusteeship.[29]

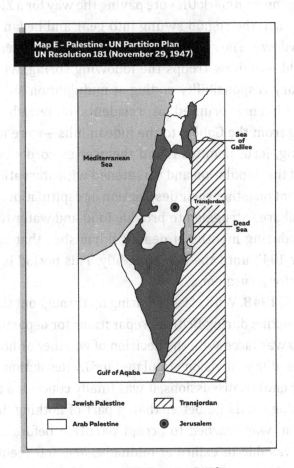

Palestine: UN Partition Plan
UN Resolution 181 (November 29, 1947)

---

[29] Chaim Herzog, *The Arab-Israeli Wars* (New York: Vintage Books, A Division of Random House, Inc., 1982), 17.

Ever faithful to a steadily consistent pattern of non-negotiation, Arab leadership claimed the land assignments were unfair and immediately instigated riots resulting in thousands of lives (Jewish, Arab, and British) lost. In this matter, the UN laid responsibility for the violence directly at the feet of the Arabs.[30]

Within a short time, the relative calm that had characterized the area from 1939 through the war years became a thing of the past. Once the landmark UN vote paving the way for a Zionist state had been cast, the region swung into gear and began preparing for a showdown. The relieved and beleaguered British announced they would withdraw troops the following spring, with all legal and military responsibility ending at midnight on May 14, 1948. Sporadic violence erupted as residents of Jewish villages—stretching from the Galilee to the Judean hills—were massacred. Before long, Jerusalemites found themselves cordoned off from the rest of the population and threatened with starvation by Arab forces intent on either their destruction or capitulation. Jews from the coastal area struggled to provide food and water to the city's residents during months of deadly skirmishes that raged from December 1947 until the following July. This period is known as the Battle for Jerusalem.

May 14, 1948. With clashes flaring up throughout the whole of Jewish Palestine during British preparations for departure, Jewish leadership was faced with the decision of whether or not to accept the proposed land division stipulated in UN Resolution 181. After seemingly endless discussions, it was finally concluded that a part of something would be better than a part of nothing. In Tel Aviv, a resolution was reached to accept partition before the British Mandate was due to expire at midnight, May fourteenth. On the afternoon of May 14, 1948, merely hours before the deadline, David Ben-Gurion, leader of both the World Zionist Organization and the

---

[30] Bard, *Myths and Facts,* P. 62 and 63.

Jewish Agency for Palestine, announced the establishment of the State of Israel.[31]

Within hours of Ben-Gurion's declaration, the surrounding nations of Egypt, Lebanon, Syria, Iraq, and Transjordan declared *jihad* (holy war) and invaded the baby nation. When the anticipated victory was not forthcoming, Arab leaders appealed to the UN. The fighting finally ended with the signing of an armistice agreement in July 1949. By then, however, the fledgling Jewish nation had fought back against astounding odds to increase the original partition plan's allotment by nearly 50 percent.

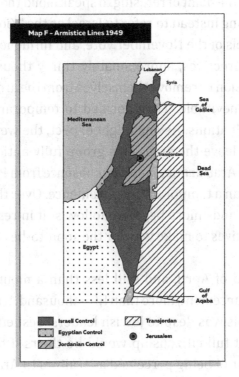

Armistice Lines 1949

---

[31] For an absorbing, firsthand account of the situation created by the 1947 UN vote, read about one family's true-life experiences in Jerusalem during the final months of the mandate. See Stephen Mansfield's *Derek Prince A Biography* (Lake Mary, Florida: Charisma House, 2005), chapter 7, "Eretz Israel: Present at the Creation," 147–167.

The refugees. Meanwhile, during the six months between the time that the UN voted on partition (November 1947) until the declaration of the establishment of the state of Israel (May 1948), Arab residents living within what had been the western part of mandated Palestine (the area on the west side of the Jordan River across from the newly-created Transjordan) were faced with the dilemma of deciding what to do and where to live. Because Arab leadership was adamantly opposed to the UN's decision regarding partition, resident Arabs were caught in the middle between a newly-recognized nation and their own leaders. And this leadership was recalcitrant to the point of refusing to speak aloud the Jewish nation's name, preferring instead to refer to Israel as the "Zionist entity."

On the heels of the November vote, and influenced by the Arab leadership's directives, approximately thirty thousand residents made the decision to remove themselves from the arena of a conflict that seemed inevitable. They decided to temporarily relocate to adjacent Arab nations. As one might expect, the wealthy were the first group to leave the area. This group fully anticipated a swift victory for the Arab armies, and their absence from Palestine would be no more than a temporary inconvenience. Over the next several months, thousands more began to follow suit in response to their leaders' directives to make way for the soon-to-be advancing Arab armies.[32]

By the end of April, and still less than a month before Ben-Gurion's announcement, more than fifty thousand Arabs had left the Haifa area. This was despite Jewish leaders' best efforts to assure the Arabs that full citizenship would be theirs if they remained. In the end, fear of being perceived as traitors to Arab nationalism caused them to turn down the offer.[33] Even though citizenship,

---

[32] Mitchell G. Bard, Mitchell G. Bard, PhD, *The Complete Idiot's Guide to Middle East Conflict* (Alpha Books, A Pearson Education Company, 1999), 174.

[33] Ibid., 176. It turns out that David Ben-Gurion actually sent Golda Meir as his personal representative to speak to the Haifa Arab community. Her best

along with all rights for participation and representation, was offered by Israel's formal Proclamation of Independence to those choosing to remain, the Arab exodus steadily grew by the tens of thousands.

The little nation of Israel desperately fought for its life as Arab armies closed in for what had been an expected and easy kill. Israel's defeat was not to be, however, and within months, the inexperienced Israeli forces were not only holding ground but also taking new territory. By the time the final armistice agreements were being signed in 1949, an estimated 550,000 Arabs had fled into the neighboring territories at the urging of their leaders. An exact population tally has never been fully agreed upon.[34] What *is* certain, however, is that 160,000 Arabs decided to throw their future in with that of the Jewish state. Choosing to remain in their homes, they put the fidelity of the new Zionist government to an ultimate reality test. Today, their descendants, Arab-Israelis, number over a million and share the full citizenship rights enjoyed by all other Israelis.

The invisible refugees. During this same period of time, another group of people was also displaced. Although this group is less well known than the Palestinians, their numbers were greater. These other refugees were the Jewish refugees, and their numbers represent the Jews living throughout the Middle East.

---

efforts to convince them to stay on were never accepted, however, and this can be primarily chalked up to their fear of being targeted as traitors, should they choose to remain as members of the "Zionist entity."

[34] Author and researcher par excellence, Joan Peters, notes figures varying between 430,000 and 650,000, due to differing census numbers and record keeping practices of the several governments and world agencies involved. Mitchell Bard cites varying figures for the Arab population as high as one million, as opposed to 472,000 from a UN mediator on Palestine. As there is no way of providing an absolutely concrete number, I have chosen 550,000 as the likely figure, as it seems to be within the range most favored by most authorities. For a further (and intensely detailed) study, I would recommend the work of Joan Peters, *From Time Immemorial: The Origins of the Arab-Jewish Conflict Over Palestine.*

Prior to the UN vote for partition, Jews had been living throughout the entire Arab region, and the existence of these communities easily predated the rise of Islam. Nevertheless, with the birth of a sovereign Jewish state, Arab nationalism boiled over, catching local Jews in the middle. Many were divested of their citizenship, their homes and property confiscated, while others left under the threat of death. Throughout the Middle East, from the countries of Morocco, Algeria, Tunisia, Libya, Egypt, Lebanon, Syria, Iraq and Yemen, eight hundred fifty thousand Jews became refugees after having been displaced abruptly from their homes.[35] The majority, approximately six hundred thousand, immigrated to Israel. The remainder was absorbed into other nations and became first-generation citizens of their new countries.

How is it then that the end-result for these two refugee groups is so strikingly different? Why are the Jewish refugees and their descendants now citizens of their own country (or countries), whereas the Arab refugees and their descendants are still refugees?

Population exchange. A better understanding of the refugee situation is to be had with a review of the geopolitical events that were taking place elsewhere in the world leading up to Israel's independence. The years between World War I and the birth of Israel in 1948 were a period of especially intense ethnic and religious conflict. As governments struggled to find solutions to myriad problems, one remedy emerged to become known as the population exchange. A prime example of this approach is the human exchange that took place between Turkey and Greece in 1923. After the defeat of the Ottoman Empire and the emergence of a modern Turkey, the Turkish and Greek governments devised a population swap to prevent further bloodshed. Basing the switch primarily on religious practice, it was agreed that the million-plus Orthodox Greeks living in Turkey should be compelled to immigrate

---

[35] Joan Peters, as cited by Frolander, K.J. in *Israel Basics* (United States of America, 2011), 132–134.

to Greece. Likewise, the approximately five hundred thousand Muslims living in Greece were to immigrate to Turkey.

A scant two decades later, in 1947, another and even larger exchange took place between India and Pakistan. At that time, British Viceroy Lord Mountbatten was grappling with the logistics of partitioning India, the English colony also known as the "Jewel in the Crown." As the attempt was made to stave off bloodshed between the two major religious groups, it was finally determined that more than seven million Muslims would evacuate India and relocate to Pakistan. Simultaneously, seven million Hindus and Sikhs would leave their homes in Pakistan and immigrate to India. In 1947, between fourteen and fifteen million people took part in this epic population exchange.

It is perhaps easier to understand the construction of the modern Middle East if one keeps in mind that it was within this standard context of diplomatic thought that boundaries for the newly emerging Jewish and Arab nations were being created. In other words, the major powers were accustomed to using very broad strokes to create a canvas to their own liking and advantage.

Refugees begetting refugees. Unlike the Jewish refugees who were welcomed and absorbed into the Jewish state, Arab refugees were left out in the cold by their brother nations. Having been told that they'd be able to return to their homes and share in the spoils of an Arab military victory, they now found themselves caught in a snare with no place to go. Israel was no longer open to them, and the surrounding Arab nations refused to allow the newly-displaced people to resettle within their boundaries.[36] Furthermore, special

---

[36] Maoz Newsletter, September, 2013. Calev Meyers, founder of Jerusalem Institute of Justice (www.jij.org.il), writes: "When these Arabs left in 1948, they went to Lebanon, Jordan, Syria, Egypt, and other countries throughout the Middle East. In 1959 the Arab League made a decision that *no Arab State in the Middle East would grant citizenship to Palestinian refugees.* This is regardless of the fact that the Palestinians are Arabs who speak the same language and have the same culture as citizens of the Arab League. And regardless of the

laws were specifically created to discriminate against them. For instance, certain professions were off-limits in the job sector; land ownership was restricted, and health and educational services were not provided. With the exception of Jordan, citizenship was also denied. With this being the case, the refugees lived in temporary camps located within the nations to which they had fled. Today, the camps are located in Lebanon, Syria, Jordan, Gaza, and the so-called West Bank.[37]

Historically, a refugee has been defined as a person involuntarily uprooted and forced to evacuate his home due to war or imminent danger because of his or her religious or political views. Since World War II, the United Nations High Commissioner for Refugees (UNHCR) has assisted millions of refugees to negotiate the relocation process. Whereas it is generally understood that a refugee is one who has been forced to flee from his or her traditional homeland, the UN has made a lone exception to this in the case of the Palestinians. At the end of 1949, the UN created a second refugee agency known as the United Nations Relief and Works Agency (UNRWA). Unlike the UNHCR, which had been responsible for refugees worldwide, this agency's sole task was designed to provide for only one demographic: the Arab Palestinians. Notably, a special stipulation as to refugee status was also added for the group now covered by the UNRWA umbrella. Palestinian refugee status was to be granted to anyone able to prove residency for two years prior to Israel's statehood.[38] The implication of course is that so many of the Arab refugees had recently relocated to Palestine's job market from surrounding Arab territories and that they would not qualify otherwise as having been driven from their *traditional* homeland.

fact that the vast majority is also Muslim." http://www.maozisrael.org/site/News2?page=NewsArticle&id=9990 - top.

[37] Danny Ayalon, *The Truth About the Refugees* (video), Rogatka Ltd. United With Israel, http://unitedwithisrael.org/the-refugees/.

[38] Joan Peters, *From Time Immemorial: The Origins of the Arab-Jewish Conflict Over Palestine* (Chicago, IL: JKAP Publications, 1984), 4.

Therefore, the two-year clause became a necessary addition in order to define this particular class of refugee as disenfranchised.

A major difference between refugees assisted by UNHCR and those by UNRWA is the stark contrast in budget and personnel. UNRWA has thirty times more staff than UNHCR, and it also spends nearly three times the amount of money per individual refugee. Another glaring difference is the projected end result. The goal of UNHCR is to bring about resettlement of refugees, whereas the result of UNRWA has been the perpetuation of a refugee people from generation to generation. Whether or not this is the stated goal, the bottom line has been the creation of a sustained refugee status for three generations of people due to a series of unique standards:

- "Refugees lose their status after receiving citizenship from a recognized country; Palestinian refugees do not.
- Refugees cannot transmit their status from generation to generation; Palestinian refugees can.
- Refugees are encouraged to settle in other countries or integrate in their host countries; UNRWA avoids such policies."[39]

This then is the answer to the mystery of 550,000 people becoming five million. After nearly seventy years, three full generations have multiplied in the way of all humanity. In this instance, however, the generations have retained a permanently inherited refugee status gene.[40]

---

[39] Ayalon, op.cit., (video). In addition to the facts cited, the video also includes an oft-mentioned and particularly illuminating quote from Sir Alexander Galloway, who was himself a former UN director of the UN refugee agency in Jordan. He said, "Arab nations do not want to solve the refugee problem. They want to keep it as an open sore ... as a weapon against Israel."

[40] Breaking the "refugee gene" facts down into an everyday situation is the following excerpt from an article printed in the Maoz Newsletter from

When contrasting the personal fortunes of the Palestinian leadership to the disconsolate masses inside the camps, also considering the immense petrol wealth of surrounding Arab nations, it becomes increasingly evident that the refugees have become pawns to their own Arab brothers.[41] Shortly after the 1967 Arab–Israeli War, also known as the Six-Day War, Arab leadership began to refer to the refugees as Palestinians, and Yassar Arafat became their acknowledged chairman. World media soon jumped onboard, and the Arab refugees were reborn as the "Palestinian People." It would appear that Chairman Arafat discovered that this new moniker gave added credibility to a battle that might better be waged in the courts of public opinion than in the field. And to an otherwise uninformed public, this has often proven to be the case. Unaware of what has actually transpired behind closed doors, the natural inclination to root for a perceived underdog has led many to mistakenly conclude that Israel's existence is the actual cause of the problem in the region.

In spite of the fact that the Arab nations control 99.9 percent of the land in the Middle East, it remains a mystery that no space has ever been brought forth to accommodate the people known as

---

September, 2013: Taken from a speech given at the University of Helsinki by Calav Meyers, founder of Jerusalem Institute of Justice (http://www.jij.org.il), Mr. Myers writes, "If, for instance, a Palestinian refugee family left Israel in 1948, and settled in Syria, and maybe the grandson of these refugees got a visa to study at the University of Helsinki. Let's say that he did well in his studies, and while he was studying, he met a beautiful Finnish girl and married her. After his studies he started a business in Finland, and executed a successful corporate exit. Now we have a multi-millionaire Finnish citizen that has been a success in a society. That person would still be recognized as a Palestinian refugee eligible for UNRWA support under the international law." For amounts and origins of UNRWA monetary funding, see the complete article at http://www.maozisrael. org/site/News2?page=NewsArticle&id=9990 - top.

[41] Tricia McDermott, *Arafat's Billions, 60 Minutes,* November 7, 2003. According to CBS correspondent, Tricia McDermott, "Yassar Arafat diverted nearly $1 billion in public funds to insure his political survival," and "All told, U.S. officials estimate Arafat's personal nest egg at between $1 billion and $3 billion." http://www.cbsnews.com/news/arafats-billions/.

Palestinians. Sadly, there has been "no room at the inn" among their own Arab brethren. And incredulously, it is only the Israelis who continue to be maneuvered and coerced into negotiating from what remains of their leftover and much-parceled smidgeon delegated by the original Balfour Declaration. This is especially peculiar in light of that other mass of humanity also reduced to refugee status as a result of the 1947 UN vote; namely, the Jews, who were resident in Arab lands prior to that time. A well-known Arab-American journalist, Joseph Farah, suggests that although "Israel represents one-tenth of one percent of the landmass ... that's too much for the Arabs. They want it all. And that is ultimately what the fighting in Israel is about today ... No matter how many land concessions the Israelis make, it will never be enough."[42]

Israel's enemies. Chapter 5 highlighted Psalm 83, with its prophetic warning against a confederation that would lay schemes against Israel. The nations mentioned in that psalm are in fact the very Arab nations that today conspire to terrorize and obliterate the Jewish nation and support the notion, "Throw the Jews into the sea!"[43] As a result, they are placing themselves on the receiving end of retribution from the one who has sworn to guard and defend Israel as the apple of His eye.

The consequences for mistreatment of Israel and lust for its land are grave. Scripture is never vague as to the severe consequences that will befall all who take part in it. Look at Joel 3:1–2 NIV, and notice that the nations involving themselves with dividing Israel's land will be taken to task. "In those days and at that time, when I

---

[42] Joseph Farah, "Myths of the Middle East", WorldNetDaily.Com, October 11, 2000. Mr. Farah is the editor and CEO of WorldNewsDaily, an independent news network. http://www.wnd.com.

[43] Larry Collins and Dominique Lapierre, *O Jerusalem!* 1972. (New York, London, Toronto, Sydney: A Touchstone Book, Simon & Schuster, 1988), 74. First attributed to the Palestine police inspector, Kamal Irekat, in the days leading up to Israel's statehood, this familiar rallying cry has been associated with many Arab leaders in the years since.

restore the fortunes of Judah and Jerusalem, I will gather all nations and bring them down to the Valley of Jehoshaphat. There I will put them on trial for what they did to my inheritance, my people Israel, because they scattered my people among the nations and divided up my land."

The believer's bottom line. Although not related by any physical DNA, both Philistines and, more recently, the Palestinians have shared the same characteristic of targeting Israel's land for themselves. The former have been blotted from the pages of history, and despite legitimate grievances, the nearly five million people known as *Palestinians* since 1967 have placed themselves in opposition to the divine will as they persist with an agenda to possess Israel's God-given land. The situation in the Middle East, as it pertains to the Palestinian–Israeli conflict, is beyond complicated, yet the essential facts and tools for a solution can be found in one source. Christians, as people of the book, must be willing to search out and then share the hard truths found in the Bible's pages concerning this dilemma. It is not a cliché to recognize that God's planned destiny for Arabs and Jews is delineated only in this one source. Any alternative must eventually fail because all other avenues for remedy or diplomatic negotiation (no matter how nobly conceived) invariably default to the current situational ethic. The Bible's sure testimony will always be the final truth.

Chapter 6 Study Guide

1. Genesis 11 and 12 refer to the land of Israel as _____.
2. After Joshua's conquest, the land is always known as _____.
3. The Jewish Israelis of today are descendants of the ancient Jewish Hebrews (T or F) _____
4. Today's Palestinians are descendants of the ancient Philistines (T or F) _____
5. The Philistines originated from _____.
6. The Palestinian peoples originated from these countries _____
   _____.
7. Displaced Arabs began to refer to themselves as "Palestinians" in what year? _____
8. Palestinians speak what language? _____
9. Religion of the vast majority of Palestinians _____.
10. Until 1950, *The Jerusalem Post* was known as _____

Chapter 7

Moed

Chapter 6 Recap: The 1920s' boundaries for the newly-created states established in the wake of the Ottoman Empire's breakup have resulted in more than one international crisis. The ongoing Palestinian–Israeli dilemma is one of these. Here, two very separate peoples contend for the same piece of real estate. The situation is fraught with conflicting versions, understanding, and interpretation of formal agreements and regional history. Adding to the confusion, the main players, and even the actual geography of the place itself, have undergone an identity makeover as their very names have been changed during the past two thousand years. Israel became Palestine, populated by Jew and Arab alike. After 1948, however, Jews were known as Israelis, and, more recently, Arabs have become the ones known as Palestinians. UN sanctions, diplomatic overtures. and wars have not been able to solve the region's problems. Students of the Bible recognize that the situation and circumstances are more than simply political; they are also spiritual in nature. The complication exists because the land in question just happens to belong to the covenant partner and guardian of Israel.

God is never blindsided. Untouched by the limitations of time and space, God lives in eternity, and His existence is without beginning or end. He is also immortal, omniscient, and omnipotent. He is all of these things, and nothing ever takes Him by surprise. According to Ephesians 1:4, He was not blindsided or shocked by Adam's fall. In fact, He already had a plan in place. As this is the case and because He so loved the world, He chose to redeem humanity in the most remarkable way. By coming into the earth as the man, Jesus, God Himself entered the dimension of time.

God's multipurpose sacred calendar. It also appears that He decided to interpose a part of Himself parenthetically into the confines of a repeating, earthly annual cycle. In other words, the great, timeless, and eternal Creator chose to reveal Himself within the limitations of an earthly calendar. It is a calendar of His own inimitable design and unrivaled by any other, for this incomparable calendar happens also to be a remarkable blueprint. In truth, it is additionally a roadmap, with guideposts along the way, marking the route toward redemption for the sons of Adam. Such unique markers are to be found in only one place, and that is in the ancient Hebrew calendar. Having been clearly set into position within the rotation of the changing seasons, signposts have been lovingly provided by a heavenly Father who knows the beginning from the end even before there was a beginning. And what better way to insure the transfer of truths from one generation to the next than from within a framework of annual repetitions?

Embedded within a yearly cycle of celebrations and anniversaries, the heavenly Father has continued to impart truth to His children. If earthly parents are aware of the need for constant repetition while training their offspring, it should come as no surprise that Father God has been aware of this principle all along.

Although the Hebrew calendar was introduced in Leviticus 23, in many instances, it tends to remain an obscure detail to the majority of the Christian world. In spite of the fact that many who have participated in programs for reading through the Bible have looked at that particular chapter, the introduction of a *living* calendar is perhaps a new concept. And, upon further inspection, this calendar– (also known as the Jewish calendar or sacred calendar) turns out to be far more than it might appear at first glance. It soon becomes evident that kingdom truths have been hidden therein and are only waiting to be discovered. Because it was originated and approved by God Himself, it is the one and only calendar to be found within all human history that serves as both a blueprint *and* roadmap.

Origins of the present Gregorian calendar. If the sacred calendar is the one given by God Himself, how then did today's calendar come to exist? This is a good question, and it turns out that the answer isn't as complicated as one might think. The present Gregorian calendar has evolved from centuries of mathematical tweaking. The ancient Romans used a solar calendar based on a year composed of 365 days. This is roughly the number of days required for the earth to orbit the sun. During the time of Julius Caesar, the Roman calendar was reorganized to reflect a more precise 364.25 days. The necessary adjustment was accomplished by simply adding an extra day every four years to the month of February. Recognize this origin of leap year? Caesar's calendar became the Church's official calendar after its adoption by the Council of Nicaea in 325 AD. Later, however, it was determined that the earth's trip around the sun was actually taking eleven minutes longer than had been previously calculated. Although eleven minutes is seemingly a small increment, by 1572, this difference of eleven minutes was responsible for an additional ten days. So in that same year, Pope Gregory XIII decided to correct the inaccuracies once and for all, and the majority of the Christian world still continues to determine the dates of holidays and anniversaries on the basis of that adjustment. His solar calendar is known as the Gregorian calendar.[1]

---

[1] Pope Gregory's astronomers accomplished the calendar change by simply deleting the extra days. The ten days were removed from the 1582 calendar so that the spring equinox would continue to fall on March twenty-first. The rest

The Jewish year, on the other hand, is regulated according to a lunar calendar. This is the calendar first given to man by God, as described in Leviticus 23. And because it was given by God, Jews continue to follow it, as dictated by the original pattern of the ancient months in their seasons. This lunar calendar determines the length of a month by the amount of time (29.5 days) it takes for the moon to orbit the earth. Remembering that a solar calendar is based on the time (365.25 days) it takes the earth to orbit the sun, one can easily see that these two calendars will not always dovetail. Because the methods for gauging time are dissimilar, the resulting dates for observing holidays and anniversaries often do not coincide. Sadly, it is these very differences for calculating the celebration of the sacred holidays that have contributed to so much of the unnecessary confusion and division between Christians and Jews over the centuries. The following chapter addresses some of these discrepancies, and it is hoped that clarity will be the result. It is also hoped that one will discover that God's intention all along was for His calendar to provide a divine blueprint for His people, both Jew and Gentile. Who knew?

Solar calendar vs. lunar calendar results in division. Man's earliest calendars were lunar and based on the lunar cycle of earth's moon. The establishment of a solar calendar, which came to be followed by the early Church, also set in motion a series of conflicting dates that still affects an understanding of scripture. That understanding (or more accurately *mis*understanding) is the reason this piece of history is important. Because they were Jewish, the earliest Christians had naturally followed the traditional lunar calendar. With the passage of time, and because they lived within the structure of a dominate Roman Empire, they began to adopt

---

of Europe slowly began to embrace this calendar, with some countries accepting it as late as the twentieth century (post revolution Russia in 1918 and Greece in 1923). It should be noted that many Orthodox churches still adhere to the earlier Julian calendar.

that empire's solar calendar. At first glance, this would seem to be a small thing, but as the two calendars' conflicting dates began to clash, a schism also developed that would eventually divide the Old Testament from the New Testament. This came about partly because the solar and lunar calendars began and ended at different intervals. Understandably, the differences resulted in discrepancies concerning the celebration of the Church festivals, and an inevitable division developed over time.

Because the observation of festivals, feasts, and anniversaries depended on an accurate dating system, the simultaneous use of *two* calendars eventually separated those who followed the solar calendar from those who continued to follow the lunar calendar. What should have been a seamless progression from the messianic prophecies contained within the Hebrew calendar to their fulfillment in Jesus became instead muddled and confusing. With an increasingly Gentile makeup of Christendom growing within the Roman Empire, many no longer related to the original lunar calendar, which eventually came to be associated only with the Jews. After the Roman Emperor Constantine's conversion and his subsequent patronage of the Church, the Roman solar calendar began to represent the Christian world, and the lunar calendar of Leviticus 23 was relegated to the Jewish world.

Let's not focus on division anymore. Let's move instead to the heartbeat of God's sacred calendar and the introduction of a wonderful Hebrew word, *moed*. The rich significance of this word provides a key to understanding and appreciating God's infinite ability to conceive and execute His magnificent plans.

Moed. When translated, the Hebrew word *moed* is used to indicate a fixed time or a fixed season. It is translated as "an appointed or ordained time." In other words, one could say that moed indicates a specifically predestined splice of time. A moed is a date or season or period that has been appointed beforehand. Additionally, it is of significance to recognize that moed is also translated as a sign or a signal.[2] When this word is used in scripture, it is the indication that a specially designated and predetermined event in cosmic time is being announced or introduced. Thus moed is the word that indicates divinely-appointed signs or events in time, and the word is also to be found when referring to a predetermined assembly or festival. "Then God said, 'Let there be lights in the expanse of the heavens to separate the day from the night, and let them be for signs and for seasons and for days and years'" (Genesis 1:14 NASB).

The word that is translated from the previous verse as *seasons* is the word *moedim,* which is the plural form of moed. This is the Bible's first mention of moed. Employing a principle known as the "Law of First Mention," scholars often trace a word or doctrine to its initial appearance in scripture in an effort to recognize patterns or comprehensive definition. Put another way, the inherent meaning of a word or doctrine often can be enhanced by studying the first time it is referenced. A word's first usage will often shed light and give clues to any subsequent occurrence. Using this concept, moed's first appearance in Genesis 1:14 is foundational because the verse explains that the purpose of the moon, sun, and stars is to point toward ordained seasons. That means that the objective given for the heavenly lights predates any established calendar while, at the same time, alluding to the appointed seasons yet to be introduced. Although the ordained festivals were as yet unidentified, God had already predetermined their appearance upon the horizon.

The fact that moed appears for the first time in the first chapter of the first book of the Bible is also noteworthy. The first chapter of Genesis describes the earliest glimpses into the deep past of creation. The lights are formed and their purpose decreed. Then man is created. Later, after God had made a covenant with a select

---

[2] James Strong, *Strong's Exhaustive Concordance of the Bible.* (Iowa Falls, Iowa: World Bible Publishers, Inc., 1986), 1201 (Strong's 4150).

branch of humanity, a whisper of the intention of His heart is heard in the cosmos as the sacred calendar is introduced. For hidden within its appointed seasons is the mystery of the coming Messiah. The calendar, as first revealed in Leviticus 23, is a virtual treasure trove of secret codes containing the marvelous plan of redemption. Remarkably, it is the calendar still used by Abraham's descendants.

The Jewish calendar is distinctly different from all other calendars. Today's secular calendars illustrate the differences between a Jewish and Gentile approach to marking time. Major contrasts are immediately evident. Consider the Gregorian calendar; it is accepted by most of the world's two billion-plus Christians and is the most widely used calendar on earth today. The first dissimilarities are obvious, as most of the days and months of this calendar are named in honor of the Greek and Roman pantheon of gods. As an example, January is named for Janus, the god of beginnings. Likewise, June is named for Juno, the wife and sister of Jupiter; March is named for Mars, the Roman god of war, and so on. As with the months, the days of the week are also similarly named to honor various deities: Monday is the day of the moon, and Saturday is the day of Saturn.

The people of the Bible, however, used a different method to track time. They used the Hebrew names and numbers for days, months, and years and followed a very different calendar than those used by the surrounding cultures. Even the Hebrew concept of a day is unique.

The Hebrew day. The difference between a Jewish and Gentile approach to something as simple as the definition of a day is found in the first pages of Genesis. To Jewish thinking, since it was God who originally created day and the *idea* of day, it would naturally follow that God is to be accorded the honor of assigning the day's title or name. The Bible records that He did indeed give names to the days:

1. *Yom Rishon* is the first day.   (Genesis 1:5)
2. *Yom Sheni* is the second day.   (Genesis 1:8)
3. *Yom Shlishi* is the third day.   (Genesis 1:13)
4. *Yom R'vi'i* is the fourth day.   (Genesis 1:19)
5. *Yom Chamishi* is the fifth day.   (Genesis 1:23)
6. *Yom Shishi* is the sixth day.   (Genesis 1:31)

The days of the week are named according to their numerical order. Since *yom* is the Hebrew word for day and *rishon* is the Hebrew word for first, Yom Rishon is first day. *Sheni* is Hebrew for second, followed by *Shlishi, R'vi'i, Chamishi* and *Shishi*. By adhering to the biblical precedent, the only day of the week to be given a name instead of a number is *Shabbat*.

7. *Shabbat* is the seventh day.   (Genesis 2:1-3)

It's written that God set apart the last of these seven days to be a day of rest, and He named this day Shabbat. The observance of this day is important enough to Him that it is included as the fourth commandment. After looking at the spelling of the two words, it is easy to see how "Sabbath" comes from the Hebrew word *Shabbat*. In modern Israel, the Sabbath greeting is always, "Shabbat Shalom!" Translation: May you have a peaceful Sabbath![3]

Also unique to Hebrew thought is the concept of each day's beginning and ending. Using the Gregorian calendar, every new day has its beginning at midnight or 12:00 a.m. This is the way time was calculated with the development of the Roman sundial, but that way of counting is predated by another—God's reckoning

---

[3] It is important to recognize that the institution of the Shabbat (Sabbath) was the *first* of the moedim to be established by the Lord in this calendar (Leviticus 23:1-3). Because this chapter focuses on the yearly moedim instead of the weekly moed, I have not chosen to go into the details concerning the weekly Sabbath.

of day and night. Look at Genesis 1:5. "God called the light Day, and the darkness he called Night. And there was evening and there was morning, the first day." Now look at Genesis 1:8. "And God called the expanse Heaven. And there was evening and there was morning, the second day." Continuing through to the end of the creation account, evening always precedes the morning, and this is why all Hebrew calendars mark each day as beginning during twilight of the prior evening. God begins the first part of each day on the previous evening.

The Hebrew month. God also created the idea of "month." Just as He had done earlier with the days, He also addresses the months by number. Notice the wording of Genesis 7:11. "In the six hundredth year of Noah's life, in the second month, on the seventeenth day of the month, on that day all the fountains of the great deep burst forth, and the windows of the heavens were opened." Or look at Genesis 8:4. "And in the seventh month, on the seventeenth day of the month, the ark came to rest on the mountains of Ararat." According to the Bible, there is only one month that is ever given a name, and that is the month of *Abib* or *Aviv*. As Israel's departure from Egypt became imminent, God introduced the month that would become that nation's inauguration, "This month shall be to you the beginning of months. It shall be the first month of the year for you" (Exodus 12:2). Later, He said, "On this day in early spring, in the month of Abib, you have been set free" (Exodus 13:4 NLT). When naming the days, God chose only the last day, but He reversed the order when He named the months. Here, He honors only the first month with an individual name.[4]

Following the years spent in Babylonian captivity, the Israelites began to embrace the calendar names from Babylon. Today's Jewish

---

[4] Three other months are referenced by name in addition to Abib, but this is in the later books. They are: *Ziv* (1Kings 6:1, 37), *Ethanim* (1Kings 8:2), and *Bul* (1Kings 6:38). Abib, however, remains the only month with a name that is specifically mentioned by God Himself.

calendar assigns a name to each of the twelve months, and *Abib* is usually referred to as *Nissan*. The use of *Nissan* instead of *Abib,* is an example of the evidence from leftover cultural assimilation from that exile. Following are the months of the current Jewish calendar:

1. *Abib/Nissan* is the first month
2. *Iyar* is the second month
3. *Sivan* is the third month
4. *Tamuz* is the fourth month
5. *Av* is the fifth month
6. *Elul* is the sixth month
7. *Tishrei* is the seventh month
8. *Heshvan* is the eighth month
9. *Kislev* is the ninth month
10. *Tevet* is the tenth month
11. *Shvat* is the eleventh month
12. *Adar* is the twelfth month

The Hebrew year. The modern Hebrew calendar year will not correlate numerically with the corresponding Gregorian year. Very generally, the latter's start date is that period of time during Jesus's life on earth, approximately two thousand years ago. In contrast and very generally, the Jewish calendar traces its start date to the time of the creation. By using a method that compiles the Bible genealogies, a total of over fifty-seven hundred years is the result when counting back from the present to Adam. As an example, the Gregorian calendar year of 2020 corresponds to 5780 on the Jewish calendar. This means that according to the sacred calendar humanity is steadily nearing the six-thousand-year anniversary of man's creation.

The sacred calendar is found in Leviticus 23. After the exodus from Egypt, God led the Israelites to Sinai where they set up camp for about a year. During this time, they were given the Ten Commandments. They were also instructed in the ways of government, sanitation, the offering of sacrifices, and the building of the tabernacle. In general, they were taught just about anything and everything pertaining to living as a people set apart and holy to their God. The very detailed specifics of this great undertaking are recorded in the book of Leviticus. In chapter 23, the Lord introduces His people to the calendar He intends for them to follow year after year. The chapter opens with these words: "Speak to the people of Israel and say to them, These are the appointed feasts of the Lord that you shall proclaim as holy convocations; they are my appointed feasts" (Leviticus 23:2). After instituting the Sabbath, the narrative then goes on to introduce Passover (v. 5), Feast of Unleavened Bread (v. 6), Firstfruits (v. 10), Pentecost (v. 15), Trumpets (v. 24), Day of Atonement (v. 27), and finally, the Feast of Tabernacles (v. 34).

Notice that the Lord makes it clear that these appointed seasons (moedim) are to be proclaimed as holy convocations. This is an important directive because the Hebrew word *miqra* or "convocation or assembly" is also translated as "rehearsal."[5] This same Hebrew word also refers to something that is specifically called out such as in a public meeting. Is it possible that God's calendar is setting forth a series of feasts that would serve as an annual *rehearsal* for the plans He had in mind for the people He'd created?[6]

Father God repeats in order to teach. Each of the special dates listed in Leviticus 23 are the appointed seasons of the Lord. They are the moedim. They are presented in calendar form so that each festival might be understood by succeeding generations through yearly repetitions. All parents and teachers know that children will only learn some things through repetition, and God is the ultimate teacher and good parent. Therefore, He repeats Himself.

---

[5] Strong, *Strong's Exhaustive Concordance of the Bible,* 292 (Strong's 4744).
[6] While in Israel, I was introduced to the idea of a hidden pattern embedded within the holy calendar. As this was a new concept to me, I was surprised to discover a goodly selection of sources for further study on the subject. Among this group of books are two that I've found to be especially interesting, detailed and helpful. Both are excellent, and the Scarlata and Pierce book is easily adapted to a school curriculum. Peter A. Michas, Robert Vander Maten, and Christie Michas, *The Rod of an Almond Tree in God's Master Plan* (Mukilteo, Washington: Winepress Publishing, 1997). Robin Scarlata and Linda Pierce, *A Family Guide to the Biblical Holidays* (Woodbridge, Virginia: Heart of Wisdom Publishing, 1997).

God's calendar is a lunar calendar. According to Genesis 1:14, the lights in the heavens are the signposts that always point to the Lord's moedim, His specially appointed seasons. This becomes evident because the phases of the moon always determine the sacred festivals. Some of the festivals, such as Passover and Feast of Tabernacles, begin at the full moon, while others are to be celebrated at the different stages of the moon. Rosh HaShanah, for instance, always begins at the new moon. In point of fact, the new moon dictates the dates of the entire month of Tishrei's festivals. "From new moon to new moon, and from Sabbath to Sabbath, all flesh shall come to worship before me, declares the Lord" (Isaiah 66:23).

The Hebrew calendar specifies three major appointed seasons: spring, early summer, and fall. The Hebrews lived in an agrarian society, and their lives revolved around seasons of planting and harvest. Before they ever entered the Promised Land, God explained that they'd need to present themselves to Him during three appointed times each year—a command performance, so to speak. To emphasize the importance of the future convocations, the moedim were announced while Israel still encamped at the base of Sinai. The reason God set these appointments was so that He could bless Israel. The feasts were to be seasons of blessing for His people, and God made it easy for them to do this because He conveniently planned the trips around their harvest seasons.

Before leaving Egypt, the Lord laid the foundation for instituting His calendar. Look at Exodus 12:

> The Lord said to Moses and Aaron in the land of Egypt, "This month shall be for you the beginning of months. **It shall be the first month of the year for you** [emphasis added]. Tell all the congregation of Israel that on the **tenth day** of this month every man shall take a lamb according to their fathers' houses, a lamb for a household. And if the household is too

small for a lamb, then he and his nearest neighbor shall take according to the number of persons; according to what each can eat you shall make your count for the lamb. Your lamb shall be without blemish, a male a year old. You may take it from the sheep or from the goats, and you shall keep it until the **fourteenth day** of this month, when the whole assembly of the congregation of Israel shall kill their lambs at twilight." (Exodus 12:1–6)

Up to this time, the month in question had not been previously recognized as the beginning of the year, so God was instituting something new here. And it has been carefully recorded for anyone reading the Bible all these years later that the father selected for his family the lamb that would become the very first Passover lamb on the tenth day of that month. It is also seen in this account that the lamb for that original Passover—well over three thousand years ago—was sacrificed on the fourteenth day of the month. It should not come as a surprise that the meticulous recording of these dates indicates a divine purpose beyond a simple attention to detail. Later, the name of the month, *Abib,* is given in Exodus 34:18. If *Abib* is introduced as the first month of the year, it is only logical that other months are to follow, and the composite of these months becomes the new calendar—God's calendar. Look at the moedim of the sacred calendar as introduced in Leviticus 23.

The first appointed time takes place during the spring of the year. The purpose of the spring feasts was to commemorate the Exodus from Egypt.

In the first month, on the fourteenth day of the month at twilight, is the Lord's **Passove**r [emphasis added]. And on the fifteenth day of the same month is the **Feast of Unleavened Bread** to the Lord; for seven days you shall eat unleavened bread. On the first day you shall have a holy convocation; you shall not do any ordinary work. But you shall present a food offering to the Lord for seven days. On the seventh day is a holy convocation; you shall not do any ordinary work." But you shall present a food offering to the Lord for seven days. On the seventh day is a holy convocation; you shall not do any ordinary work." "Speak to the people of Israel and say to them, When you come into the land that I give you and reap its harvest, you shall bring the sheaf of the **firstfruit**s of your harvest to the priest, and he shall wave the sheaf before the Lord, so that you may be accepted. On the day after the Sabbath the priest shall wave it." (Leviticus 23:5–11)

The second appointed time for Israel to meet with God in Jerusalem takes place fifty days later. "You shall count seven full weeks from the day after the Sabbath, from the day that you brought the sheaf of the wave offering. You shall count fifty days to the day after the seventh Sabbath. Then you shall present a grain offering of new grain to the Lord" (Leviticus 23:15–16). *Pentecost* is Greek for fifty days. Pentecost takes place seven full weeks plus the day after the last Sabbath.

The third appointed time of meeting with the Lord takes place during the fall.

And the Lord spoke to Moses, saying, "Speak to the people of Israel, saying, In the seventh month, on the first day of the month, you shall observe a day of solemn rest, a memorial proclaimed with blast of **trumpets** [emphasis added], a holy convocation. You shall not do any ordinary work, and you shall present a food offering to the Lord." And the Lord spoke to Moses, saying, "Now on the tenth day of this seventh month is the **Day of Atonement**. It shall be for you a time of holy convocation, and you shall afflict yourselves and present a food offering to the Lord." (Leviticus 23:23-27). "And the Lord spoke to Moses, saying, 'Speak to the people of Israel, saying, On the fifteenth day of this seventh month and for seven days is the **Feast of Booths** to the Lord." (Leviticus 23:33–34)

Reading through the book of Acts, and following along behind the apostles and early believers, one cannot miss the fact that they continued to celebrate the Jewish feasts even after Jesus had ascended to heaven. They faithfully carried on with the yearly cycle of traveling to Jerusalem for observance of the moedim. Just as Jesus had "opened the scriptures" to the two disciples on the road to Emmaus, the leaders of the early church also interpreted the deeper meaning of the festivals. Acts 2 records how Peter's sermon explained the fullness of the purpose for Pentecost as he quoted the prophets Joel, Samuel, and Isaiah, as well as the Psalms. He "opened the scriptures" to a transfixed crowd as he taught about God's original intention for instituting the moed of Shavuot, known to later Gentile generations as Pentecost.

Today's Christians have had the distinct advantage of being taught by that great Jewish lawyer, the apostle Paul. His commentary is available to anyone with access to a New Testament. He, along with the author of the letter to the Hebrews, made the case that the priestly duties and the Jewish feast days not only had symbolic value but that they also foreshadowed what was to come, namely, Jesus.[7]

With this in mind, as well as remembering that the word *convocation*, can also be translated as "rehearsal," the Old Testament pages unfold with startling clarity in regard to the annual feasts. With the advantage of hindsight, inherent truths located within the annual feasts come into sharp focus for those living in the twenty-first century. Beginning chronologically with the first of the moedim, it becomes clear that Jesus fulfilled all three parts of the sacred calendar's spring feasts.

- **Passover** *(Pesach)*
- **Unleavened Bread** *(Hag Ha Matzot)*
- **Firstfruits** *(Yom Ha Bikkurim)*

He is *the* Passover lamb sacrificed for the world. He is the only man to never sin; therefore, there was no leaven found in Him. He is the first of many brethren; therefore, He is the first fruits. Jesus fulfilled the spring feasts.

From today's vantage point, it also becomes apparent that the feast known as Pentecost has similarly been fulfilled.

- **Pentecost** *(Shavuot)*

Fifty days following the resurrection, the Holy Spirit fell on the 120 who were gathered in the upper room. Prior to the Lord's dramatic victory over death, Jews had obediently gathered in Jerusalem during this festival to commemorate the giving of the law at Sinai some fourteen hundred years earlier. That the Holy Spirit

---

[7] Both Paul and the writer of Hebrews explain that the Tabernacle and its contents, as well as the other established Jewish *moedim*, are shadows of things to come (Colossians 2:17 and Hebrews10:1), as well as the pattern of things existing in Heaven (Hebrews 8:5 and Hebrews 9:23).

should be imparted to believers on this very date's anniversary is yet another example of how God planned to use the feasts as a connection between Himself and His people. With the Holy Spirit's entrance into individual believers, it now became possible for God's law to be *inside* the hearts of His people, as well as etched on stone tablets. Jesus prayed: "That they may all be one, just as you, Father, are in me, and I in you, that they also may be in us, so that the world may believe that you have sent me" (John 17:21). Jesus fulfilled the Feast of Pentecost by sending the Holy Spirit.

Prophetic significance of Passover and Pentecost is fulfilled. The preceding centuries of Passover and Pentecost observation were in fact *rehearsals* for the coming of Jesus and for the coming of the Holy Spirit. God had given the first clue about the coming Messiah when He prophesied that the seed of the woman would crush the serpent's skull. This veiled allusion is found in Genesis 3:15. In turn, the Messiah Himself cloaked the coming of the Holy Spirit with "code talk" during His final hours with the twelve. Their last meal was a Passover dinner known as a *seder*. During the evening, Jesus repeatedly assured the disciples that though He would be leaving them for a time, He would be sending a special comforter and helper to take His place. Because His death and resurrection were not yet accomplished, the Lord chose His words carefully so as not to give away the plan that had been determined from before the creation of the world.[8]

Prophetic significance of the fall feasts is yet to come. If the first four moedim of the sacred calendar have proven to be reliable harbingers of specific events, it stands to reason that the remaining three moedim might also foretell of God's dealings with

---

[8] The dinner conversation from that night has been recorded faithfully for us by John in chapters 13–17 of his Gospel. Specific references to Holy Spirit are found in John 14:16–17, 26, John 15:26, and John 16:7, 13. At that time, the disciples were not able to fully understand the meaning of the Lord's words because they were couched in "code talk."

mankind. Put another way, if the spring and summer feasts of the Lord have provided an accurate foretelling of events that have already taken place, it seems reasonable to expect that the fall feasts might provide insight for the future. The three fall feasts have as yet to be prophetically fulfilled.

- **Jewish New Year** (Yom Teruah or Rosh HaShanah)
- **Day of Atonement** (Yom Kippur)
- **Feast of Tabernacles** (Succot)

The believer's bottom line. The plan and purpose for God's feasts, as celebrated in the sacred calendar, have been largely lost on the Christian world. This loss happened over many years and came about as the lunar calendar was exchanged for a solar calendar and because of language translation. There were also, undeniably, efforts by the Church's leaders during the third and fourth centuries to distance the "Christian" Gospel from its earlier Jewish roots. The result is that the majority of Christians are not even aware that the Hebrew calendar exists. This has been a great loss for the Church. There is, however, a renaissance taking place in the Christian world as its genealogy is traced back to its Jewish origin. While exploring the Hebrew calendar, one discovers that God continually operates and reveals Himself within its special moedim, and that it is a calendar intended for both Jews and Christians.

The next three chapters will focus on the three groups of moedim:

Spring: Passover, Unleavened Bread, and Firstfruits.
Late Spring/Early Summer: Pentecost.
Fall: New Year, Day of Atonement, and Feast of Tabernacles.

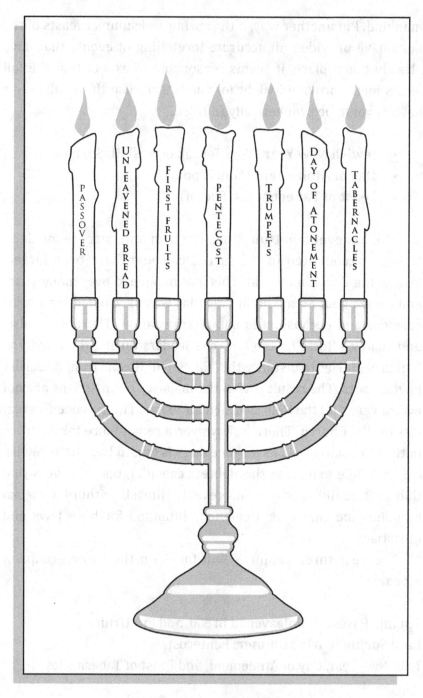

The Menorah Calendar

Chapter 7 Study Guide

1. The Jewish day begins at sundown on the previous day for this reason: _____ ' _____

   _____ .

2. According to the Bible, the only day to be given a name instead of a number _____

   _____ .

3. According to Exodus 34:18, the first month of the Jewish year is _____ also known as

   _____ .

4. The first month of the sacred calendar commemorates this event in Israel's history

   _____ .

5. Moed is the Hebrew word for _____

6. Miqra is the Hebrew word for_____ . It can also be translated _____ .

7. The Bible introduces God's calendar in this book and chapter: _____ .

Chapter 8

The Spring Feasts

Chapter 7 Recap: In the beginning, God introduced the concept of days and months. He also introduced the moed, a specially fixed, appointed, and ordained season. God directed that these special seasons should be proclaimed as holy convocations. The convocations or rehearsals, the miqra, were placed within the framework of a sacred calendar found in Leviticus 23. This unique calendar is unlike any other in the history of mankind. It not only serves as an annual reminder for special memorials, anniversaries, and celebrations, but since the convocations are also rehearsals, it is a prophetic blueprint of God's plans concerning His creation's redemption and destiny.

The beginning of the months. Essentially, calendars are social contracts that act to unify a society with a common agenda organized around specific dates and events. One of the first things God did after bringing the children of Israel out of Egypt was to introduce them to a calendar unlike any other that had existed. In doing so, He reorganized Israel's previously celebrated dates and anniversaries within the context of His own special agenda. Significantly, He meticulously arranged the festivals of the new calendar around the planting and harvest seasons of the (as yet) unfamiliar Promised Land. It was with the sacred calendar's presentation that Israel's new beginning was formalized, and the introduction of this alternative timetable provided the means with which to make a clean break from past tradition. Henceforth, the month of the departure from Egyptian captivity was decreed to be the first month of the year. "This month shall be for you the beginning of months. It shall be the first month of the year for you" (Exodus 12:2). Thus the first month of each succeeding year would be known always as the month of Abib. From this point forward, God begin to ratchet up the phases for His ultimate plan—humankind's redemption.

According to Genesis 46, Israel went down to Egypt as a single family but emerged as a mighty people. A nation had been forged during the years of enslavement, and the Messiah, as yet still hidden in the mind of the omnipotent and eternal Creator, was already destined to come forth from the DNA of that very nation. The sacred calendar—that freshly inaugurated annual agenda—was to become one of several tools God would use to teach His people about Himself. The new calendar was free from the former pagan influence of Egyptians, Canaanites, and Sumerians. It would prove to be an excellent classroom for a people developing into their unique and God-given identity.

Having been provided with a fresh beginning, the people looked forward to meeting with the Lord on the dates He set aside for worship and celebration. Israel was instructed to gather as a nation before the Lord three times during the year, and already the dictates of the calendar were setting them apart from the surrounding nations. The first annual meeting, according to God's calendar, was slated to take place always during the spring, in the month of Abib, around the time of the barley harvest.[1]

---

[1] The word *Abib* translates as the "young barley grain," which would indicate the time of year in relation to harvest. After the Babylonian Captivity, the month of Abib came to be called Nissan.

This spring gathering, the first of the three major annual convocations, is actually composed of three distinct divisions. Over the years, however, it has come to be most commonly referred to by only one name: Passover. Although the three spring feasts are known collectively as Passover, they are more accurately placed into the three separate feasts of Passover, Unleavened Bread, and Firstfruits. This chapter examines the three parts of Passover, as they are introduced in scripture. Played out against the backdrop of God's sacred calendar, it becomes remarkably clear that the life of Jesus perfectly fulfilled and was the literal embodiment of each aspect of the spring feasts.

The Spring Feasts are divided into three parts:

1. Passover (Pesach)

From the study of the feasts of the Lord, as introduced in Leviticus 23, notice that Passover, which is actually a memorial of Israel's final night of Egyptian captivity, always takes place in the month of Abib. Today's Jews continue to follow the same sacred calendar, and they have been observing the Passover for well over three thousand years. Modern Hebrew calendars, however, usually refer to the month of Abib as Nissan, a name that was picked up during the Babylonian Captivity.

According to Leviticus 23:5, Passover is always Nissan 14. "In the first month, on the fourteenth day of the first month at twilight, is the Lord's Passover." Since the first month is also known as Abib, or more recently Nissan, this means that Passover occurs in the spring, in the March/April period. In Israel, the month of Nissan signals the end of the rainy season, the beginning of the growing season, and the time when the new lambs are being born. Spring comes to the land of Israel during this loveliest of months when the warm breezes blow over fields that wave with barley, and wild flowers burst forth from their winter's sleep, blanketing the hills with a riot of color. It is in fact the optimum month for a visit to Israel.

Origin of Passover. It was God who introduced the idea of Passover. The original account of the story is found in the book of Exodus, with the opening scenes taking place in ancient Egypt. After having been subjected to slavery for four generations, the Jews find themselves witnessing a series of plagues brought upon their Egyptian oppressors by the God of Israel. It so happens that the plagues have come about as a consequence to the Egyptian Pharaoh's stubborn refusal to acquiesce to God's command of "Let My people go." As each plague becomes progressively worse than the previous one, Egyptians grow anxious and fearful as the power of the Hebrew God persistently decimates a helpless pantheon of Egyptian deities. Meanwhile, the Israelites watch the confrontation with growing wonder and hope, as the words of Moses are consistently backed up by the one known as "I Am."

Finally, in that long ago Abib of the great Exodus, Moses issued instructions for what would come to be known as Passover. The head of every household was directed to select an unblemished male lamb on the tenth of the month and then to care for it until the fourteenth. On that day, the lamb was to be killed and its blood smeared above and on both sides of the outside door to each dwelling. Then the entire lamb was to be roasted. The meat was to be eaten with unleavened bread and bitter herbs, making sure to burn any inedible parts and bones on the following morning. Moses instructed all family members to present themselves at this meal fully dressed and with their feet shod for a journey. It was explained to the people that God would pass through the land of Egypt, executing judgment about midnight. "For I will pass through the land of Egypt that night, and I will strike all the firstborn in the land of Egypt, both man and beast; and on all the gods of Egypt I will execute judgments: I am the Lord" (Exodus 12:12).

The story continues that after the Jews had marked their doors with the lamb's blood and had partaken of their Passover meal, the Lord passed throughout the entire land of Egypt, slaying every firstborn. This included the firstborn of Pharaoh, the firstborn of prisoners in jail, and even the firstborn of the livestock. The Bible says there was not a single household without one dead family member. Imagine. By the next day, Abib 15, the people of Israel, numbering six hundred thousand men began their journey out of Egypt. The account relates the Exodus beginning exactly 430 years *to the day* that this event first had been prophesied. Including women and children, the number of people departing was in the millions. The account specifically records that they left with their baked unleavened bread and that, apparently, Egyptians also joined the mass exit as a "mixed multitude."[2]

Notice the wording of the text. God passed *through* the land of Egypt, but He passed *over* the homes marked with the lamb's blood. "The blood shall be a sign for you, on the houses where you are. And when I see the blood, I will pass over you, and no plague will befall you to destroy you, when I strike the land of Egypt" (Exodus 12:13). This then was the first great Passover.

Passover practiced throughout the centuries. The celebration of Passover is mentioned many times in both the Old and New Testaments. For instance, exactly one year after their dramatic departure, the Israelites can be found camped in the Sinai wilderness and celebrating the first anniversary of their deliverance from Egypt (Numbers 9). At this time, God reviews again with Moses the specifications of the feast so that the meal might be properly observed. Thirty-nine years of life in the desert pass, and on the eve of the famous march around Jericho, the Israelites are seen to be keeping the Passover on the fourteenth day of Abib (Joshua 5). By the seventh century BC, King Hezekiah actually had

---

[2] Exodus 12:37–41.

to reinstitute the observation of Passover after a particularly dark chapter of wicked behavior in Israel's history (2 Chronicles 30). A little over one hundred fifty years after Hezekiah's reign, Jews, recently returned home from their Babylonian exile, are celebrating Passover under Ezra's leadership (Ezra 6). Moving ahead another five hundred years, Jesus and the disciples are sharing the same feast. Is the average Christian aware that the Lord's last meal before His crucifixion was a Passover seder?

The Seder. The traditional Passover meal is called the seder because the Hebrew word *seder* is translated as "arranged in order." There is an orderly progression to this dramatic and symbolic meal. Over many centuries, certain arrangements for the meal developed and have come to be incorporated. For instance, specific scriptures are always read, and special foods are always served. Also, traditional questions and roles have come to be an anticipated part of the seder. Today, Jews continue to observe this meal, and a growing number of Christians are joining them. Clearly, it has special meaning for both groups. As a believer looking at Passovers stretching across a thirty-five-hundred-year history, one cannot help but be impressed with the unparalleled majesty and brilliance of a God who would institute such a meal for a slave nation. It's a meal that invites the participants to recall the story of their Egyptian deliverance and, on another level, take part in the grand master plan for humanity's deliverance. As it turns out, the Passover seder is not only a dinner commemorating the Exodus; it is also a symbolic rehearsal dinner for the triumph of the cross.

Scripture states simply that the lamb for Passover was killed on the fourteenth of the first month. As God passed through the land on that fateful night so long ago, the salvation of each home depended upon one thing and one thing only. Before the midnight reckoning, every Hebrew household shared a common act of obedience; each home's door had been strategically marked with blood. As horrible judgment was being executed, it was only the blood from the lamb that staved off the death that befell the whole of Egypt.

Jesus is the Lamb of God. The major part of each seder is always the lamb. Today, a lamb shank is present on the seder plate, even if another meat is being served to the guests. The scriptures speak for themselves as they indicate the clear association of Jesus as the Lamb of God.

- The Passover lamb was to be without blemish. When John the Baptist saw Jesus coming toward him, he acknowledged, "Behold, the Lamb of God, who takes away the sins of the world!" (John 1:29). Upon hearing these words, John's Jewish audience would have immediately been aware of the terminology as referencing Passover; there would have been no other inference. Jesus never sinned, and there was never a word of deceit from His lips (1 Peter 2:22). Jesus was sinless and without blemish.
- The Passover lamb was to be inspected for four days (Exodus 12:3–6). The cross-referencing of the Gospel accounts of Jesus's activities in the days leading up to the crucifixion provide extensive documentation that He presented Himself for inspection in the temple at Jerusalem on the tenth of Nissan. The Gospels record how the religious leaders conspired to trick Him and tried to find fault with Him. They didn't succeed (Matthew 21–25; Mark 11–14; Luke 19–21; and John 12). The actions and testimony of Jesus remained unassailable and defect-free throughout four days of scrutiny by both Pharisees and Sadducees.
- The Passover lamb was slaughtered on the fourteenth day of Abib, and Jesus was crucified on the Passover. According to Josephus, the Passover lambs were sacrificed between

3:00 and 5:00 p.m.[3] Three of the four Gospel accounts are careful to include the important connection that Jesus died around the ninth hour, or 3:00 p.m. (Matthew 27; Mark 15; and Luke 23:44–47). Jesus died on Passover, Abib 14.

- The Passover lamb was required to be without blemish and have no broken bones. The instructions given in Exodus and Numbers are very clear that not one bone of the Passover lamb was to be broken (Exodus 12:46; Numbers 9:12). Referring to the coming Messiah, David prophesized that His bones would remain intact (Psalm 34:20). In spite of a practice for accelerating the death process by shattering the legs of the crucified, Jesus was spared this final assault. According to John's eyewitness account, Jesus had died by the time Roman soldiers began to carry out this stage of the execution, and so it was not necessary to break his legs (John 19:31–36). The bones of Jesus's body were not broken.
- The Passover lamb was sacrificed so that God's judgment would pass over each household marked with blood. In later years, each family selected a special lamb for the annual Passover sacrifice. Representing his household, the father of the family brought the sacrifice into the temple courtyard. Here, the lamb was slaughtered, with its blood carefully collected by the priests and then dashed against the foundation of the altar. The father of each household was responsible to provide and present the lamb.[4]

---

[3] William Whiston (1737 translation), *The Works of Flavius Josephus: The Jewish War 6.9.3,*
Courtesy of *The Flavius Josephus homepage* and edited by G. J. Goldberg. (www.josephus.org). Flavius Josephus was a first-century Jewish historian who was present during the siege of Jerusalem and at its destruction in 70 AD. His writings about Roman and Jewish history provide one of the best-known contemporary accounts of the times.
[4] Animals were identified and tagged with the family's name. *The Priesthood and the Blood,* Global MissionaryChurchMinistries. http://www.hissheep.org/special/hebrew/the_priesthood_and_the_blood.html.

Father God did no less than He required of His children. There would be no humane death for His lamb, however, as crucifixion was the brutal and public form of capital punishment favored by the Romans to keep a conquered people in line. For this very reason, it was usually carried out at a congested and well-traveled crossroads or city entrance. Due to its festival-swollen population, Jerusalem was bursting at the seams during Passover, insuring a glaringly public presentation of God's own Passover lamb.

Luke's genealogy ends with "Adam, the son of God" (Luke 3:38). Adam and his descendants were God's family on earth. Jesus was presented as God's Passover sacrifice for the family of Adam. The great heavenly Father demonstrated His ultimate love as His lamb's life and blood were offered in exchange for the errant household of humanity.

Abib 14: a unique window in time. Having seen that Jesus Himself was the fulfillment of Passover, it should not be surprising to find that He was also obedient to go up to Jerusalem for the observance of Passover, just as other faithfully observant Jews did every year. Each one of the Gospel accounts carefully reports this detail; the Savior was an observant Jew. As messianic prophecies unfolded and became literally epitomized in Jesus, God's spectacularly wondrous attention to detail is brought sharply into focus when one looks at the twenty-four-hour period of Abib 14. Not only did Jesus *fulfill* Passover; He also *observed* the Passover.

Back in Egypt, the first Passover had taken place on Nissan 14 (Exodus 12), and the Old Testament accounts of subsequent Passovers also describe a Nissan 14 observance. By the first century, however, the Seder dinner was being held on Nissan 15. The reason for changing the date can be found in a scripture from Deuteronomy, "But at the place that the LORD your God will choose, to make his name dwell in it, there you shall offer the Passover sacrifice, in the evening at sunset, at the time you came out of Egypt" (Deuteronomy 16:6). "Came out of Egypt" is the key phrase in this passage. At some point after the Jews returned from the Babylonian exile in 458 BC, rabbinical interpretation dictated that the seder observation should be moved from the fourteenth day to the fifteenth. As the rabbis studied the previously mentioned passage in Deuteronomy, they came to the conclusion that in order to follow God's instructions to the strictest degree, the Passover meal should be eaten on the fifteenth, since they "came out of Egypt" on the fifteenth. [5] At the first Passover, the Israelites had observed the meal on Nissan 14, and departed (came out of) Egypt on Nissan 15. By the time of Jesus, however, many had begun to follow this rabbinical interpretation.

Modern Judaism, known as Rabbinic Judaism, is descended from the Pharisaic beliefs instead of from the Sadducees. Today, the majority of Jews follow ritual and liturgical practices as interpreted by the Pharisees. For this reason, the seder meal is held on the fifteenth of Nissan instead of the fourteenth. A modern Hebrew calendar will also indicate that Nissan 15 is the first day of Passover.

Jesus and the disciples, however, adhered to the pattern originally instituted during the Exodus. Jesus lived on earth during a window of time when He could both celebrate a seder with His disciples on Nissan 14, as well as be slain *as the lamb* on Nissan 14. This is yet another of the many marvels of divine timing.[6]

---

[5] With the blessing of Persia's King Darius, Jews returned to Israel in 458 BC. Ezra 6:19 records that the newly-returned exiles kept the Passover on the fourteenth day of the first month. From this account, we can discover that the date change for observing the Passover seder must have taken place during the approximately four hundred years between Ezra and the advent of the Lord. All recorded seders previous to the New Testament accounts were observed on the fourteenth of the first month. An exception providing for special circumstances is found in Numbers 9:1–12, but, in this case, the day remained the same, and the meal simply moved to the second month.

[6] K.J. Frolander, *Israel Basics* (United States of America, 2011), 183–9. The author introduces several of the explanations for the two dates of seder observance and includes profiles of the different sects and groups impacting the affairs of first century Israel (Sadducees vs. Pharisees; Galileans vs. southern Israelites, etc.).

The *Akeidah.* In the Genesis account of the *akeidah*—the binding of Isaac—God did not require Abraham to actually sacrifice his son, Isaac. God never asks man to give more than He himself is willing to give, and this event is the perfect example of that very fact. Although God didn't require the life of Abraham's son, He did not spare the life of *His* only son. The American Standard Version of Genesis 22:8 reads, "Abraham said, God will provide himself the lamb for a burnt offering, my son. So they went both of them together." *Himself the lamb.* As an example of the Old Testament's accuracy at providing shadows of what would be coming in the future New Testament, note the similarities between the binding of Isaac and the crucifixion of Jesus:

- Wood for the sacrifice was laid on Isaac's shoulders. Jesus carried a wooden cross or crossbeam on His shoulders (John 19:17).
- Isaac was the much-desired and long-awaited son. Jesus was the much-desired and long-awaited Messiah (Luke 2: 21–35).
- Isaac was the only son of covenant. God's only begotten son was sacrificed *as* the new covenant (1 Corinthians 11:24–26).
- The horns on the head of the ram were caught in a thicket. Thorns and thistles were a result of Adam's disobedience. The Lord had this cruel reminder of man's sin, a crown of thorns, brutally forced down onto his head (Matthew 27:29).
- The binding of Isaac was located in the region of Moriah. The crucifixion took place in the region of Moriah (John 19:20).

Abib 14 is Passover. Jesus is crucified on Passover

(1Corinthians 5:7 and John 1:29)

2. **Feast of Unleavened Bread** *(Chag HaMatzot)*

A look at any Jewish calendar will show a week during the spring marked as "Unleavened Bread." Over the years, the Feast of Unleavened Bread has come to be referred to as Passover. Although it begins on Nissan 15, its name has become interchangeable with Passover, and it is also called the second day of Passover. The Feast of Unleavened Bread, as introduced in Leviticus 23, states that no leaven should be found in any household food during this time. "And on the fifteenth day of the same month is the **Feast of Unleavened Bread** [emphasis added] to the Lord; for seven days you shall eat unleavened bread. On the first day you shall have a holy convocation; you shall not do any ordinary work. But you shall present a food offering to the Lord for seven days. On the seventh day is a holy convocation; you shall not do any ordinary work" (Leviticus 23:6–8).

After God passed throughout the land of Egypt on that first Passover at midnight, terror-stricken Egyptians desperately urged the Israelites to leave the country. Because the departure was so sudden, their bread had no time to rise. The Bible record is implicit that they "took their dough before it was leavened, their kneading bowls being bound up in their clothes on their shoulders" (Exodus 12:34). Why does the account seem to go into such great detail with all of the information about bread making procedure and apparatus? As with all the feasts, one discovers that unleavened bread clearly points to Jesus. For those who have eyes to see and ears to hear, the feasts are windows into God's ultimate plan for mankind. They are His holy *moedim.*

Leaven is equated to sin. The scriptures abound with examples of this analogy.

- Matthew 16:11-12 AMP states, "How is it that you fail to understand that I was not talking to you about bread? But beware of the leaven (ferment) of the Pharisees and

Sadducees. Then they discerned that He did not tell them to beware of the leaven of bread, but of the teaching of the Pharisees and Sadducees."

- Galatians 5:9 states, "A little leaven leavens the whole lump."
- First Corinthians 5:7–8 states, "Cleanse out the old leaven that you may be a new lump, as you really are unleavened. For Christ, our Passover lamb, has been sacrificed. Let us therefore celebrate the festival, not with the old leaven, the leaven of malice and evil, but with the unleavened bread of sincerity and truth."

Traditional preparation for unleavened bread. Throughout the centuries, getting a household ready for this *moed* has always required effort, time, and labor. Weeks before Passover, families begin the preparation by ridding their homes of all *chametz* or leavening. *Chametz* is the name given to something that is the result of biological fermentation. That is, *chametz* is the product that appears when water, along with one of five types of grain, is allowed to stand raw for more than eighteen minutes. This timetable is according to rabbis' best understanding of all the rules concerning fermentation. On the other hand, the required wine for the seder meal is made from fermented grapes. In this case, however, wine is exempt, since no grain is involved. It is due to such stringent specifications as these that many Orthodox Jewish homes have two complete sets of kitchenware (cooking utensils, dishes, pots, and pans) to help them keep from breaking the rabbinical laws.[7]

Getting rid of the leaven. Beginning with the first week of Nissan, a thorough housecleaning is initiated in Orthodox Jewish homes. This is conveniently timed to coincide with "spring house cleaning." Perhaps this is that event's origin? Typically, furniture

---

[7] Foods made with baking soda are allowed to remain because they result from a chemical fermentation rather than a biological one.

is moved, and kitchen cabinets are carefully emptied, cleaned, and restocked. All that can possibly be done to insure a *chametz*-free zone is carried out. On the night before Passover, the father conducts a formal search for any trace of leavening, and many families let the children participate in what becomes a great adventure. A special prayer is recited, and then a room-to-room search is begun. The head of the household carries several items. Traditionally, they are a feather, a wooden spoon, a candle, and a disposable container (usually a sack). Due to the wonders of technology, a flashlight now often replaces the candle. It is also customary for some small pieces of leavened material to be left out so that they can be "discovered." After all the lights are turned out, the search begins. Once the light from the candle falls upon an item of *chametz,* the feather is used to carefully whisk it into the wooden spoon. Gingerly, the contents of the spoon are emptied into the sack, and the search continues. The candlelight (or flashlight) must be shone in every corner, nook, and cranny, and at the end of the evening's quest, the sack is tied shut and set to the side. On the following morning, a special prayer is said as the sack and its contents are burned. Finally, the house can be declared kosher for Pesach. In other words, every law and rule has been followed; all requirements are met, and the home is pronounced clean for Passover. For centuries, this ritual, or one very similar to it, has been practiced in Jewish homes.[8]

Like every good parable, this earthly recital has a heavenly meaning.

- The home's occupants do everything humanly possible to make the house clean. Likewise, one can try earnestly

---

[8] I'd heard about this tradition regarding the *chametz,* and Robin Scarlata and Linda Pierce also include it in *A Family Guide to the Biblical Holidays* on pages 171–172. According to my Israeli friends, this hunt for the *chametz* is mainly practiced in the Orthodox community. It is a poignant enactment of God's great care for His children and a beautiful parable of the Holy Spirit's activity within the human heart.

to clean up and show only the good side to others and to God. This is like our game face with which one attempts to conceal what is actually going on internally.

- The father, the head of the family, searches for *chametz* just as the heavenly Father searches the hidden recesses of all hearts. The Creator of the universe requires that only those who are totally sin-free can live in His presence, for sin is neither allowed nor can it be tolerated by a holy God.
- Like the candle's illumination of the *chametz*, the word of God exposes and reveals sin (Hebrews 4:12–13).
- Just as the feather sweeps away the *chametz*, the Holy Spirit gently convinces one's heart of sin and causes the sinner to want to be rid of it.
- The wooden spoon is the receptacle of the leavening, just as Jesus, while nailed to that wooden cross, received sin's consequence by actually becoming sin. "Christ redeemed us from the curse of the law by becoming a curse for us—for it is written, 'Cursed is everyone who is hanged on a tree'" (Galatians 3:13).
- The sack is representative of the grave. The body of Jesus was laid in a grave, but the believer's sins are buried with Christ and removed forever, as far as the east is from the west (Psalm 103:12).
- Finally, the burning of the sack is a visual reminder that the heavenly Father chooses to forget sins forever. They no longer exist; they vanish like ashes from the celestial rear view mirror and are forever forgotten throughout all the eternities by a loving Father (Hebrews 10:17).

Unleavened bread or *matzah*. Matzah is the only bread consumed at the Passover seder and also during the entire week of Unleavened Bread. This means that an observant household will be dining on *matzot* (plural of *matzah*) from Nissan 14–21. Most grocery stores sell the product throughout the year in specialty food sections, but usually there is a matzah display during the actual festival. The matzah is made from flour and water and requires quick work so that no fermentation can take place inadvertently. After being rolled flat, it is pricked with a fork, knife, or special instrument rolled over the dough to make tiny holes. It is then cooked at high heat until the rows of pricks are scorched dark. The end product remains without leaven and is a reminder of the crucified body of Jesus. without sin, pierced, and covered with the stripes of His whipping.

Abib 15 is Unleavened Bread. Jesus, the bread of life, was without leaven

(1 Corinthians 5:7–8 and 1 Corinthians 11:23–24).

3. Firstfruits *(Yom HaBikkurim)*

This feast was one that encouraged the participants to look ahead to the future. "And the Lord spoke to Moses, saying, "Speak to the people of Israel and say to them, When you come into the land that I give you and reap its harvest, you shall bring the sheaf of the **firstfruits** [emphasis added] of your harvest to the priest, and he shall wave the sheaf before the Lord, so that you may be accepted. On the day after the Sabbath the priest shall wave it" (Leviticus 23:9–11). After all, it was by faith that they originally believed they'd come into the Promised Land, and so it would be by faith that they believed they'd reap a harvest once there. The future harvest would come from these first fruits. It is easy to see that a man's participation in this feast required faith.

Firstborn from the animal and plant kingdoms.

Bekowr is the Hebrew word for "firstborn," and *Bikkurim* is the Hebrew word for "firstfruits." Both words come from the same root and are masculine, with the former being singular and the latter being plural. *Yom HaBikkurim* translates as "Day of the First Born or Firstfruits."[9]

The people of Israel had been taught to give the first part to the Lord. They recognized that the firstborn son, as well as the firstborn of any animal, belonged to the Lord. They remembered the fate of Egypt's firstborn and understood the gravity and principle of the firstborn. Furthermore, it was clear that the first fruits from the ground also belonged to the Lord. The entire chapter of Deuteronomy 26 detailed the importance of keeping this law. During the time of Jesus, the Pharisees were scrupulous about observing this rule, even to the tithing of their spices.

Firstfruits in ancient Israel. As the barley crop grew, the farmer eagerly watched for its maturation and selected a particular sheaf to be marked as the firstfruits. It is said that a red cord was used for this purpose. Then, the farmer would gather the bundle of specially-marked grain and bring it to the priest. The priest would then wave it before the Lord, as instructed in Leviticus 23. In this way, the farmer acknowledged his gratitude to the Lord for providing the seed, the soil, and for sending the sunshine and rain that enabled his crop to grow. He was also, in another sense, thanking God in advance for the rest of the harvest to come. He was, in truth, giving thanks for the crop that would follow after the evidence of this firstfruit.

Firstfruits are indicative of the coming harvest. One reaps what one sows. Scripture warns that God will not be mocked and that everything that has been sown will eventually reap a harvest. The sowing of specific seed in order to reap a desired result is a principle that was first initiated by God. The grand design for His carefully planned and patiently awaited personal harvest reached a critical point with the crucifixion of His own son. The Lord had

---

[9] Strong, James, *Strong's Exhaustive Concordance of the Bible* (Iowa Falls, Iowa: World Bible Publishers, Inc., 1986). *Bekowr* (1060), *Bikkuwr* (1061). *Bikkurim* is the plural of *Bikkuwr*.

included all that He could safely say on the subject when He spoke to Philip and Andrew. "Jesus replied, 'The hour has come for the Son of Man to be glorified. Very truly I tell you, unless a kernel of wheat falls to the ground and dies, it remains only a single seed. But if it dies, it produces many seeds'" (John 12:23–24 NIV). Until His death had become actual fact—something that He'd only surreptitiously mentioned in the conversation recorded here—Jesus was mindful to speak in "code talk." In this conversation, He was obviously equating His life with the sowing of a seed. Christians of course understand His words and remember that God had spoken of the seed from the woman who would bruise the head of the serpent. And with the hindsight that comes from living on this side of the cross, it is clear that His death was necessary for the triumphant harvest of humankind redeemed!

To the believers in Rome, Paul explained that God had known each one from the beginning and that His plan had always been to mold them into the image of His Son. But how had He determined to accomplish this? That very same Son would of necessity become the firstborn among many brethren. He would become the pattern to the mold (Romans 8:29). A few years earlier, Paul had been delivering this same teaching to a different group of believers in Corinth when he wrote, "But now [as things really are] Christ (the Messiah) has *in fact* been raised from the dead, [and He became] the first fruits [that is, the first to be resurrected with an incorruptible, immortal body, foreshadowing the resurrection] of those who have fallen asleep [in death]. For since [it was] by a man that death *came* [into the world], it is also by a Man that the resurrection of the dead *has come*. For just as in Adam all die, so also in Christ all will be made alive. But each in his own order: Christ the first fruits, then those who are Christ's [own will be resurrected with incorruptible, immortal bodies] at His coming. (1 Corinthians 15:20-23 AMP).

John 20:1 states, "Now on the first day of the week Mary Magdalene came to the tomb early, while it was still dark, and saw that the stone had been taken away from the tomb." As far as the Jewish calendar goes, the first day of the week—then and now—is Sunday. Because the seventh day of the week is Shabbat, the first day of the following week is always Sunday. The Bible record is clear that Jesus's resurrection had taken place by early dawn of the first day of the week. It is also clear that Jesus accurately prophesied the duration of time between His death and resurrection. Matthew 12 gives the account of how the Pharisees, fresh from having witnessed a blind mute's complete healing, challenged Jesus to work a miracle in order to prove His God-mandated credentials. The Lord refused, and chiding them for continuing to demand miracle after miracle, He told them that the only sign they would be given would be the "sign of Jonah." For just as Jonah spent three days and three nights in the belly of the great fish, so He would also be in the heart of the earth. And with these words, He gave credence to the literal veracity of the book of Jonah.

Working backward from the point of a Sunday resurrection, certain scriptures begin to emerge in a new light. For instance, "Now it was the day of Preparation, and the next day was to be a **special** [emphasis added] Sabbath. Because the Jewish leaders did not want the bodies left on the crosses during the Sabbath, they asked Pilate to have the legs broken and the bodies taken down" (John 19:31 NIV). Keeping in mind that the Jews referred to each of the seven annual feasts as Sabbaths, one understands that the Sabbath mentioned in the previous verse is not necessarily referring to the usual weekly Shabbat. It is easy to see how it could be assumed that this verse was referring to the weekly Sabbath; however, this Sabbath was a *special* Sabbath, one of the High Holy Days, and not the weekly Sabbath.

It is written that the Lord was already raised by dawn of the first day of the week. The Jewish Shabbat concludes at dusk on Saturday, which is the end of Shabbat. This makes Sunday the first day of the week, and the earliest Christians celebrated Sunday as the day of resurrection. Sometime between the end of the previous day, which began at twilight on Saturday evening, and the earliest light of Sunday dawn, marks the interval of His Resurrection. Counting back three days from Firstfuits, which occurs on Nissan 17, one arrives at Passover, Nissan 14. [10]

Abib 17 is Firstfruits. Jesus is the firstfruits of resurrection (John 12:23–24; Romans 8:29; 1 Corinthians 15:20–23).

Psalm 22. During Bible times, copious amounts of scripture were diligently studied and committed to memory. As any guide in Israel can tell a visiting tour group, entire books of the Bible were memorized before the age of twelve, with rabbis and scribes reciting the entire Tenach by memory. Scripture was honored and discussed among even the common men. The ample evidence of his extensive Bible knowledge is demonstrated in Peter's address, as recorded in Acts 2. During his famous sermon delivered on the day of Pentecost, Peter cited passages from Joel, Isaiah, and Samuel, in addition to numerous psalms. It is apparent from the reaction of his audience that they were also familiar with the verses quoted and well understood his intended meaning. In those days, upon hearing a line from a well-known scripture, listeners would have recognized the source of the quotation, and it would not have been necessary to recite the entirety of the referenced scripture. According to one authority, it was well-understood at the time that reference to the first and last words of any scripture were in fact recognized as referencing the entirety of that scripture. "According to Hebraic understanding, a reference to the first and last words of

---

[10] Instructions from Leviticus 23:11 (AMP) state that the sheath of the firstfruit shall be waved before the Lord on "the next day after the Sabbath the priest shall wave it." The word *Sabbath* can be interpreted either as the weekly Sabbath or as one of the special Sabbaths or moedim of the Hebrew calendar. Not surprisingly, different sects disagree along these lines. I believe "the next day after the Sabbath" refers to the day immediately following the weekly Shabbat (Saturday is Shabbat), as all of the first-century accounts report that Jesus was resurrected on the first day of the week.

a particular text denotes the entire text. With this understanding, Yeshua's final words are of the utmost significance."[11]

A modern frame of reference, for instance, might be the words, "Fourscore and seven years ago, our fathers brought forth ..." This phrase is easily identified by most twelve-year-olds as belonging to the introduction of Lincoln's famous Gettysburg Address. Similarly, lines from certain scriptures would have been immediately recognized during the time of Jesus. With this in mind, read through Psalm 22, written by King David, who was himself an ancestor of the Lord. (Bold text has been added.)

> Psalm 22 (NIV)
> **My God, my God, why have you forsaken me?**
> Why are you so far from saving me, so far from my cries of anguish?
> My God, I cry out by day, but you do not answer, by night, but I find no rest.
> Yet you are enthroned as the Holy One; you are the one Israel praises.
> In you our ancestors put their trust; they trusted and you delivered them.
> To you they cried out and were saved;
> in you they trusted and were not put to shame.
> But I am a worm and not a man, scorned by everyone, despised by the people.
> **All who see me mock me; they hurl insults, shaking their heads.**
> **"He trusts in the Lord," they say, "let the Lord rescue him. Let him deliver him, since he delights in him."**
> Yet you brought me out of the womb;

---

[11] Peter A. Michas, Robert Vander Maten, and Christie Michas, *The Rod of an Almond Tree in God's Master Plan* (Mukilteo, Washington: Winepress Publishing, 1997), 184–185.

you made me trust in you, even at my mother's breast.

From birth I was cast on you; from my mother's womb you have been my God.

Do not be far from me, for trouble is near and there is no one to help.

Many bulls surround me; strong bulls of Bashan encircle me.

Roaring lions that tear their prey open their mouths wide against me.

I am poured out like water, and all my bones are out of joint.

My heart has turned to wax; it has melted within me.

My mouth is dried up like a potsherd, and my tongue sticks to the roof of my mouth;

you lay me in the dust of death.

Dogs surround me, a pack of villains encircles me; **they pierced my hands and my feet.**

All my bones are on display; people stare and gloat over me.

They divide my clothes among them and cast lots for my garment.

But you, Lord, do not be far from me. You are my strength; come quickly to help me.

Deliver me from the sword, my precious life from the power of the dogs.

Rescue me from the mouth of the lions; save me from the horns of the wild oxen.

I will declare your name to my people; in the assembly I will praise you.

You who fear the Lord, praise him! All you descendants of Jacob,

honor him! Revere him, all you descendants of Israel!

For he has not despised or scorned the suffering of the afflicted one;

he has not hidden his face from him but has listened to his
cry for help.
From you comes the theme of my praise in the great
assembly;
before those who fear you I will fulfill my vows.
The poor will eat and be satisfied; those who seek the Lord
will praise him - may your hearts live forever!
All the ends of the earth will remember and turn to the
Lord,
and all the families of the nations will bow down before him,
for dominion belongs to the Lord and he rules over the
nations.
All the rich of the earth will feast and worship;
all who go down to the dust will kneel before him - those
who cannot keep themselves alive.
Posterity will serve him; future generations will be told
about the Lord.
They will proclaim his righteousness,
declaring to a people yet unborn: **He has done it!**

Those standing within earshot of the cross heard Jesus cry
out the first and last lines from what was universally regarded
as a messianic psalm, a psalm pointing toward the long-awaited
Messiah. Three of the Gospel writers, Matthew, Mark, and John,
carefully record these words as spoken from the cross; they are
words so accurately put to verse many centuries before by the
psalmist David. After reading accounts of the Lord's final hours,
some find it difficult to believe that Psalm 22 was written one
thousand years before the crucifixion, and yet, this is the case.
The Holy Spirit so precisely guided David's pen that his psalm is
practically a script for those momentous hours. Abandoned by the
ones He'd nurtured and led, Jesus trod the lonely corridor that He
alone could travel. Within sight of the eternal goal, He doggedly

endured the brutality of beating and whipping, the humiliation of being stripped and hung naked, the agony of His bones ripping from their joints, and the awful conscious separation from His Father and God. But He did it and was able to cry, "It is finished!"

What was finished? The master plan for redeeming mankind had found completion; it was finished. In Eden, a rescuing savior/ Messiah had been promised to mankind. "He will bruise and tread your head underfoot"(Genesis 3:15 AMP). Later, another facet of God's master blueprint was spoken into earth's atmosphere by His covenant partner and friend. "Abraham said, God will provide himself the lamb for a burnt offering, my son" (Genesis 22:8 ASV). Truly, God had provided Himself as the lamb for an offering. His lamb was without sin, just as the matzah was without leaven. On Firstfruits of that year, God's lamb, His Son, was resurrected by the invincible power of the Holy Spirit. With His glorified body eternally intact, Jesus strode forth from the realm of the dead as the firstborn of many brethren, holding in His precious, nail-pierced hand the keys of death and hell. (Revelation 1:18). Jesus: the firstborn of many!

The seder was always a rehearsal for the cross. Just as Psalm 22 points to only one man from history, the seder meal also reveals Jesus of Nazareth. To better appreciate the meal's resemblance to the life of Christ, many Christians have begun attending communal seders in recent years. Usually hosted by messianic congregations, more and more traditional churches also are beginning to provide such events.

The Passover seder follows a loosely organized program, and, depending on the age of the participants, it can be extremely detailed or not. The main theme, however, is always a recounting of the original Passover and God's faithfulness to deliver His people. Every year, each generation has the opportunity to be reminded about the events of the Exodus. The story unfolds throughout the meal; prayers are offered at different intervals, and all the diners participate in activities designed to keep everyone on their toes.

A special Pesach platter is placed in a prominent position on the table. Many of these decorative platters have a design of pre-formed indentations that hold samples of the traditional foods. Among the foods always included are:

- *karpas:* parsley or celery that is dipped into salty water to symbolize the tears that were shed in Egypt
- *maror:* romaine lettuce or some other bitter vegetable that is eaten to recall the bitterness of slavery
- *beitzah:* boiled egg, which is symbolic of mourning over the destruction of both the first and second temples. There is no evidence, however, that the egg was present until sometime after the Roman destruction of the second temple in 70 AD.
- *z'roah:* shank bone of a lamb, which is the reminder of the Passover lamb, even when fish or chicken is served
- *charoset:* a mixture of chopped dates, apples, nuts, honey, cinnamon, and red wine. This combination symbolizes the mortar used by the Jewish slaves to hold bricks together for Pharoah's building projects.
- *chazeret:* horseradish—another reminder of the bitterness of slavery.

Each table is furnished with plates piled high with matzah. A traditional Jewish seder will also follow a prescribed order of prayers and activities. The program is printed into a book known as the *Haggadah.* The leader for the evening (usually the father of the family if he enjoys telling the story) will refer often to his copy of the Haggadah, especially if the seder he is presiding over is a formal, detailed affair. Each seder also includes drinking an obligatory four glasses of wine. Orthodox homes that follow a traditional Haggadah will observe the prescribed prayers, questions, washing of hands, and blessings at the appropriate time during the evening. As mentioned earlier, however, the meal may be intensive or fairly brief; it may be detailed or cover only the most basic facts; it may be formal or casual. Ultimately, style and ritual depend on the individual family. While incorporating traditions from the past, the seder is a meal that is constantly evolving to include relevant, modern mores.[12]

The Lord's Last Supper broke the seder mold. As a result of having participated in this meal from their earliest youth, all of the disciples were well acquainted with the prescribed order for each prayer and blessing. It is evident from reading the Gospels that Jesus, as leader for the evening's celebration, made it clear that it was no ordinary Passover. Accordingly, Matthew, Mark. and Luke record that after the traditional blessing and breaking of bread (matzah), He added, "This is My body which is given for you" If any one of the disciples had not been paying close attention up to this point, he certainly was now, for these words were not part of any Haggadah script. Some twenty years later, Paul shares that Jesus had included also the poignant request, "Do this to remember me" (1 Corinthians 11:24 NLT).

During the next year's Passover seder, following the crucifixion, it doesn't take much to imagine the thoughts and emotions of the eleven as they once again listened to the traditional, centuries-old blessing of the matzah. This time, a full year had elapsed since their beloved teacher had led that last seder; a big difference was that *now* they fully understood what He'd been saying to them.

---

[12] An example of the innate adaptability of a modern Seder is the recent addition of an orange segment to some Passover plates. It is symbolic of feminism and the gay community. My favorite Haggadah, *The Temple Haggadah*, was purchased in Jerusalem at the Temple Institute. It is a beautifully illustrated book that tells the story of the Passover as it was celebrated during the time of the second temple. It is not uncommon for a Haggadah to remain in use for many years. Many families pass a treasured copy from generation to generation, and these much-loved heirlooms will frequently exhibit small wine stains on the pages!

The four cups. Time-honored prayers were offered before each of the four Passover cups of wine. Due to the purpose and sequence of each cup, they have come to be known as:

1. The cup of sanctification
2. The cup of judgment or plagues
3. The cup of redemption
4. The cup of praise or restoration

The rabbis explain that there are four cups because of the four different descriptions of the Exodus redemption in the following scripture:

> Say therefore to the people of Israel, "I am the Lord, and **I will bring you** [emphasis added] out from under the burdens of the Egyptians, and **I will deliver you** from slavery to them, and **I will redeem you** with an outstretched arm and with great acts of judgment. **I will take you** to be my people, and I will be your God, and you shall know that I am the Lord your God, who has brought you out from under the burdens of the Egyptians. I will bring you into the land that I swore to give to Abraham, to Isaac, and to Jacob. I will give it to you for a possession. I am the Lord." (Exodus 6:6–8).

As He'd done with the matzah, Jesus followed the pattern of formal blessings over the cups of wine, that is, until it came time for Him to bless the third cup. The third cup is not to be drunk until the meal is finished, and this is why Luke specifies that it is during the blessing of the third cup that Jesus equated His own life's blood with the cup of redemption (Luke 22:20). Later, while writing to the believers in Corinth, Paul shared the additional words Jesus had attached to the blessing concerning the third cup. "In the same way also he took the cup, after supper, saying, "This cup is the new covenant in my blood. Do this, as often as you drink it, in remembrance of me" (1 Corinthians 11:25). Yet again, Jesus chose to amend the time-honored formal blessing. For the rest of their lives, His disciples would recall always His words over this third cup, the cup drunk after the meal. No doubt, each year's succeeding Passover brought a bittersweet remembrance. The Amplified Bible even says that Jesus told them to *affectionately* remember Him when, in future years, they would drink the third cup—the cup of redemption.

The symbolism of the seder is rich in the news of the Gospel. Messianic Jews often express incredulity that they didn't recognize the true meaning of the meal until after they were born again. There is still so much more to the symbolism and content of a traditional Seder; in fact, entire chapters could be devoted easily just to the meal itself. There remains, however, one final part that cannot be left out: the *afikomin*.

This feature of the seder was probably introduced during the centuries of Greek influence that followed Alexander the Great, and it continues on as a major part of the meal today. Afikomin is derived from a Greek word that translates as "to come after." During the meal, the evening's leader lifts up a cloth bag that has been divided into three "pockets." The pockets are rather like the divisions of a billfold. This bag is known as the *Matzah Tash* and contains three pieces of matzah, each piece tucked into its own individual pocket. Usually, the bag has been sitting on the table in front of the leader throughout the telling of the story. After reciting a blessing, he removes the piece of matzah from the center pocket of the bag (tash) and breaks it. This broken piece, known as the afikomen, is then carefully wrapped into a clean, linen napkin and placed aside. When the children aren't looking, it is hidden. At the end of the meal, with its traditional desserts, the children are allowed to hunt for the afikomen, and the search is always eagerly anticipated, for they are rewarded with either candy or money. Once discovered, everyone receives a small bite of it so that the last taste from the seder will be matzah. The afikomen is the seder's finale.

Since the purpose of this tradition has never been fully explained, the rabbis speculate as to the meaning of this part of the seder. Could the three pieces of matzah represent Abraham, Isaac, and Jacob? If so, why then is Isaac broken? This separating of the patriarchs is but one of several explanations offered over the centuries for the division of the afikomen. Of course, any messianic Jew easily guesses that the three pieces of matzah represent the Trinity: Father, Son, and Holy Spirit. Jesus, the middle of the three, was broken, carefully wrapped in linen grave clothes, and hidden away until the third day. Ever so much better than candy or money is the actual, real-life prize of discovery, for the reward for finding Jesus is eternal life! Certainly the Passover seder is truly a marvel of precision as the rehearsal's true purpose becomes evident.

The believer's bottom line. All three of the spring feasts on God's sacred calendar—God's moedim—have been gloriously and perfectly fulfilled in Jesus. It is no wonder then that the angels rejoiced as the Creator's ultimate master plan of redemption dawned as a tangible reality for His beloved human family during a momentous spring two thousand years ago.

Homework for this chapter: read Exodus 12.

Chapter 8 Study Guide

1. Passover is divided into ____ separate spring feasts.
2. Pesach is about _____.
     (John 1:29) and (1 Corinthians 5:7b)
3. Hag haMatzah is about_____
     (1 Corinthians 5:7a–8) and (1 Corinthians 11:23–24)
4. Yom HaBikkurim is about _____.
     (John 12:23–24) (Romans 8:29) and (1 Corinthians 15: 20–23)

After reading the chapter, meditate on and discuss the following scriptures:

5. Hebrews 1:1–6
6. Colossians 1:13–22
7. Revelation 1:5
8. Isaiah 53:7–10
9. John 1:29
10. Psalm 22

Chapter 9

Shavuot

Chapter 8 Recap: The three spring feasts or moedim were introduced to the Israelites at the beginning of their new life of freedom from Egyptian slavery. Passover, Unleavened Bread, and First Fruits are the first of the holy calendar's seven annual festivals. As a Jew, Jesus would have participated in all three from His earliest childhood. During His final days on earth, the Lord demonstrated that He was the actual physical embodiment of the Passover and the unleavened bread. At His resurrection, He became the first fruits. Jesus is the Lamb of God, slain from before the foundation of the earth. Jesus is the unleavened bread of life, broken for the sake of Adam's family. And Jesus is also the first fruits of God's great harvest and the firstborn of many brethren. Yeshua HaMashiach—Jesus the Messiah—is the perfect fulfillment of the sacred calendar's spring holy days.

Shavuot **is Pentecost.** Following the three spring moedim, the next feast to be reckoned on God's calendar occurs as the spring and summer seasons merge. Shavuot, or "weeks," is the festival that marks the end of the barley harvest and the beginning of the wheat harvest. The scriptures assign the third month (Sivan) for this celebration, and it is always observed seven weeks after Passover. The Festival of Shavuot, also known as the Festival of

Weeks, is rich in historical tradition, as well as being imbued with prophetic promise. Christians will recognize it by its more familiar Greek name of Pentecost. Shavuot and Pentecost are one in the same.

Exodus 19:0 NIV states, "On the first day of the third month after the Israelites left Egypt--on that very day--they came to the Desert of Sinai." This third month is known as the month of Sivan and it falls into its place on the calendar during the equivalent months of May/June. Jewish commentaries explain that Moses brought the people to the area of Sinai on the first day of Sivan.[1]

More than three thousand years later, Jews continue to observe this feast by its Hebrew name: *Shavuot.* The festival is also known as *Matan Torah* or "the giving of the Torah." Because the book of Acts was written in Greek, the festival is introduced in the New Testament as Pentecost. Pentecost is the Greek name for Shavuot.

Uniquely positioned between the spring festivals and the fall festivals, Shavuot serves as the middle convocation in God's yearly calendar of events. It is preceded by the three spring holidays: Passover, Unleavened Bread, and Firstfruits. It is followed by the three fall holidays: Trumpets, Day of Atonement, and Tabernacles. Like all the other dates listed within the sacred calendar, Shavuot, the anniversary for the giving of the Ten Commandments, seems to convey or represent a purpose far beyond the obvious.

The Israelites set up camp and remained at the base of Mount Sinai for about a year. Most everyone knows that Moses

---

[1] Rabbi Nosson Scherman. *The Stone Edition Chumash.* (Brooklyn, NY: ArtScroll Mesorah Publications, 1993). This book, a translation of the Torah, includes the Hebrew and English text, along with explanation and rabbinic commentary. Pages 400–403 include an explanation for how the Jewish sages settled on the specific date(s) that honor the giving of the Torah at Mt. Sinai. That being said, although the Bible doesn't name the specific date for Shavuot, an analysis of the Exodus story, along with rabbinical tradition, certainly seems to indicate that the two coincide. My copy was purchased at the M. Pomeranz Bookseller in Jerusalem, and although I often disagree with the rabbinic commentators, I certainly appreciate reading their many detailed insights.

climbed the craggy heights of Mount Sinai to receive the Ten Commandments. Indeed, the famous encounter between God and the lawgiver, Moses, is possibly the best-known story from the Old Testament. Most Christians, however, are not aware that Jewish tradition teaches that the event occurred some fifty days after the children of Israel passed through the Red Sea. This means that within less than two months, God had successfully guided the recently liberated horde of former slaves out of Egypt into the plain surrounding a mysterious mountain known as Horeb. With camp set up around Horeb, which is also known as Mount Sinai, He introduced them to a radical new way of life. Here, He charged Moses to present a set of commands written on stone tablets that would forever define Jewish life. The tablets were, of course, the Ten Commandments. To commemorate the anniversary of this momentous event, a feast has been celebrated throughout the subsequent years during the month of Sivan.

In addition to being given the Ten Commandments, it was during this same time that the young nation was instructed in the ways of government, social and familial interaction, sanitation laws, dietary rules, and ordinances pertaining to ritual sacrifices within the tabernacle. In short, Moses taught Israel about everything concerning the daily existence of a people chosen to live a life set apart—set apart *from* the rest of humanity, as well as set apart *to* God. God's peculiar "chosen people" were deposited into a remote desert wilderness where they were placed into a fast-track course of learning. It would see them coalesce into the mighty nation that would eventually succeed in conquering the Promised Land. The specifics of this epic undertaking are recorded in the book of Leviticus. There, it is clearly laid out that God intended to issue a clean slate to His people, one that would begin with the starting point of a brand-new calendar, and one ordered and tailored toward creating special times of connection and intimacy between God and His beloved Israel. In Leviticus 23, the Lord introduced the calendar, detailing and defining the annual cycle of ceremonial events that were to be faithfully followed by succeeding generations. The chapter opens with these words: "The Lord spoke to Moses, saying, 'Speak to the people of Israel and say to them, These are the appointed feasts of the Lord that you shall proclaim as holy convocations; they are my appointed feasts'" (Leviticus 23:1–2). The narrative then goes on to introduce the annual events: Passover (v. 5), Unleavened Bread (v. 6), Firstfruits (v. 10), Pentecost (v. 15), Trumpets (v. 24), Day of Atonement (v. 27), and finally the Feast of Tabernacles (v. 34).

Shavuot is determined by counting the Omer. Upon closer inspection of the fine print, it is noticeable that both the spring feasts and the fall feasts begin with definite commencement dates. For instance, the spring holidays begin on the fourteenth day of the first month, Abib (Nissan) 14. Likewise, the fall holidays begin on the first day of the seventh month, Tishrei 1. However, standing alone in a category by itself, the Feast of Shavuot has no specified date for the exact day of its beginning. Instead, the Torah teaches that the beginning of this middle moed is to be determined by counting seven weeks from the waving of the firstfruits by the priest. "From the day after the Sabbath, the day you brought the sheaf of the wave offering, count off seven full weeks. Count off fifty days up to the day after the seventh Sabbath, and then present an offering of new grain to the Lord" (Leviticus 23:15–16 NIV). Once the seven weeks are counted off, the next day, or the fiftieth day, is celebrated as Shavuot. Understanding the language of this instruction is not an easy thing, and even seasoned Bible scholars struggle to comprehend the nuance of the wording. The controversy centers upon one's perception of what type of Sabbath the passage is intending to mention. Is it referring to the weekly Sabbath or to the Sabbath of Unleavened Bread? This determination is a sticking point that has remained a contentious argument within the different movements of Judaism since biblical times.[2]

The interval of time that elapses while counting the number of days between Passover and Shavuot is also known as the counting of the omer. The word *omer* is unusual, and it is mentioned in the Bible text in only one place: Exodus 16:16–36. In this passage, it is recorded that the Israelites gathered about an omer of manna per person each morning. By comparing ancient weights and measurements, the omer amount is revealed to be equivalent to either a heap when collecting the manna into bowls, for instance, or a sheath of grain when used as a wave offering. "The word (omer) implies a heap, and secondarily a sheath."[3]

Back in the spring during the Feast of Firstfruits, each farmer would have gone into his fields to cut the individual shock of barley that had been determined to be the firstfruits of his entire barley harvest. The selected shock or sheath was then tied off and brought to the priest. The priest waved the designated sheath (omer) before the Lord as an offering and as thanksgiving for the coming harvest. Thanksgiving and faith walked hand in hand during this ceremony because the firstfruits sheath was representative of the entire

---

[2] Today, the Samaritans, the Karaite movement of Judaism, and Rabbinic Judaism continue the very same debate. In ancient times, three distinct views developed concerning the interpretation of Leviticus 23:15–16. The debate centered upon whether or not the Sabbath in question was the weekly Sabbath or the Sabbath of Unleavened Bread. Pharisees, Essenes, and Sadducees held *three* different opinions concerning this matter. Two of the three, Essenes and Sadducees, disappeared from history after the destruction of the second temple in 70 AD. Rabbinic tradition that descended from Pharisaic laws has had the biggest influence in molding the character of modern Judaism. Hence, the modern Jewish calendar denotes Nissan 16 (following the *special* Sabbath of Unleavened Bread) as the beginning of the omer countdown to Shavuot. As might be expected, this is the same ruling shared by the Pharisees of old. On the other hand, most messianic Jews choose to align with the camp that places Firstfruits following the *weekly* Sabbath.

[3] William Smith, LLD (Author), Rev. F.N. and M.A. Peloubet (Editor). *A Dictionary of the Bible, Teacher's Edition* (Chicago, Philadelphia, Toronto: The John C. Winston Company, 1884 edition), 741.

future harvest. By waving the omer, the farmer was recognizing God as the ultimate provider of the coming harvest. The farmer trusted Him for the bounty, and acknowledged Him as that same harvest's supreme protector from both drought and blight. On the day following the ceremony of waving the first omer before the Lord, the farmer eagerly began counting off seven weeks. He would have said, "Today is the second day of Omer," and "Today is the third day of Omer," and "Today is the fourth day of Omer," and so on. Because seven times seven equals forty-nine, the day following the completion of the counting of the Omer would be the fiftieth day or Shavuot. The New Testament's language of Greek would have translated the name for the festival from Hebrew into Greek, and it would have read "Pentecost" (fifty).

Shavuot (Pentecost) during the Old Testament. Arriving fifty days after Firstfruits, Shavuot formally signified the end of the barley harvest, as well as the beginning of the following wheat harvest. "You shall count seven weeks. Begin to count the seven weeks from the time the sickle is first put to the standing grain. Then you shall keep the Feast of Weeks to the Lord your God with the tribute of a freewill offering from your hand, which you shall give as the Lord your God blesses you" (Deuteronomy 16:9–10). It is easy to see how the Israelites would have eagerly looked forward to this festival, for it was the culmination of months of arduous labor in the fields. Just as a teenager eagerly counts off the days until that sixteenth birthday—when a driver's license may be obtained—the Israelites counted the days until the special freewill offering would be given to the Lord on Shavuot. On this occasion, two large bread loaves made from the firstfruits of the wheat crop, along with leaven, were to be brought to the priest as a wave offering. Again, thanksgiving and faith were walking hand in hand. "You shall bring from your dwelling places two loaves of bread to be waved, made of two tenths of an ephah. They shall be of fine flour, and they shall be baked with leaven, as firstfruits to the Lord" (Leviticus 23:17). These two loaves were not the austere flatbread of the Passover but the happy result of freshly-risen dough, fragrant and delicious. Shavuot was the time to give an offering that would be over and above what the law required. Indeed, Shavuot presented the perfect opportunity to give the Lord a gift straight from the heart.

Shavuot is multifaceted. The harvest feast of Shavuot represents more than one interaction between God and His people.

- **Shavuot commemorates the anniversary of the giving of the law: Matan Torah.** According to Jewish scholarship, the giving of the Ten Commandments came fifty days after the Israelites had crossed through the Red Sea. It is believed also that the motive for introducing Shavuot by way of a fifty days' countdown was for the purpose of making an intentional connection between the Exodus and Sinai. While it is true that with the Exodus God had redeemed His people, it was not until the giving of the law at Sinai that the purpose for that freedom was finally revealed. Throughout the centuries, the law would remain the irrefutable moral frame upon which the people would lean as they continued the ongoing synthesis toward nationhood. As one wise rabbi said, "Freedom without rules is anarchy."[4] And so it was that at Sinai, the heavenly parent established definite boundaries for His children, and it is those very boundaries that have served to set Israel apart from all the surrounding nations throughout the succeeding millennia.

---

[4] The wise rabbi is Dr. Neil Lash. Rabbi Lash has served both as president and rabbi of Temple Aron HaKodesh, a messianic congregation in Fort Lauderdale, Florida. With his wife, Jamie, he cohosts the award-winning television series, *Jewish Jewels*. www.JewishJewels.org.

In Israel, the holiday is observed on the sixth day of Sivan. For Jews living within the Diaspora, Shavuot is celebrated on the sixth and seventh of Sivan because this variance also accommodates the difference in time zones.[5] It is not unusual for devout Jews to spend the entire night studying the Torah. During the Shavuot observances in congregations spanning the globe, Exodus 19 and 20 are read aloud. This portion of the Torah recounts the meeting that took place as the Hebrews, standing assembled on the desert floor at the base of Mount Sinai, actually witnessed the descent of God on to the mountain. Congregants listen to the account that describes a terrifying scene on that day: the enveloping thick cloud and the thunder and lightning accompanied by an increasingly loud blast from a heavenly *shofar* ("trumpet" or "horn"). Scripture says that as the Lord descended with fire to the top of the mountain, smoke began to ascend from the site like a furnace. It is recorded that the entire area was encompassed with smoke as the earth quaked and a trembling people stood transfixed. Within the context of this dramatic scenario, Moses introduced the Ten Commandments, as given to him by God:

1. I am the Lord your God. You shall have no other gods before Me.
2. You shall not make for yourselves any graven image.
3. You shall not take the name of the Lord your God in vain.
4. Remember the Sabbath to keep it holy.
5. Honor your father and mother.
6. You shall not murder.
7. You shall not commit adultery.
8. You shall not steal.
9. You shall not witness falsely against your neighbor.
10. You shall not covet.

---

[5] Jews living outside of Israel are known collectively as the Diaspora.

- **Shavuot is the birthday of the nation of Israel.** Before this time, God had made covenant with individuals. At Sinai, however, He made covenant with an entire nation. "Now if you obey Me fully and keep My covenant, then out of all nations you will be My treasured possession. Although the whole earth is mine, you will be for Me a kingdom of priests and a holy nation" (Exodus 19:5–6 NIV). It is recorded that the people responded, "'We will do everything the Lord has said.' So Moses brought their answer back to the Lord" (Exodus 19:8 NIV). With the stipulations from God having been clearly stated and then agreed upon by the people, an entire nation was now in formal covenant with the God of Abraham, Isaac, and Jacob.

- **Shavuot commemorates the anniversary of Israel's *Ketubah.*** It is said that the Feast of Weeks is also the anniversary of the wedding contract presented by God (the groom) to Israel (the bride). In ancient times, the groom would present a formal and legally binding document to the bride during the wedding ceremony. This document, known as a ketubah, specified the commitments made by the groom to the bride as they entered into the marriage covenant. The certificate was the groom's gift to his bride as her guarantee of his sworn obligations to her. Clearly, the ketubah was for the bride's protection and benefit, particularly as there was no reciprocal instrument provided to the groom.

In addition to reciting the customary scriptures reserved for this celebration, many Sephardic congregations include the reading of a special ketubah.[6] This lovely tradition recognizes the giving of the Torah at Sinai as God's ketubah given to Israel. The Lord, as the

---

[6] The term *Sephardic* denotes the descendants of Jews settling in the regions surrounding the Mediterranean Sea and includes the areas of Spain and Portugal (Iberian Peninsula), northern Africa (Maghreb), and the Middle East. The term

groom, obligated Himself to honor, support, and provide shelter and refuge for His bride, Israel. The gift of the Torah was the heavenly ketubah, carefully written for future reference. Addressing Israel, the Lord said, "And I will betroth you to me forever. I will betroth you to me in righteousness and in justice, in steadfast love and in mercy. I will betroth you to me in faithfulness. And you shall know the Lord" (Hosea 2:19–20).

- **Ruth.** Along with portions from the book of Exodus, the book of Ruth is also read on Shavuot. It is appropriate that the story of this Moabite widow and convert to Judaism is honored on this holiday. Just as Ruth had pledged her love and loyalty to her mother-in-law, Naomi, and to Naomi's God, the children of Israel promised love and allegiance to the Lord at Sinai.

Gleaning at the corners of a newly harvested field, Ruth benefited from the generous provisions of the law. After all, it was the law that provided for the poor by directing the harvesters to leave behind bits of the harvest. Ruth was a recipient of grace because this ordinance was practiced.

Ruth 1:22 states, "So Naomi returned, and Ruth the Moabite her daughter-in-law with her, who returned from the country of Moab. And they came to Bethlehem at the beginning of barley harvest." Boaz, Naomi's close relative, acted upon his legal right to rescue the women when he entered a marriage covenant with Ruth. As the kinsman redeemer or *go-el*, Boaz was a type and shadow of the coming Messiah redeemer.

The story of Ruth not only took place during a harvest season, but the narrative goes on to explain that she eventually became the great-grandmother of David, Israel's beloved psalmist king and

---

also refers very broadly to the customs, Hebrew language accent, liturgies, and even recipes for special dishes, and so forth.

an ancestor of the promised Messiah. Tradition teaches that King David was born and also died on Shavuot, the Feast of Weeks that is celebrated during a season of harvest. For these reasons, the story of Ruth is remembered at Shavuot.

Jesus introduces the Holy Spirit. Twenty-eight generations after David's time, his descendant, Jesus, the eternal *go-el*, was hosting a pivotal Pesach celebration. At the final seder dinner with His disciples, the Lord Jesus began to initiate anticipation for a future encounter with the very spirit of the Jewish law. During the annual meal commemorating the great exodus, Jesus confided to the disciples that He would very soon be leaving them. As the evening progressed, He repeatedly referred to a "comforter" who would come to replace the void left by His absence. He explained that this spirit of truth would teach them everything they'd ever need to know. He assured them that in spite of His eminent departure, His Father would send Holy Spirit to earth in response to His request and that this *person* would never leave them.

It is evident from reading the account of the evening's conversation, as recorded in chapters 13–17 of the Gospel of John, that the men reclining around the seder table that night were unable to grasp the full intent of the Lord's words. Indeed, as mentioned earlier, Jesus was also careful to couch His words in "code-talk," and this is because the magnificently executed plan of the ages was actually *in process* as He was speaking. As only He could have done, the Lord skillfully unveiled the impending events without giving away any of heaven's secret. It is written that "None of the rulers of this age understood this, for if they had, they would not have crucified the Lord of glory" (1 Corinthians 2:8). Perfectly planned before the foundations of the earth, the Creator Himself had carefully hidden the great mystery of the cross that would soon come to fruition during the hours that followed this last meal (Ephesians 1:4–5).

After the resurrection and for the next forty days, Jesus appeared multiple times, not only to the disciples but many others as well. He paid a series of visits to His followers in Jerusalem when they were still cowering behind locked doors. He proved that He was neither ghost nor apparition and bolstered their faith when He invited them to examine His punctured side and touch the open wounds in His hands. One morning at daybreak, on the shores of the Sea of Galilee, He greeted them with a specially prepared grilled breakfast. On another occasion, He demonstrated that His glorified body was capable of ingesting food. Luke 24:41-43 NLT states, "Then he asked them, 'Do you have anything here to eat?' They gave him a piece of broiled fish, and he ate it as they watched." At one point, He was seen by a crowd of more than five hundred.[7]

It was during this same interim that the faithful shepherd continued to love, encourage, and teach, just as He always had done. He specifically commissioned His followers to carry the Gospel into every corner of the earth but admonished them to remain in Jerusalem until they'd received the Father's promised gift of the Holy Spirit. At the end of the forty days, following along the same route that had been their path on the night of the recent seder, He conducted them once more out across the Kidron Valley to the Mount of Olives. This time, however, instead of entering into an agonizing period of prayer, He lifted up His hands and invoked a blessing upon them. "But you will receive power when the Holy Spirit has come upon you, and you will be my witnesses in Jerusalem and in all Judea and Samaria, and to the end of the earth" (Acts 1:8). In the midst of this blessing, the disciples marveled to see their beloved rabbi and Messiah being lifted up and received into Heaven. Luke reports that after the Lord disappeared into

---

[7] First Corinthians 15:6. As further verification, Paul states that the majority of people in that crowd were still alive at the time his epistle to the brethren at Corinth was being written.

the clouds, they returned to Jerusalem with great joy to await the promise (Luke 24:49–53).

Shavuot fulfilled in the New Testament. Ten days later, it happened! "When the day of Pentecost came, they were all together in one place. Suddenly a sound like the blowing of a violent wind came from heaven and filled the whole house where they were sitting. They saw what seemed to be tongues of fire that separated and came to rest on each of them. All of them were filled with the Holy Spirit and began to speak in other tongues as the Spirit enabled them" (Acts 2:1–4 NIV). Acts chapter 2 also informs the reader that, in addition to the local population, many foreign Jews were in the city for the purpose of celebrating Shavuot. Shavuot was, after all, one of the three pilgrimage moedim. The location and the timing for the momentous appearance of the Holy Spirit coincided with the Jewish festival of Shavuot. The Amplified Bible reads, "And when the day of Pentecost had fully come …" In the absence of a specific date, Shavuot can be ascertained only by counting the fifty days, and the one who created those days arranged for the Holy Spirit to enter hearts on the fiftieth day after the resurrection. This is in perfect accord with God's own celestial, eternal calendar. Amazing.

- **Tongues of fire.** During the holiday on which Jews from the surrounding nations were in Jerusalem to celebrate the giving of the law, Matan Torah, God sent the Holy Spirit to the earth. On this first Shavuot after the resurrection, however, God's law was no longer limited to words etched upon the surface of stone tablets. When the day of Pentecost had fully come, the very spirit of the law came to reside within the human heart. Just as the fiery flashing of lightning had accompanied the event on Sinai, Luke records that tongue-like flames of fire separated and then settled upon each of the one hundred twenty persons present.

- **A mighty rushing tempest.** In both instances, the manifestation of fire was accompanied by high-decibel sound. At Sinai, a heavenly trumpet blast grew increasingly louder as God's presence descended upon the mountain. Many centuries later, in Jerusalem, the sound of a sudden violent, rushing wind heralded the arrival of the Holy Spirit.
- **Three thousand souls.** During the time that Moses was meeting with God upon the heights of Sinai, the people rebelled and convinced Aaron to forge a golden calf. As they sang and worshiped the idol, Moses descended the mountain. Carefully, he bore the two stone tablets whereupon the Ten Commandments had been written with God's own finger. Arriving at the foot of the mountain and witnessing the raucous scene before him, Moses angrily hurled the tablets to the ground. He stationed himself at the gate of the camp and issued the summons, "All of you who are on the Lord's side, come here and join me." His own tribe, the tribe of Levi, joined him. Strapping on their swords and setting off from the gate, the Levites went throughout the camp, slaying fellow Israelites who had participated in the pagan idol worship. It is recorded that three thousand died on that day (Exodus 32 NLT).

Fifty days after the Lord's resurrection, the Holy Spirit descended with power. An unusual phenomenon accompanied this wondrous event. Pilgrims who had traveled to Jerusalem for Shavuot suddenly found themselves confronted in their native languages with noisy, animated testimony that extolled the mighty works of God. Luke reports that visitors from the modern day countries of Iran, Iraq, Turkey, Egypt, Libya, Italy, Crete, Arabia, and areas surrounding the Black Sea *all* heard the Gospel in their own language as it was preached by the apostles. The unusual circumstances drew thousands of curious onlookers. Emerging from the commotion, Peter stood to speak. Surrounded by the other eleven apostles, he addressed the crowd and preached with remarkable anointing—skillfully and earnestly quoting from the prophets and the psalms. To the listening multitude, Jesus was presented as Messiah, and, as the Holy Spirit opened hearts, many believed. Significantly, the number of new believers added to the brethren and those baptized on that particularly momentous anniversary of the giving of the law is recorded as three thousand. The law brought death as sin's consequence; the Holy Spirit brought life.[8]

- **The waving of the two loaves.** On the very day that the Holy Spirit fell upon those gathered inside an upper room in the city of Jerusalem, a time-honored ceremony was conducted at the nearby temple. Two large loaves consisting of wheat bread prepared with yeast (leaven) were being waved before the Lord as a freewill offering. Although an explanation for waving *two* loaves was never given, the people nonetheless brought their offerings in obedience.

After coming to faith in Jesus as their Messiah, many Jews recognize that the two loaves are representative of the two people groups: Jew and Gentile. The apostle Paul expressed the mystical union of the two groups in his letter to the believers in Ephesus. "By setting aside in his flesh the law with its commands and regulations, His purpose was to create in himself one new humanity out of the two, thus making peace" (Ephesians 2:15 NIV). In another letter, Paul instructed the Church that upon receiving Jesus as savior, there no longer existed Jew or Gentile, for they had become one in Christ.[9] What was once considered sinful, as represented by the leavened bread, was justified in Christ and acceptable to the Father.

---

[8] Acts 2:41; Romans 7:10; 2Corinthians 3:7–8.
[9] Galatians 3:28.

In Jesus, Jew and Gentile have become one, the one humanity born out of the cross.

Pentecost is the realization of God's promise. From the very beginning, God desired to have a family whose hearts would belong to Him. Written a little over six hundred years before the birth of Jesus, the following scripture captures a glimpse into God's longing for family and clearly foretells the reason for a new covenant.

> Behold, the days are coming, declares the Lord, when I will make a new covenant with the house of Israel and the house of Judah, not like the covenant that I made with their fathers on the day when I took them by the hand to bring them out of the land of Egypt, my covenant that they broke, though I was their husband, declares the Lord. For this is the covenant that I will make with the house of Israel after those days, declares the Lord: I will put my law within them, and I will write it on their hearts. And I will be their God, and they shall be my people. (Jeremiah 31:31–33)

The necessity of understanding that the new covenant is a possibility for all humanity—Jew and Gentiles alike—is emphasized as Paul quotes Jeremiah, word for word, in his letter to the Church at Corinth (2 Corinthians 3:3).[10]

Just as He'd promised, the Lord Jesus sent the Holy Spirit to baptize and indwell His followers during the convocation known as Shavuot. The highly anticipated event occurred fifty days after His resurrection, at the precise time when the nation of Israel

---

[10] Hebrews 10:16 is another example of a direct quotation from Jeremiah 31:31–33.

was observing the feast that commemorated the giving of the Ten Commandments. With the coming of the Holy Spirit's power, God's law was no longer relegated to words etched into stone tablets, but the very Spirit of God indwelled the hearts of God's family.

Sivan 6–7 is Shavuot (Pentecost). The Holy Spirit is given on Shavuot, the anniversary of Matan Torah (Exodus 19; Leviticus 23; Acts 2).

The believer's bottom line. The early summer feast of Shavuot followed Firstfruits by seven weeks, plus a day, and celebrated the anniversary of the giving of the Torah at Sinai. In the same year that Jesus was crucified on Passover, buried during Unleavened Bread, and resurrected on Firstfruits, a world-changing event also took place during Pentecost. His faithful followers gathered in Jerusalem and waited for the mysterious helper Jesus had promised. Then it happened "when the day of Pentecost arrived." From out of the godhead, and with explosive, sovereign power, the Holy Spirit fell on the 120 who were there in the upper room. True to the pattern, a previously appointed time on the sacred calendar now took on a new and even greater significance. At Sinai, God's presence had been *on* the mountain. At Shavuot, the same Spirit that had raised Christ from the dead, came to dwell *in* His children.

Chapter 9 Study Guide

1. Shavuot is the Hebrew name for _____.
2. Pentecost occurs _____ days after Firstfruits.
3. Shavuot commemorates _____.
4. The feast of Shavuot is given no specific date; therefore, its celebration is determined by _____.
5. The Shavuot wave offering is composed of this grain _____.
6. On Shavuot, instead of waving a sheath of grain before the Lord, the priest waved _____.
7. What is a Ketubah? _____
   _____.
8. As the kinsman–redeemer (go-el), how is Boaz like Jesus?
   _____
9. The day of Pentecost is described in this chapter of the book of Acts_____.

Chapter 10

The Fall Feasts

Chapter 9 Recap: God met with the Israelites at Mount Sinai after leading them out of Egyptian captivity. Jews celebrate this event every year during the annual feast of Shavuot, a moed known as Pentecost to the Gentile community. Shavuot commemorates this special time as the giving of the law, the birthday of the twelve tribes as a nation, and as the anniversary of God's making covenant with all of Israel. Some fourteen hundred years after that first Shavuot and while gathered in an upper room in Jerusalem, one hundred and twenty disciples were filled with the Holy Spirit. That day is recorded in the second chapter of Acts and it is recognized as the birthday of the Church.

God's divine blueprint. Before proceeding with the third and final group of moedim (the fall feasts), a short review may be helpful. For centuries, the Hebrews were obligated to appear before the Lord at three separate times during the year. These assemblies were required meetings, and they seemed to be a type of anniversary in that they were repeated yearly on precisely the same dates of the Hebrew calendar. But there was something more to these meetings—much more than initially met the eye. God was revealing to His children (if they would but open their eyes to see) the very plan He had worked out for their salvation. "Even as [in His love] He chose us [actually picked us out for Himself as His own] in Christ before the foundation of the world, that we should be holy (consecrated and set apart for Him) and blameless in His sight, even above reproach, before Him in love" (Ephesians1:4 AMP).

This little verse, which can so easily fly under the radar, lets us in on a marvelous revelation, namely, that the divine architect had already conceived the entire blueprint for man's redemption before the events of Genesis 1:1 ever took place. "Before the foundation of the world" necessarily indicates an action taking place before Genesis 1:1, does it not? More importantly for every believer, it means that the plan—that incredibly wonderful divine blueprint for man's salvation—was conceived long before those sad events recorded in the third chapter of Genesis. And this means of course that, as far as God is concerned, there is nothing in your existence or mine that has ever been an afterthought. This fact is extraordinary and provides a reason for great rejoicing.

The Hebrew calendar appears to be God's own encoded preview to His secret strategy for redeeming His creation. Through annual repetitions, the God of Israel led His people through a series of rehearsals for future divine events. As Leviticus 23:2 states, "Speak to the people of Israel and say to them, These are the appointed feasts of the Lord that you shall proclaim as holy convocations; they are my appointed feasts." Keeping in mind that the Hebrew word for convocation, *miqra,* can be translated as "rehearsal," it seems that the Lord chose to conceal His master blueprint within the feasts themselves.[1]

The purpose for rehearsals is to prepare participants for the actual performance. First responders rehearse various crisis scenarios; a rehearsal dinner celebrates the wedding party's practice for the actual nuptials; sports teams repeatedly drill before the big game, and so on. Through a series of rehearsals, God's

[1] James Strong, *Strong's Exhaustive Concordance of the Bible.* (Iowa Falls, Iowa: World Bible Publishers, Inc., 1986) 292 (Strong's 4744).

calendar incorporated His plan into the feasts. It has already been seen that the Passover was actually a rehearsal for the Crucifixion and that Shavuot was a rehearsal for the coming of the Holy Spirit. The Lord thoroughly rehearsed His people for these events.

Following this same line of reasoning, the apostle Paul explained to the believers in Colossae, a town located in modern-day Turkey, that the feast days were shadows of things to come. He taught that they had symbolic value and pointed to the future.[2] To Christians, it becomes obvious that the spring and summer convocations were in fact rehearsals for the coming of Jesus and the Holy Spirit. Those living in the twenty-first century have had the advantage of looking back through history with respect to the first two moedim. From this vantage point, one is granted the ability to view the circumstances of Jesus's life as past tense, and see how clearly and precisely Passover and Pentecost were fulfilled. With this perspective, it is sometimes difficult to understand how anyone could have failed to recognize that Jesus was the Messiah, and yet, many did. In retrospect, one cannot help but acknowledge that all the promises for the Messiah were fulfilled, promises foretold with veiled accuracy in Genesis 3:15. History really *is* His story.

Every aspect of the first four annual convocations, from Passover through Pentecost, has been fulfilled, and this is what makes the fall feasts so full of promise and fascination. Since the earlier moedim appear to evidence a blueprint pattern of divine prophesy, it stands to reason that the last three feasts are also revelatory. But herein lies a great difference; the fall feasts have *not* been completed, and, regarding the fall moedim, there is no longer the advantage of any hindsight lens. Realizing that God often speaks in "code talk," these fall feasts hold special interest and appeal for many believers. Thus the final feasts are introduced in this chapter by way of the month known as Elul.

---

[2] "These are a shadow of the things that were to come; the reality, however, is found in Christ" (Colossians 2:17 NIV).

Elul—**month of introspection and preparation.** Each of the three fall assemblies is observed during Tishrei, the seventh month on the sacred calendar. Elul is the month directly preceding Tishrei. The purpose of the entire month is to help everyone get ready for the somber, spiritual nature of the fall feasts. To be in Israel during Elul is a wonderful experience. The normally hectic traffic conditions of rush-hour Jerusalem give way to a considerate, almost polite Israeli driver. Passersby on sidewalks actually acknowledge each other with a smile and friendly greeting. Bankers, grocers, and -clerks behind counters all show an extra measure of patience. What could possibly be the reason for this sudden inclination to become a kinder, gentler human being? It is nothing less than the time of the year; it is Elul.

Due to the solemn nature of Rosh HaShanah and Yom Kippur, it is during Elul that the majority of Israel's people try to reconcile any breach in relationships that may have occurred during the year. Because tradition holds that God reviews the book of life during the month of Tishrei, an observant Jew is inclined toward repentance during the preceding month of Elul. Jews envision the Creator–judge of the earth as sitting in heaven's court, reviewing each man's life and deciding whether or not to write his name into the book of life for another year. Most are seriously introspective and seek to set about righting any wrongs before the High Holy Days begin. Elul is set apart from other months by the daily blowing of the shofar during morning prayers, the reading of Psalm 27, and special prayers of repentance recited known as *Selichot*.[3] In fact, a full forty days are dedicated to repentance. The forty days begin

---

[3] The shofar is traditionally a ram's horn that has been hollowed out and is used as a ritual and liturgical instrument. Ancient Jews utilized the shofar to announce special occasions and sacred events, and, in times of war, it was used to confuse the enemy (read about Gideon in Judges 7 or the fall of Jericho in Joshua 6). The shofar is still blown at the beginning of each month. Today, many shofar aficionados favor the long and imposing horn of the African Kudu over the smaller traditional ram's horn.

on the first of Elul and run through the tenth day of Tishrei. They are known collectively as *Tishuvah* (repentance).

The Jewish month of Elul holds meaning for Christians. Since the High Holy Days begin with the blast of a trumpet, it is noteworthy that the previous month is set aside for peacemaking, repentance, and preparation. If, as Paul proposes, the convocations are shadows of things to come, it seems reasonable that one would pay attention to such signs. So as the month of Elul focuses on self-examination and preparation, one's thoughts naturally turn toward the gravity of the present. With most believers becoming increasingly aware that the hour grows late, the concept of keeping short accounts with God and man makes good sense. With the return of the Lord coming closer every day, believers rightly endeavor to keep spiritually prepared and take seriously their calling to be ministers of reconciliation and workers in the harvest. Similar to the daily shofar blasts of Elul, an inner witness of the Holy Spirit is alerting many to shake off a slumbering spirit and wake up. "This is all the more urgent, for you know how late it is; time is running out. Wake up, for our salvation is nearer now than when we first believed. The night is almost gone; the day of salvation will soon be here. So remove your dark deeds like dirty clothes, and put on the shining armor of right living" (Romans 13:11–12 NLT).

As the month of Elul ends, Israel enters the season of the fall moedim. The first ten days of Tishrei are known by the different titles of "Days of Awe," the "Ten Days of Repentance," and "High Holy Days." Beginning with the first day of Tishrei, the sacred calendar moves into the third and final group of appointed meetings: the fall feasts.

> And the Lord spoke to Moses, saying, "Speak to the people of Israel, saying, In the seventh month, on the first day of the month, you shall observe a day of solemn rest, a memorial proclaimed with blast

of **trumpets** [emphasis added], a holy convocation. You shall not do any ordinary work, and you shall present a food offering to the Lord." And the Lord spoke to Moses, saying, "Now on the tenth day of this seventh month is the **Day of Atonement**. It shall be for you a time of holy convocation, and you shall afflict yourselves and present a food offering to the Lord. And the Lord said to Moses, 'Say to the Israelites: 'On the fifteenth day of the seventh month the Lord's **Festival of Tabernacles** begins, and it lasts for seven days." (Leviticus 23:23–27 and 33–34 NIV)

The Fall Feasts are divided into three parts:

1. **Jewish New Year (Yom Teruah or Yom HaZikaron or Rosh HaShanah)**

   The advent of fall's High Holy Days begins on the first day of Tishrei and is known by several different names. The Bible calls this day *Yom Teruah,* literally, "Day of the Blowing of the Trumpets" (Leviticus 23:24–25). From these verses one learns that the festival is a memorial, for *Yom HaZikaron* is Hebrew for "Day of Remembering."

   The day is also known as Rosh HaShanah, literally, "Head of the Year." *Rosh* is Hebrew for "head," and *Shanah* is the word for "year." This third description that refers to the festival is one that was picked up during the Babylonian Captivity. Although Rosh HaShanah is not the scriptural name for the moed, it is, nevertheless, the one most commonly used in modern times. Even though the sacred Hebrew calendar begins with the release of the Israelites from Egypt during the month of Abib, the month of Tishrei is traditionally considered to be the first month of the *civil* year. Just as a school's academic calendar begins in the fall or taxes are paid on a particular date within the fiscal calendar, Israel has both a religious and civil year. The rabbis teach that God created the world in the month of Tishrei, thereby making Tishrei the first month. For this reason, Jews celebrate the world's birthday during Tishrei.

Yom Teruah is a memorial. Although much tradition is attached to the observance of this High Holy Day, there is mystery to its deepest meaning. It turns out that even though God instructed that trumpets should announce the beginning of the seventh month as a memorial, He did not tell the people what or whom the memorial was honoring. Rabbinical tradition teaches that the trumpets (shofar) are blown in remembrance of the completion of earth's creation, but scripture is strangely silent about a definitive meaning.

Due to this lack of precise information, rabbis have postulated that it is possibly a memorial to the Akeidah, or the binding of Isaac. The scriptures tell how Isaac's life was spared, and a ram was sacrificed instead. Because the ram was provided when its horns became entangled in a thicket, the incident is memorialized today by the blowing of a ram's horn, also known as a shofar. And to this day, the blowing of the shofar is associated with Rosh HaShanah. This dramatic event, detailed in Genesis 22, demonstrates God's enormous mercy for His people. And just as a merciful God showed His lovingkindness to Abraham and Isaac, Jews hope that God will be merciful to them too because the books are opened in the court of heaven during this season.

Yom Teruah has more than one theme. There are varied themes emphasized during the commemoration of this date. Following are three:

- **Creation:** Jewish tradition holds that God created the world on this day. Because He is the Creator, He is also the king of the universe. One of His titles is *Melech HaOlam:* "King of the Universe."

- **Coronation:** In ancient times, the coronation of the kings of Israel was announced with the blowing of a shofar: 1 Kings 1:34; 2 Kings 9:13; 2 Kings 11:12–14.
- **Judgment:** Jewish tradition teaches that in the heavenly court of the universe the books are opened on this day. It's when God judges individual men and women to see whether or not they should be included with the righteous, the wicked, or the intermediate.

The Shofar. The fact that the blast of the trumpet is associated with Yom Teruah cannot be missed. The dramatic sound of a shofar always commands attention. When the Lord summoned His people for the giving of the law, a heavenly trumpet was sounded. God's descent to the smoking, quaking mountain was announced by a blasting trumpet whose volume grew increasingly louder as Moses brought the Israelites to stand at the base of Mount Sinai (Exodus 19 and 20).

In addition to announcing the imminent presence of God, the shofar was associated with wartime (Joshua 6:20; Judges 3:27 and Judges 7:18–22). Moreover, the shofar was sounded as a warning in times of danger (Amos 3:6).

One reads from both the Old *and* New Testaments that the shofar will sound in the day of the Lord. Isaiah 27:12–13 states, "In that day from the river Euphrates to the Brook of Egypt the LORD will thresh out the grain, and you will be gleaned one by one, O people of Israel. And in that day a great trumpet will be blown, and those who were lost in the land of Assyria and those who were driven out to the land of Egypt will come and worship the LORD on the holy mountain at Jerusalem." While speaking about the protection for His people Israel, the prophet Zechariah says that the Lord Himself "shall be seen over them and His arrow shall go forth as the lightning and the Lord God will blow the trumpet and will go forth in the windstorms of the south ... to defend and protect them" (Zechariah 9:14–15 AMP). Lastly, when the dominion of this world finally comes into the formal possession of the one true and returning king of kings, a mighty angel will announce the moment by the blowing of a trumpet (Revelation 11:15).

Observance of Yom Teruah today. The month of Elul comes to its end, and Tishrei begins with the blast of a trumpet. On this date, temple and synagogue services feature one hundred dramatic blasts from the shofar, and the congregation is reminded that the clock is ominously ticking toward the day of Yom Kippur. There are now only ten days remaining to set straight everything in one's life, and the time for repentance is short. These ten days, from Yom Teruah (Tishrei 1) until Yom Kippur (Tishrei 10), are known as the "Days of Awe" *(Yamim Nora'im)*. At this point, the righteous have been inscribed already in the book of life for another year, and the wicked and intermediate have a final ten days to repent and make peace with God.

"Shanah Tovah!" is the daily greeting as people are wished a good year, and it means "Good Year!" Every home will have apples and honey to offer a visitor because to dip an apple slice into honey evokes the hope for a sweet new year. Beautiful, large pomegranates are sold in the markets because it is hoped that during the coming year, one's life will be as full of good deeds as there are seeds in this fruit.

Prophetic fulfillment of Yom Teruah. Many believe that this holy day will be fulfilled just as surely and completely as Passover, Unleavened Bread, Firstfruits, and Pentecost have been. It would seem that God has certainly established this pattern with the other feasts. If this is the case, what then does this particular memorial about blowing of trumpets symbolize? Will its fulfillment come with the Rapture? The Second Coming? With reference to the latter, scripture records that Jesus told His disciples no one but the Father could know the exact day or hour when He would return. In fact, He confided that even He didn't have this information. It does seem, however, that God has given clues.

Meanwhile, one continues to prayerfully search the scriptures and ask for the Holy Spirit's truth on the matter. One thing *is* clear: a trumpet is calling for each heart to repent while the Lord still tarries. Believers can be assured that a loving heavenly Father will see to it that His plans are accomplished and that He watches over us each moment of each day. Some might be fearful when looking toward the future, but God's children are not among that number.

2. **The Day of Atonement (Hebrew: Yom Kippur)**

The day of atonement takes place on Tishrei 10. It is the second of the two High Holy Days and the most solemn twenty-four-hour period in the Jewish year. It is not a feast day; it is a day of affliction (fasting), and work is strictly forbidden. The day is known as Yom Kippur because *kippur* comes from the Hebrew word that means "to cover or hide." Likewise, the *kippah,* or head covering worn by many Jewish men, also comes from the same Hebrew root word. Thus, Yom Kippur could be said to be the day of the covering of sin: the Day of Atonement.

> Now on the tenth day of this seventh month is the Day of Atonement. It shall be for you a time of holy convocation, and you shall afflict yourselves and present a food offering to the Lord. And you shall not do any work on that very day, for it is a Day of Atonement, to make atonement for you before the Lord your God. For whoever is not afflicted on that very day shall be cut off from his people. And whoever does any work on that very day, that person I will destroy from among his people. You shall not do any work. It is a statute forever throughout your generations in all your dwelling places. It shall be to you a Sabbath of solemn rest, and you shall afflict yourselves. On the ninth day of the month beginning

221

> at evening, from evening to evening shall you keep
> your Sabbath. (Leviticus 23:27–32)

The high priest in ancient Israel. Resting inside the temple's Holy of Holies, was the Ark of the Covenant. This was a specially made box, covered with pure gold. The site of the mercy seat, it was the one place on earth that had been promised by God, "There I will meet with you."[4] Except for the times when the Ark was being transported, it was always separated from the people and kept inside of the holy of holies. The word *holy* comes from the Hebrew word *kadosh*, which means "sacred, hallowed." Thus, the Holy of Holies is sacrosanct and separated from all else as "the sacred of the sacred." On one day of the year, the high priest was permitted to enter this holy and separated enclosure with the purpose of making atonement for the nation of Israel. The day was the one time that God's personal name was allowed to be uttered, and then only by the high priest. His responsibility was immense, and whether the people would live or die depended upon his being able to carefully and precisely carry out each part of his duties. Unless the high priest correctly fulfilled the specifications for each element of the complicated ritual, he also risked losing his own life. On the Day of Atonement, he entered the Holy of Holies to sprinkle the blood of sacrificial animals upon the mercy seat, thereby making atonement for the entire nation of Israel.

After first presenting a sin offering for himself, his family, and for the other priests, the high priest then cast lots to see which of two selected goats should be sacrificed to the Lord and which one would become the scapegoat. Once the choice was made, the blood from the goat sacrificed to the Lord was sprinkled on the mercy seat. Leviticus 16:15 includes these details: "Then he shall kill the goat of the sin offering that is for the people and bring its

---

[4] Exodus 25:22.

blood inside the veil and do with its blood as he did with the blood of the bull, sprinkling it over the mercy seat and in front of the mercy seat." When this part of the ceremony was completed, the high priest laid his hands on the head of the goat for Azazel, also known as the scapegoat, and confessed over him all of the sins of Israel. Now bearing the nation's sin, the goat was led away and dismissed forever into the Judean wilderness. The people looked on and took heart as this activity symbolized God's removal of Israel's sin for the duration of another year. Atonement for the entire nation depended solely on the high priest's being able to fulfill his duty on this Day of Judgment. The intricate procedure would of course need to be repeated again the following year and every year thereafter. This is where Jesus, the great high priest, differs from Israel's high priests of the past.

Jesus is the heavenly and eternal high priest. In Psalm 110, one reads prophecy about the awaited Messiah, a priest forever according to the order of Melchizedek. Later, the book of Hebrews, written to the first generation of messianic Jewish believers, would also speak of this same king/priest, Melchizedek, as being a shadow or type of the coming Christ. The writer beautifully explains the transaction that took place two thousand years ago.

> So Christ has now become the High Priest over all the good things that have come. He has entered that greater, more perfect Tabernacle in heaven, which was not made by human hands and is not part of this created world. With his own blood- not the blood of goats and calves- he entered the Most Holy Place once for all time and secured our redemption forever." [and] "And he did not enter heaven to offer himself again and again, like the high priest here on earth who enters the Most Holy Place year after year with the blood of an animal. If that had been

necessary, Christ would have had to die again and again, ever since the world began. But now, once for all time, he has appeared at the end of the age to remove sin by his own death as a sacrifice. (Hebrews 9:11–12, 25–26 NLT)

The cohen gadol (high priest) was required to sprinkle animal blood seven times upon the mercy seat. Jesus, as the eternal high priest, offered His own blood seven separate times and literally became the nation's sin offering:

- Blood ran from the stripes on His back. (1)
- Blood poured down His face from the crown of thorns. (2)
- Blood dripped from both hands. (3 and 4)
- Blood dripped from both feet. (5 and 6)
- Blood flowed from the piercing of His side. (7)

Every sin ever committed, all iniquity, and each transgression was heaped upon the Lord as He became the scapegoat. Galatians 3:13 NLT explains, "But Christ has rescued us from the curse pronounced by the law. When he was hung on the cross, he took upon himself the curse for our wrongdoing. For it is written in the Scriptures, 'Cursed is everyone who is hung on a tree.'"

As high priest, Jesus covered the heavenly mercy seat with His own blood, thereby obliterating the consequences of sin from His own forever. Hebrews 10:14 states, "For by a single offering he has perfected for all time those who are being sanctified." Sin was removed as far as east is from west. With His own blood, Jesus redeemed the human race; Yeshua is the ultimate cohen gadol.

Observance of Yom Kippur today. According to Jewish teachings, God makes His final decision concerning each individual's fate on Yom Kippur. Ten days earlier, on Yom Teruah, the names of the righteous have been inscribed in the book of life, but now the time has come to make a final decision about the rest of humanity. On Yom Kippur, the books are sealed for another year, and Jews worldwide spend this twenty-four-hour period in solemn fasting and prayer.

In Israel, the entire country enters into the Shabbat. Beginning in the early afternoon, shops and offices close as traffic begins to dwindle on the streets. People wearing the traditional white greet each other with the words *Gmar Hatimah Tovah,* which means, "May your final sealing (in the book of life) be good." Most, and certainly the Orthodox, will not be wearing any leather on their feet, as rubber-soled canvas shoes peek out from underneath dressy white attire.[5] As twilight begins to fall, with no vehicles moving along the normally busy thoroughfares, the Shabbat siren sounds to announce that Yom Kippur is beginning. Modern observance begins in the evening, with the somber *Kol Nidre* service, during which God is asked to release His people from any vows they might make in the coming year.

After Titus destroyed the temple in 70 AD, the priesthood was no longer able to continue the prescribed ritual sacrifices. Nevertheless, the observance of Yom Kippur continues, even though the temple no longer exists, and the hereditary high priesthood is no longer in operation. Because of the absence of high priests and their crucial role, Judaism has developed a service that compensates for the loss. Modern services place emphasis on the rituals surrounding the national repentance that took place long ago during the time of the temple. It is explained that one benefits spiritually from this focus, even without having experienced the

---

[5] Although the explanations vary, the most common reason given for not wearing leather shoes is that Yom Kippur is a day of *affliction*; therefore, the luxury of leather shoes is to be foregone. Another reason offered is the honoring of the animals that lost their lives following humankind's original sin. Additionally, nobody wants to wear something that reminds God about the Genesis 3 episode, particularly on this day—the last chance for appeal before the book is sealed for another year.

actual ritual participation. Prayer services are held throughout the day, and the book of Jonah is read because it is a reminder of God's mercy toward one who repents. At the conclusion of the final prayer service, the entire congregation recites the *Shema*.[6] A very long shofar blast—known as the *tekiah gedolah*—signals the end of yet another Yom Kippur.

Prophetic fulfillment of Yom Kippur. As with each of the other fall convocations, there is speculation about the relationship of Yom Kippur to end-time events. Is Yom Kippur a symbolic rehearsal for the Second Coming? Does Yom Kippur prophetically speak about the final judgment? With the emphasis on having one's name written in the book of life, a judgment scenario certainly seems plausible when considering this scripture:

> Then I saw a great white throne and him who was seated on it. From his presence earth and sky fled away, and no place was found for them. And I saw the dead, great and small, standing before the throne, and books were opened. Then another book was opened, which is the book of life. And the dead were judged by what was written in the books, according to what they had done. And the sea gave up the dead who were in it, Death and Hades gave up the dead who were in them, and they were judged, each one of them, according to what they had done. Then Death and Hades were thrown into the lake of fire. This is the second death, the lake of fire. And if anyone's name was not found written in the book of

---

[6] The opening lines of this prayer are found in Deuteronomy 6:4: "Hear O Israel, the Lord our God, the Lord is One." The words of the Shema are part of a longer prayer that is prayed twice daily, on Shabbat, during many other Jewish services, and as the final prayer of one nearing death. *"Shema Yisrael, Adonai eloheinu, Adonai echad."*

life, he was thrown into the lake of fire." (Revelation
20:11–15)

3. The Feast of Tabernacles (known in Hebrew as Succot)

The Feast of Tabernacles takes place during the week of Tishrei
15–21. This is the last moed on God's sacred calendar. Known as *Ha
Hag* or "The Feast," it is the greatest of the feasts. Like the Feast of
Unleavened Bread, this festival also continues for seven days. Succot
is the plural form of the Hebrew word *sukkah*, which is a booth or
temporary shelter. It is a week-long feast that commemorates the
faithfulness of God as He brought the Israelites out of Egypt, and
they lived in temporary shelters. Succot is a joyous time to be in
Israel because family and friends enjoy sharing festive meals in
booths that are known as sukkahs. It is a time of extreme and
jubilant celebration.

> And the Lord said to Moses, Say to the Israelites, The
> fifteenth day of this seventh month, and for seven
> days, is the Feast of Tabernacles or Booths to the
> Lord. On the first day shall be a holy convocation;
> you shall do no servile work on that day. For seven
> days you shall offer an offering made by fire to the
> Lord; on the eighth day shall be a holy convocation
> and you shall present an offering made by fire to
> the Lord. It is a solemn assembly; you shall do no
> laborious work on that day. These are the set feasts
> or appointed seasons of the Lord, which you shall
> proclaim to be holy convocations, to present an
> offering made by fire to the Lord, a burnt offering
> and a cereal offering, sacrifices and drink offerings,
> each on its own day. This is in addition to the
> Sabbaths of the Lord and besides your gifts and all
> your vowed offerings and all your freewill offerings

which you give to the Lord. Also on the fifteenth day
of the seventh month [nearly October], when you
have gathered in the fruit of the land, you shall keep
the feast of the Lord for seven days, the first day and
the eighth day each a Sabbath. And on the first day,
you shall take the fruit of pleasing trees [and make
booths of them], branches of palm trees, and boughs
of thick (leafy) trees, and willows of the brook; and
you shall rejoice before the Lord our God for seven
days. You shall keep it as a feast to the Lord for seven
days in the year, a statute forever throughout your
generations; you shall keep it in the seventh month.
You shall dwell in booths (shelters) for seven days:
All native Israelites shall dwell in booths, that your
generations may know that I made the Israelites
dwell in booths when I brought them out of the land
of Egypt. I am the Lord your God." (Leviticus 23:
33–43 AMP)

Visit Israel during Succot. This is *the* time to be in Eretz
Israel—the land of Israel. As soon as the shops reopen at the close of
Yom Kippur, several special items immediately appear at sidewalk
kiosks throughout the land: freshly cut palm fronds and the *lulav.*
The palm fronds will be used to make the roof of the sukkah. The
lulav, on the other hand, resembles a bouquet composed of native
plant branches accompanied by an *etrog.* The etrog is an unusual,
lemony type of citrus fruit that is indigenous to the region. The
sudden appearance of these items can be easily compared to the
Christmas tree lots that spring up toward the end of November in
America. The sound of hammering can be heard for the next several
days as each family builds its own sukkah. It is a busy time because
the Feast of Succot will arrive in a mere five days, on the fifteenth
of Tishrei.

The sukkah is associated with Succot. Happy childhood memories are made from evenings spent in the family sukkah. The average sukkah is constructed so that it can be put up and taken down easily. It must be sturdy enough to last for the entire celebration and large enough for the family to gather inside for meals. Imagine a rectangular frame made from two-by-fours that has sheets or some type of lattice enclosing three of the four sides. Cover the frame with a "roof" fashioned from palm branches loosely laid across the top, and a sukkah emerges—voilà! Once the sukkah is erected, festive colored lights are strung throughout, and the walls are often decorated with fruit or drawings or photographs of Israel's produce. Do not forget that this is a harvest festival, and the land boasts the most amazingly beautiful dates, olives, figs, pomegranates, grapes, and wheat during this season. Many family sukkahs are decorated with simple, interlocking paper chains that are handmade from colorful construction paper and paste.

The palm frond roof of each sukkah is carefully arranged so that the stars can easily be seen when looking up into the night sky. The scriptures gives clear instruction to "dwell in booths (shelters) for seven days ... that your generations may know that I made the children of Israel dwell in booths when I brought them out of the land of Egypt: I am the Lord your God." (Leviticus 23) Most families recognize this time as a wonderful opportunity to teach and remind their children about the Bible stories from the Exodus. As the nation continues to *dwell*—taking meals and sometimes spending the whole night under the stars in the sukkah—ordinary thoughts begin to turn to thoughts of God. This festival reminds the people of God's faithfulness and His ability to accomplish what He says He'll do. Frequently, friends and family will gather in the sukkah to sing hymns throughout the night. It is the best camp-out experience ever!

The lulav is also known as "the four species" associated with Succot. The four species are the four types of trees referred to in Leviticus 23:40. Traditionally, they are the myrtle, willow, date palm, and etrog. To make a lulav, branches from the first three are held together as a cluster and accompanied by the fruit of the etrog. Outside of Israel, the etrog is known as citron. During each day of Succot, the lulav is shaken toward six directions: up, down, and to the four points of the compass. The shaking ritual symbolizes bringing in the harvest. This ceremony always accompanies the prayers for rain—uppermost in everyone's mind during this season.

There is a traditional teaching that each of the different species is representative of the four different types of people. It is understood that although the species are vastly different from each other when looked at individually, there is unity when they are joined into the single lulav.[7] Leviticus 23:40 AMP states, "And on the first day, you shall take the **fruit** [emphasis added] of pleasing trees [and make booths of them], **branches** of palm trees, and **boughs** of thick (leafy) trees, and willows of the brook; and you shall rejoice before the Lord your God for seven days."

1. Etrog: It is believed that the etrog is the "pleasing tree." This tree bears fruit throughout every season and has a lovely fragrance. Over the years, people in the Middle East have attributed various medicinal qualities to its fruit. The etrog traditionally symbolizes the person who studies the Torah and also does good deeds known as *mitzvot*. One could say that the etrog and its fruit represent a person

---

[7] Christians have begun joining in this celebration. During the Feast of Tabernacles, an annual event sponsored by the International Christian Embassy Jerusalem (ICEJ), the lulav is waved in a special ceremony on the first day of Succot. For most of the Gentile pilgrims traveling to Jerusalem for the Feast, this will be the first time that they have heard about the ritual and significance of the lulav. Ezra, the priest, is responsible for reinstating the practice of celebrating the Feast of Tabernacles. He instructed the exiles returning from Babylon to gather branches from olive, pine, myrtle, palm and other leafy trees for the Succot celebration (Nehemiah 8). Today, however, the only species that are considered permissible by the rabbis for the lulav are myrtle, willow, date palm, and etrog.

who is a blessing, always exuding love, joy, peace, patience, gentleness, goodness, kindness, faithfulness, and self-control. This person knows scripture and practices what he or she preaches. The best kind of person is like the etrog.

2. Date Palm: This beautiful tree certainly has tasty fruit but has no lovely fragrance.. This is the person who studies the Torah and has a form of wisdom but then fails to perform any good deeds. A person touting the law without any acts of compassion isn't very attractive or inspiring.

3. Myrtle: Although this tree is fragrant, it produces no fruit. The myrtle is like the person who performs good deeds yet neglects the study of the Torah. This person is always lacking in the true wisdom that comes from studying the word of God.

4. Willow: This tree has neither fragrance nor fruit and is analogous to the person who fails to study the Torah and fails to perform any good deeds. This is someone with neither wisdom nor kindness to show others. Surely no one aspires to be like the "weeping" willow.

Rain is associated with Succot. Anyone who has been in Israel during the fall months knows that the last rains of the year begin at this time. Ideally the final harvest has been brought in, and families have already enjoyed special time in their sukkahs. People are relieved and thankful to have moved on from the days of Yom Teruah and Yom Kippur, with their emphasis upon repentance and judgment. Now is the time for rejoicing as the rainy season arrives to quench a dry and thirsty land. These rains are desperately needed in order to replenish water supplies after the heat of summer and to soften the ground for the next plantings that will be harvested in the spring.

Moses prepared the people to watch for the special rains from heaven. He had described the Promised Land to the Israelites by comparing the way Egyptian crops received water to the method God would provide for Israel's water supply: rain.

> For the land which you go in to possess is not like the land of Egypt, from which you came out, where you sowed your seed and watered it with your foot laboriously as in a garden of vegetables. But the land which you enter to possess is a land of hills and valleys which drinks water of the rain of the heavens, a land for which the Lord your God cares; the eyes of the Lord your God are always upon it from the beginning of the year to the end of the year. And if you will diligently heed My commandments which I command you this day - to love the Lord your God and to serve Him with all your [mind and] heart and with your entire being - I will give the rain for your land in its season, the early rain and the latter rain, that you may gather in your grain, your new wine, and your oil. (Deuteronomy 11:10–14 AMP)

While in Egypt, the Jewish slaves used their feet to operate the water wheels that brought the Nile's water into the fields. In Israel, however, the people learned to depend upon God's favor; in response to their obedience, He promised to send the rains of heaven. God's favor is interwoven with the harvest celebration of Succot.

Jesus chose to associate Himself with Succot because He is the source of living water. The seventh chapter of the book of John opens with a discussion on making the trip to Jerusalem for the Feast of Succot.

After having learned that the Feast of Tabernacles is one week in duration, verse 14 takes on new importance. "About the middle of the feast Jesus went up into the temple and began teaching"

(John 7:14). In other words, Jesus began to teach on the nineteenth or twentieth of Tishrei. These dates can be established, since the sacred calendar provides the exact dates for the holiday of Succot. One can also reckon that the Lord made use of the traditional ceremonies taking place during Succot as illustrations for His lessons. Priestly teachings during this week always emphasized scriptural references to water and to the coming Messiah. This is because the Gihon Spring, which is the source of water found in the Siloam pool, was associated with the coronation of Israel's kings. Additionally, the Jews were looking forward to the coming of Messiah as the king of the kings. Also at this time, pilgrims would gather just south of the temple each day during the feast to watch a priest proceed down the steps to the Pool of Siloam (today this area is known as Silwan). The priest would then fill a golden pitcher with the pool's water and return through the Water Gate back into the temple complex. The water, along with wine, was poured then on the base of the altar. This occasion was known as the water libation or drink offering. Throughout the week, the atmosphere was exuberantly festive and accompanied by singing, musical instruments, blowing of the shofar, and dancing. "With joy you will draw water from the wells of salvation!" (Isaiah12:3)[8]

The last day of the feast is known as *Hoshanah Rabbah. Hoshanah*, or *Hosanna*, translated as "save us!" or "rescue us!" During the days of the second temple, this was the climax of the feast, and everyone looked forward to the day's drama and emotion. Amid

---

[8] Alfred Edersheim, *The Temple: Its Ministry and Services* (Peabody, Massachusetts: Hendrickson Publishers, Inc., 1994), 220–222. Another valuable resource is *The Holy Temple of Jerusalem,* by The Temple Institutes' Chaim Richman. This book is also beautifully illustrated with scenes from the various feasts. Additionally, the Jewish Talmud provides a detailed account of the festivities during Succot. In October 2014, the Water Libation was reenacted in Jerusalem for the first time since the Roman destruction of the temple. To get a sense of the excitement surrounding the ceremony, watch it on YouTube: Festival of the Water Libation 5775,https://www.youtube.com/watch?v=oK4GDsDuOSA. Accessed 10/13/2014.

the chanting of Psalm 118 and cries of "Hoshanah," the priests concluded the final water libation by walking seven times around the altar.⁹ Meanwhile, there was one standing in the crowd by the name of Yeshua. The throngs cried out, "Hoshanah, save us!" In Hebrew, Yeshua means "salvation," and He chose that specific moment to make His identity known to those gathered for the libation ceremony. "On the last day of the feast, the great day, Jesus stood up and cried out, 'If anyone thirsts, let him come to me and drink. Whoever believes in me, as the Scripture has said, 'Out of his heart will flow rivers of living water'" (John 7:37–38).

Jesus chose to associate Himself with Succot because He is the light of the world. After citing the Talmud, Rabbi Lash describes the scene:

> There was another ceremony of the Feast of Tabernacles called the Illumination of the Temple. Four huge golden candlesticks were set up in the court of the women in the Temple. Four youths of priestly descent filled the candlesticks with pure oil. The light that shone from these four candlesticks was so bright that, according to rabbinic sources, 'There was no courtyard in Jerusalem that was not lit up with the light." (Sukkah 5:3).

> Now picture Yeshua, the young rabbi, walking in the midst of the great celebration surrounded by Levitical musicians, the Levitical choir and religious leaders dancing, singing songs of praise and holding burning torches. Jerusalem shone brightly with a light that was seen from miles around. In this setting, Yeshua proclaimed, "I am the light of the world; he

⁹ Ibid., 223.

who follows Me shall not walk in the darkness, but shall have the light of life." (John 8:12)[10]

In both cases, the Lord's claims were substantiated when He healed the man who had been blind from birth (John 9:1–41). Jesus put mud on the man's sightless eyes and then sent him to the Pool of Siloam to wash. On that occasion, He who *is* the light of the world gave light to blind eyes. Furthermore, He who *is* the source of living water brought healing through washing in water. As He was mixing the mud, perhaps He was remembering how Adam had been formed from that same earth.

Prophetic fulfillment of Succot. It is possible that this feast foretells details of the millennium to come. Or maybe it speaks of the future eternity in heavenly Jerusalem. As it is the finale among the festivals of God's sacred calendar, Succot has many special elements that bear further study. This chapter, however, is limited to commentary on only two such possibilities.

1. **The Nations.** Jesus was sent to the Jews first, but after the resurrection, He instructed His disciples to take the Gospel to the nations. God so loved the *world* that He sent His only begotten Son.

"Nations" is the Hebrew word *goyim* and indicates all peoples not descended from Abraham, Isaac, and Jacob. The goyim are the Gentile nations. In the Old Testament, all non-covenant people are referred to as the "nations" or Gentiles.[11]

Numbers 29 records that seventy bulls were offered for sacrifice during the week of Succot. The rabbis reason that this number is representative of the seventy nations listed in Genesis 10. It was

---

[10] Neil and Jamie Lash, *Jewish Jewels* (Fort Lauderdale, Florida; October, 2003), 3.
[11] Strong, *Strong's Exhaustive Concordance of the Bible* (Strong's 1471).

the descendants from these seventy nations who would repopulate the earth after the flood of Noah's generation.

Read Zechariah 14. This enlightening chapter speaks of that future age when the Lord will have already returned to the Mount of Olives and established His throne in Jerusalem. One learns that He will firmly and judiciously deal with the nations that had earlier encircled and fought against His holy city. Then, with a jolt, one reads that this same ruling monarch expects for the remaining nations to present themselves by coming to worship during the annual celebration of Succot. It will be a command performance.

> Then the survivors from all the nations that have attacked Jerusalem will go up year after year to worship the King, the Lord Almighty, and to celebrate the Festival of Tabernacles. If any of the peoples of the earth do not go up to Jerusalem to worship the King, the Lord Almighty, they will have no rain. If the Egyptian people do not go up and take part, they will have no rain. The Lord will bring on them the plague he inflicts on the nations that do not go up to celebrate the Festival of Tabernacles. (Zechariah 14:16–18 NIV)

It appears that Succot will continue to be celebrated by Jews and Gentiles alike during the Lord's future reign from Jerusalem. Could the sacrifices of the seventy bulls mentioned in Numbers 29 have been a rehearsal for this future millennial Succot?

2. **Is Succot a birthday celebration?** It is an intriguing conjecture to speculate that the nations will be summoned each year during the millennium to Jerusalem to commemorate the birthday of the great king/Messiah. Although the birth of Jesus has been traditionally celebrated on December twenty-fifth, a

number of Bible scholars speculate that Joseph and Mary were in Bethlehem during Succot and that Jesus was in fact born during the Feast of Tabernacles. One can simply turn to the scriptures for information on this theory. Luke relates that Caesar Augustus ordered a census of his vassal territory, Israel. As the population was to report to their tribal cities, Joseph was required to travel to Bethlehem, the city associated with the tribe of Judah. Both Joseph and Mary were members of this tribe. Luke's account describes a town so crowded that the couple from Nazareth could find no place to stay. "And while they were there, the time came for her to give birth. And she gave birth to her firstborn son and wrapped him in swaddling clothes and laid him in a manger, because there was no place for them in the inn" (Luke 2:6–7).

Because the Lord's first crib was a manger, it has been assumed that he was born in a stable or barn, but there is another possibility. Taking into consideration the "law of first mention,"[12] one finds that the Hebrew word for stable is the very same word used for a booth or temporary shelter. It is in fact the same word used by Israelis to describe their family's sukkah during the week of Succot. The first time the word appears in scripture is found in Genesis. "But Jacob journeyed to Succoth, and built himself a house and made booths for his livestock. Therefore the name of the place is called Succoth" (Genesis 33:17). The word used here for the booth or stable that Jacob built is translated "sukkah."[13] With the celebration

---

[12] The law of first mention is a principle of Bible scholarship and teaches the importance of finding the initial use of a word in scripture. The word's first reference or placement will reveal basic or fundamental meaning of the word or doctrine.

[13] Strong. *Strong's Exhaustive Concordance of the Bible* (Strong's 5521). While overlooking Shepherd's Field just outside Bethlehem, our group was engaged in discussion about the possibility that Mary and Joseph had been offered the use of a sukkah; our Israeli guide, Gideon, verified this as a very good probability.

of Succot in full swing, it is possible that Joseph and Mary, unable to find normal accommodations at an inn, would have been offered the option of a sukkah. Today, Israeli hotels often build a large communal sukkah for the feast, and most patrons will choose to dine "sukkah-style" if given the option. Jerusalem would have been a crowded place during any of the feasts, and Bethlehem, a mere five miles away, would have been one of the several outlying areas to handle a spillover of families looking for accommodations.

Another consideration is the census. The Romans wanted an accurate accounting and would have initiated such an undertaking during a part of the year when travel was easy. Expecting a country's population to travel over cold and icy roads would not have facilitated Rome's desired goal and may well have elicited a revolt. Israel can experience snow and sleet during the cold winter month of December.

There is also Luke's description of shepherds and their flocks out in the fields. Pasture grasses would not be available during this time, and shepherds would have kept their flocks protected inside caves and stables. Israel's winter is cold and often rainy, whereas the weather in Bethlehem during Succot is usually warm if not downright hot. Even today, shepherds let their sheep graze and sleep out in the open fields during the fall of the year. No, a December birth date is simply not credible.

The schedule for the priests' assigned duty times in the temple proves to be another source of information about the season of the Lord's birthday. It is recorded that the mother of John the Baptist and the mother of Jesus were relatives and that John was conceived six months before Jesus (Luke 1:26, 1:36). If one were to discover the time of John's conception, it would be a simple thing to count six months ahead thereby deduce the time of Jesus's birth. As though to help with such a quest, Luke gives a bit of additional information concerning this very thing. He includes the detail that John's father, the priest Zachariah, served during the division of Abia (Luke

1:5). Abia is also known as *Abijah.* Since the course divisions are listed in 1 Chronicles 24, it can be seen that Zachariah's family was assigned to serve during the eighth course out of a total of twenty-four courses (v. 10).

Each course or division was assigned to serve for two weeks during each year, once at the first part of the year and once in the second part of the year. Because of the additional amount of work required during the three major festivals, all the divisions would serve simultaneously during those feasts. Armed with this information, it can be ascertained as to which weeks of the year the division of Abia would be in service. By using parallel dating, it can be shown that the angel Gabriel appeared to John's father during the service of his second course. If one then takes into account the purity laws and the time needed for Zachariah's return home, John's conception can be determined.[14] Considering an average gestation time for both babies and counting forward will show that the Lord's conception would have taken place during Hanukkah. Because Hanukkah is known also as the Feast of Dedication or the Festival of Lights, this means that the light of the world was conceived during the Festival of Lights.[15]

By using the same method of calculation, it follows that the Lord was born during the fall and in the week of Succot. It is fitting that Jesus would have been born during the Feast of Tabernacles. John 1:14 YLT states, "And the Word became flesh, and did tabernacle among us, and we beheld his glory, glory as

---

[14] E.W. Bullinger, *Appendixes to the Companion Bible* (Windber, Pennsylvania: Bible Student's Press, 2010), 230–234.

[15] Hanukkah is not mentioned in Leviticus 23 as one of God's appointed feasts. Hanukkah celebrates an event that took place during the four hundred "silent years" that fell between the Old and New Testaments. Known as the Festival of Lights, it commemorates the cleansing and rededication of the temple, as well as the Jewish victory over the Seleucids. Those events took place in 165 BC, and it is recorded that Jesus was in Jerusalem during this festival's anniversary (John10:22).

of an only begotten of a father, full of grace and truth." The one who came to tabernacle among men was born during the Feast of Tabernacles.

Without even knowing it, the many generations of pilgrims going up year after year to Jerusalem to celebrate Succot have been honoring the birthday of the king. For generations, Jews have rehearsed this most celebratory of festivals. In recent decades, the people who have been "grafted in" (Romans 11:17) have joined with the thousands who stream into Jerusalem during the fall months to celebrate the Feast of Tabernacles.

The believer's bottom line. Yom Teruah, Yom Kippur and Succot are the final moedim according to the Hebrew calendar. Among the seven annual holidays, four have been fulfilled, but the final three have not. Although there is ample speculation about what each of the fall's holy assemblies may symbolize or predict, no one knows the answers with absolute certainty. It has been seen that the convocations of Passover, Unleavened Bread, and Firstfruits were rehearsals pointing to the atoning work of the Savior. Shavuot was the rehearsal for the gift of the Holy Spirit. Paul taught that the moedim are patterns of what is to come; therefore, the child of God can safely look forward to whatever the future holds, knowing that God is good and His plans are also good.

Chapter 10 Study Guide

The Fall Feasts

1. The month of Elul precedes the High Holy Days. It is a time for _____.

2. There are ___ feasts (moedim) during the fall; all are in the month of _____.

3. Yom Teruah (Tishrei 1) is also known as _____ and _____.

    (Exodus 19:19–20) (1 Kings 1:34) (Isaiah 27:13) (I Thessalonians 4:16–17)

4. Yom Kippur (Tishrei 10) is also known as _____.

    (Leviticus 16) (Hebrews 9: 11–12) (Hebrews 10:12–14) (Matthew 27:50–51)

5. Succot (Tishrei 15–21) is also known as _____.

    (Leviticus 23:40–43) (John 1:14) (John 7:2, 14, 37–38) (Zechariah 14:16–18)

6. Sukkah can be translated as _____.

    (Genesis 33:17)

7. According to Zechariah 14, which of the fall feasts will be celebrated during the millennium?

    _____.

Chapter 11

Jerusalem

Chapter 10 Recap: As examples of types and shadows to come, four of the seven annual feasts present a clear precedent for their spiritual and physical fulfillment in the life of Jesus. Based on this emerging pattern of prophetic actualization, the three fall feasts are the only moedim of the sacred calendar that remain to be fulfilled. For the believer, speculation about this final part of God's calendar holds special fascination and anticipation. Ultimately, however, the end result (with regard to the various possibilities considered) is that one simply stands in awe and reverence at how precisely and perfectly Jesus fulfilled His role as the eternal high priest. The book of Hebrews takes on deeper meaning as Yeshua is compared to the Cohen Gadol of Yom Kippur. Meanwhile, the entire creation stands on tiptoe, waiting for the trumpet blast of Yom Teruah in that day, with its promise of an eternal Feast of Tabernacles.

Jerusalem (ירושלים): city of the great king. Jerusalem is the eternal city destined to become the world's capital during the future millennial reign of the Prince of Peace. The scriptures disclose that it be replaced only upon the arrival and appearance of heavenly Jerusalem. Mentioned over eight hundred times in the Bible, Jerusalem is here to stay, and her presence in the world's headlines will only increase as the birth pangs of the Second Coming intensify.

Not many would deny that Jerusalem occupies a significant position in the Creator's vast and eternal panorama. Furthermore, activity pertaining to this strife-torn city seems to be somehow uniquely personal to Him. Having once been an important fixture in the distant past, Jerusalem's role has again emerged to be reckoned with, and it appears as though it will remain so into the foreseeable future. Is there in fact an ultimate purpose for Jerusalem? Is her destiny somehow bound up with the eventual resolution for peace in the region? A look at Jerusalem's pedigree and history are a reasonable starting point for answers. In this case, God Himself has unfolded the mystery of Jerusalem as He has progressively disclosed the details and identity of His chosen city.

First introduced as *Salem*, one reads the account of Melchizedek who, as king of Salem, brought bread and wine to Abraham following the latter's military victory.[1] Later, and then throughout the years under Joshua and the judges, the Israelites unsuccessfully fought with the Amorites for Jerusalem. Around 1000 BC, David finally wrested Jerusalem from the Jebusite occupants. Thus it came to be known as the city of David and has remained Israel's capital for the past three thousand years.[2] To date, Jerusalem has been conquered and reconquered over forty times. It has been destroyed three times: by the Babylonians under Nebuchadnezzar in 586 BC, by the Romans under Titus in 70 AD, and finally by the Emperor Hadrian in 135 AD. In spite of horrific and repeated devastation, David's city remains.

Although the famed temple no longer exists, its former location is uppermost in the minds of the thousands of pilgrims, Jew and Gentile alike, who visit yearly. Today, all that remains of this famous landmark is the retaining wall that once supported the platform upon which the former temple stood. Most frequently referred to as the Western Wall, it is also known as the *Kotel* or Wailing Wall. And

---

[1] Genesis 14:18.
[2] Second Samuel 5:6–9 and I Chronicles 11:4–8. Prior to David's victory, the city was also known as Jebus.

it is to this place that today's Jews come to pray. They believe that God's eyes are ever upon it, and He is attentive to each prayer offered from this precise location. Streaming from every corner of the globe, pilgrims come to Jerusalem, bringing written prayers to be carefully folded and tucked between the ancient stones of the Kotel.

Modern Jerusalem. Today, Jerusalem is nestled high in the Judean hills, a mere thirty miles from the Mediterranean coast. The city stands stalwart, occupying the same space as she has for millennia. Sitting alone at over twenty-four hundred feet above sea level, ever so slightly west of the Great Rift Valley, Jerusalem is sandwiched between two very different climate and vegetation zones. The result of this unique elevation and location is a repeating pageant of dramatic skies as overhead clouds from the Mediterranean sweep west to east during the day; they are followed by clouds swiftly moving from east to west during the night.

Jerusalem is spread like a blanket over topography composed of a series of hills known by such names as *Moriah, Zion, Ophel, Olives,* and *Scopus.* And although these closely-compacted mountains are covered with architecture ranging from Crusader-era to ultra-modern styles, the overall landscape appears to be homogenized by the exclusive use of a light-colored limestone known as Jerusalem stone. Ever since the time of the British Mandate, the municipality has required this local limestone to be used as the surface facing for every building. Consequently, from a distance, the entire city seems to be one vast cloud of pale pink or gold or white or gray, with the exact hue depending on weather conditions and time of day. Nevertheless, despite the city's irresistible beauty, first-time visitors are usually surprised at Jerusalem's relatively modest size. Understandably, most are expecting it to be significantly larger due to the amount of news coverage it garners. The population of Israel's capital is just over 801,000.[3]

---

[3] *World Atlas.* Last modified August 14, 2015, http://www.worldatlas.com/webimage/countrys/asia/israel/ilfacts.htm.

The size of the city's population is not the only thing that is unexpected, for Jerusalem has none of the special characteristics that would normally qualify or indicate a place's potential to become one of the great cities of the world. At the time David made it Israel's capital, it even lacked a secure water supply. And it would be another three hundred years before one of his descendants, King Hezekiah, would finally fortify the city's lone water source with a wall and tunnel. Additionally, Jerusalem has no harbor. It is not located on or even near a navigable river or canal. Furthermore, the city has never been easy to defend. For instance, the Temple Mount's position on Moriah has always been decidedly vulnerable, surrounded as it is by mountains of a higher elevation. As if these disadvantages were not obvious enough, the site of the city wasn't even conveniently located along either of the region's two ancient trade routes—the Via Maris or the King's Highway. In truth, Jerusalem's position has always been located near nothing more than "a little, higgely-piggely path that was used by the patriarchs to schlep back and forth from Shechem to Beersheva."[4] When judged by the usual standards easily claimed by other major world cities, there is simply nothing to recommend fame and greatness for Jerusalem. And yet, in spite of these deficiencies, Jerusalem has a destiny of eternal significance.

Significant from the beginning. Because Jerusalem and her king are inexplicably bound together throughout the eternities, one must first return to the garden where a conversation of great significance took place "in the beginning." From the time Satan first heard God's decree that one of Eve's offspring would bruise his head, he began an intense scrutiny of humanity, lying in wait for

---

[4] At an international conference in Israel, I first heard the distinguished Bible scholar and author, Lance Lambert, speaking about Jerusalem's decidedly unspectacular beginnings. Lance described the ancient rock strewn route between Beersheva and Shechem as a "little higgily-piggily path," accurately noting that it was followed by few except for the nomadic patriarchs. (Permission to quote was graciously granted by Lance Lambert.)

the advent of this promised savior. When the covenant was made with Abraham, this patriarch's future offspring became clearly identified and targeted as the family of the messianic recipient. Immediately, Satan's relentless stalking of this specific branch of humankind was set into motion. As the centuries progressed, God began to disclose more clearly the identity of the future champion; believers are familiar with these clues by another name: messianic prophecies. Little by little, under the unction of the Holy Spirit, God's prophets began to reveal the details concerning the promised Messiah: His tribe (Genesis 49:10); His family (Jeremiah 23:5); and His place of birth (Micah 5:2).

As might be expected, history is replete with evidence of demonic onslaught and repeated attempts to thwart God's plan as babies from different generations of this family were born and then murdered. Two examples of the adversary's heinous schemes were the pharaoh's consignment of Jewish newborns to the Nile and the slaughter of every little boy under the age of two in Bethlehem, so ordered by the vicious despot, Herod. Both of these horrors were orchestrated in a satanic effort to counter the entrance of the one who would bruise the serpent's head.

For the Messiah to be safely born, God chose to disguise the Savior's identity in the language of prophecy. In the same way, God cloaked the identity and even the location of Jerusalem with veiled words. And what is the explanation for such mystery? Jerusalem and the Messiah share in a joint destiny. Indeed, it is from Jerusalem that the king of kings, Jesus the Messiah, will reign for one thousand years.[5] Much as a developing baby is safely guarded within its mother's womb, Jerusalem was hidden from view until God determined the perfect timing for her debut.

"Code Talk." In the same way as parents sometimes resort to talking over the heads of their children with "code talk," God was

---

[5] Revelation 20:2–4.

doing that very thing through His prophets. While speaking in code, adults might refer to going to the movies as a "cinematic experience" or identify mom as the "maternal parental unit." In other words, by using vocabulary that is more complex and unfamiliar than the ordinary everyday usage, words become a sort of code that is communicated only to the intended recipient, even in the presence of others. It could be said that only those who have ears to hear will be able to unravel the mystery. And so as time went on, the clues from such "code talk" began falling into place for God's people who studied the prophecies and had ears to hear. Yet even as glimmers of the anticipated promise continued to be divulged, the Lord wisely guarded His secret, remaining careful about where and how the information was shared. This is because He knew an enemy was also listening for clues. Therefore, information concerning the Messiah (as well as Jerusalem) remained cloaked in mystery and was decipherable only by revelation. Brilliant!

***Ha'Makom* is code for Jerusalem**. God vigilantly protected the secret location He predetermined to be the place of His very own presence on earth. The Hebrew word *makom* is interpreted as "the place" and can refer to an area or to a specific spot.[6] It is intriguing to retrace how the Lord ever so carefully began to introduce the place or ha'makom. Although it would be disclosed eventually as Jerusalem, one notices that He did not immediately announce the name of the city or its exact location. The Lord guarded Jerusalem by referring to it only as "the place." With this information in mind, look at three early clues and descriptions that speak of Jerusalem:

- **"The place" is located within the region of Moriah (Genesis 22).** Decades after the covenant was introduced in Genesis 15, God spoke once again to Abraham. "Some time later God tested Abraham. He said to him, 'Abraham!' 'Here

---

[6] Strong, James. *Strong's Exhaustive Concordance of the Bible.* (Iowa Falls, Iowa: World Bible Publishers, Inc., 1986). (Strong's 4725)

I am,' he replied. Then God said, 'Take your son, your only son, whom you love--Isaac--and go to the region of Moriah. Sacrifice him there as a burnt offering on a mountain I will show you'" (Genesis 22:1–2 NIV). Notice that the place is also mentioned in the following verses: "On the third day Abraham lifted up his eyes and saw the place from afar" (v. 4); "When they came to the place of which God had told him, Abraham built an altar there" (v. 9); "So Abraham called the name of that place 'The Lord Will Provide'" (v. 14).

- **"The place" would be inhabited by God's presence (Deuteronomy 12).** Shortly before the Israelites' entry into the Promised Land, God revealed His intention to actually dwell in a special place within that land. From this chapter in Deuteronomy, one learns that the place was within the boundary of one of the tribes and that all sacrifices and offerings were designated for this location only. Eventually, it would be disclosed that the chosen territory lay within Benjamin's allotment.[7]

> But you shall seek the place which the Lord your God will choose out of all your tribes to put his name and make his habitation there. There you shall go ... then to the place that the Lord your God will choose, to make his name dwell there, there you shall bring all that I command you: your burnt offerings and your sacrifices, your tithes and the contribution that you present, and all your finest vow offerings that you vow to the Lord. Take care that you do not offer your burnt offerings at any place that you see, but at the place that the Lord will choose in one of your tribes, there you shall offer your burnt offerings, and there

---

[7] Joshua 18:28.

you shall do all that I am commanding you. If the
place where the Lord your God will choose to put
his name there is too far from you..." (Deuteronomy
12: 5, 11, 13–14, 21)

- **"The place" is the chosen venue for the three annual
feasts (Deuteronomy 16).** Before His people ever took
up residence in the land promised to them, God gave
instructions as to where they should celebrate His feasts.
It was clear from the outset that the place of God's dwelling
would be the only acceptable location for commemorating
the sacred holidays. From Deuteronomy 16, one learns that
the place is the physical site where the name of God would
dwell within the Promised Land—that unique portion of
the land where He vowed to meet with His people three
times during the year. "For seven days you shall keep the
feast to the Lord your God at the place that the Lord will
choose, because the Lord your God will bless you in all your
produce and in all the work of your hands, so that you will
be altogether joyful. Three times a year all your males shall
appear before the Lord your God at the place that he will
choose: at the Feast of Unleavened Bread, at the Feast of
Weeks, and at the Feast of Booths. They shall not appear
before the Lord empty-handed" (Deuteronomy 16:15–16).
- **"The place" is imprinted with God's name.** *HaShem* is
Hebrew for "the name." Traditionally, the single Hebrew
letter *Shin* represents *Shaddai. El Shaddai* (God Almighty) is
one of the names of God. Maps show that the topography of
the city's valleys actually connect to one another in the shape
of the letter Shin. When viewed from above, the conjunction
of the Valley of Hinnom, the Tyropoeon Valley, and the Kidron
Valley is shaped in such a way as to clearly form a Shin;
therefore, it can be said that God's name dwells in that place.

D. H. Withers

First Kings 11:36 states, "Yet to his son I will give one tribe, that David my servant may always have a lamp before me in Jerusalem, the city where I have chosen to put my name." Second Kings 21:4 adds, "And he built altars in the house of the Lord, of which the Lord had said, 'In Jerusalem will I put my name.'"

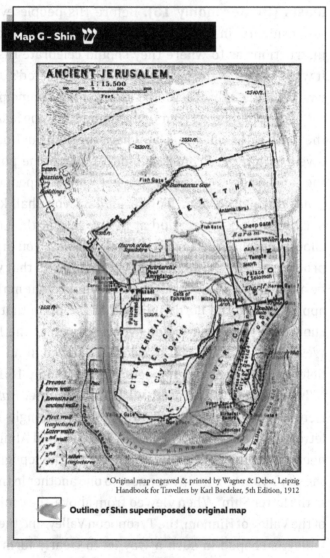

Map of Jerusalem with Shin superimposed

Jerusalem is the location of the Holy of Holies (2 Chronicles 5). Approximately four hundred years after Moses led the Israelites out of Egypt, their descendants had successfully inhabited the land, and the site for "the place" had been determined to be Jerusalem. From David's bequest of building materials and beautiful things dedicated and reserved for the Lord's temple, Solomon built a resplendent edifice. The newly completed temple sat upon Mount Moriah, and all of Israel assembled for its formal dedication. The location of ha'makom was no longer shrouded in mystery. For as the priests brought the ark to its resting place and as musicians and singers began to praise the Lord—accompanied by the blast of one hundred twenty trumpets—the temple filled suddenly with a cloud of glory. According to the official account, the priests were no longer able to remain standing under the tangible weight of this cloud. True to His word, God's very presence had come to dwell above the mercy seat of the Ark of the Covenant as it was placed inside of the Holy of Holies.

Second Chronicles 5:7 states, "Then the priests brought the ark of the covenant of the Lord to its place, in the inner sanctuary of the house, in the Most Holy Place, underneath the wings of the cherubim."

Prayers from Jerusalem are heard in heaven (2 Chronicles 6). As King Solomon knelt during the dedication prayer, he acknowledged that no earthly building could ever possibly contain the God of the universe. He did ask, however, for the prayers offered in this place to be heard from heaven. Solomon's words in his prayer established the precedent for facing Jerusalem while offering prayers: "That your eyes may be open day and night toward this house, the place where you have promised to set your name, that you may listen to the prayer that your servant offers toward this place. And listen to the pleas of your servant and of your people Israel, when they pray toward this place. And listen from heaven your dwelling place, and when you hear, forgive" (2 Chronicles 6:20–21).

Throughout the world, Jewish houses of worship are typically built so that the congregation faces toward Jerusalem. If for some reason the synagogue or temple is unable to be constructed in this way, the congregation turns to face Jerusalem when engaged in prayer. With respect to one's location regarding this holiest of areas, many visitors to the Western Wall demonstrate their respect by backing away from the place after having said their prayers. In this way, they remain facing the site where the Holy of Holies once stood.

God's attention, His heart, and His name are forever tied to Jerusalem. At the end of Solomon's prayer, fire fell from heaven and consumed the offerings and sacrifices. It is little wonder that after witnessing this phenomenon the people fell to their faces, and the priests were not able to enter the temple because the cloud of the Lord's glory fell upon it. Twenty-two thousand oxen and one hundred twenty thousand sheep were sacrificed on the day of the temple's dedication. One reads that at the end of the celebration—held during the fall at the time of Succot—God personally appeared to Solomon by night. It was during this visitation that He specifically answered Solomon's earlier prayer and gave further explanation about how His favor and protection would be contingent upon certain steps taken by the Israelites. Second Chronicles 7:14 is well-known by nearly anyone who has ever prayed for his or her nation, but few realize the words were originally spoken in relation to Israel's beloved first temple.

> Then the Lord appeared to Solomon in the night and said to him: "I have heard your prayer and have chosen this place for myself as a house of sacrifice. When I shut up the heavens so that there is no rain, or command the locust to devour the land, or send pestilence among my people, if my people who are called by my name humble themselves, and pray

and seek my face and turn from their wicked ways, then I will hear from heaven and will forgive their sin and heal their land. Now my eyes will be open and my ears attentive to the prayer that is made in this place. For now I have chosen and consecrated this house that my name may be there forever. My eyes and my heart will be there for all time. (2 Chronicles 7:12–16)

The divine purpose for guarding Jerusalem. Not only did the Father guard the specifics of the coming of His Son until it was an accomplished fact, but it can be seen from the following scriptures that He also guarded ha'makom, Jerusalem. From the beginning, He had purposed this city to play an integral part in the divine blueprint for humanity's ultimate destiny, and under no circumstance would anything be allowed to interfere with His plan. Three clear purposes emerge for safeguarding the identity and location of ha'makom:

- **Jerusalem is the spiritual capital of all mankind**. During the future millennium, the nations of the world will look to Jerusalem for leadership in all areas. The city will be established as the clearly acknowledged world capital where international judicial disputes will be settled. More importantly, Jerusalem has been ordained to become the official residence of the unchallenged and reigning world monarch, "King Jesus," Yeshua ha'Melech. Isaiah 2:2–4 explains:

  In the last days, the mountain of the Lord's house will be the highest of all--the most important place on earth. It will be raised above the other hills, and people from all over the world will stream there to

253

worship. People from many nations will come and say, 'Come, let us go up to the mountain of the Lord, to the house of Jacob's God. There he will teach us his ways, and we will walk in his paths.' For the Lords teaching will go out from Zion; his word will go out from Jerusalem. The Lord will mediate between nations and will settle international disputes. They will hammer their swords into plowshares and their spears into pruning hooks. Nation will no longer fight against nation, nor train for war anymore.

- **God is the founder of Jerusalem, and He loves Jerusalem above all other cities.** He guarded and protected this location until He determined the timing for the city's foundation. It was done in His way and on His terms. He has set it apart from all other cities and lets it be known that Jerusalem is His favorite city. "On the holy mount stands the city he founded; the Lord loves the gates of Zion more than all the dwelling places of Jacob. Glorious things of you are spoken, O city of God" (Psalm 87:1–3).
- **Jerusalem is personal to the Lord; He speaks to this city as a husband would speak to his wife.** The sixteenth chapter of Ezekiel opens a door to the unique relationship God shares with Jerusalem. The chapter is a parable of His relationship with Israel, as represented by Jerusalem, and it is clear that His involvement with her is personal. In His blazing anger, He reminds her of her inglorious origin; He enumerates her adulterous behavior with other gods; and He decrees a judgment of shame and disgrace. Yet, in spite of her treacherous and inexcusable behavior, the Lord— the everlasting God—promises to restore relationship for the sake of the covenant. The covenant. There can be no doubt that God alone is the God of merciful redemption

and magnificent restoration. Many great cities of antiquity have disappeared, yet Jerusalem still stands, and she stands because she is from God's own heart. In spite of her actions, He loves her very foundation, and has foreordained and established her eternal destiny as the city of God. The following is a summary of Ezekiel 16.

Her origin and early years. To better understand Ezekiel's story, it is important to know that the Amorites who lived in the area of Canaan, as well as people from Phoenicia (modern-day Lebanon) and Syria, were known as "barbarians" to the civilized Sumerians (modern-day Iraq). The Hittites from Anatolia (modern-day Turkey) worshiped a myriad of gods. The parable opens to find the offspring from this union of Amorite and Hittite discarded and left alone, abandoned in an open field, callously thrown away.

Ezekiel 16:3–5 AMP states, "Your [spiritual] origin and your birth are thoroughly Canaanitish; your [spiritual] father was an Amorite and your [spiritual] mother a Hittite. And as for your birth, on the day you were born your navel cord was not cut, nor were you washed with water to cleanse you, nor rubbed with salt or swaddled with bands at all. No eye pitied you to do any of these things for you, to have compassion on you; but you were cast out in the open field, for your person was abhorrent and loathsome on the day that you were born."

But God was passing by and spoke life to this infant—abandoned, bloody, naked, and unwanted. He betrothed her to Himself and then anointed her wounds and washed her clean. Clothing her with fine linen and silk, He lavished her with exquisite ornaments of gold and silver. All the while, He fed her with the finest of foods and honey. Nothing was withheld from her, just as He had freely bestowed His own majesty and splendor on Jerusalem. Read verses 6–14 of Ezekiel chapter 16.

255

Her adulterous behavior. Alas, beautiful Jerusalem (representing Israel) was snared by pride and forsook her faithful husband. Turning to other lovers (idols), she brazenly ran after them, sinking so low as to sacrifice the Lord's own children in the process. Read verses 15–34 of Ezekiel chapter 16.

Her judgment. As one continues reading in Ezekiel 16, God finally calls a halt to Jerusalem's harlotry. With wrath and jealousy, she is judged and turned over to the cruelty of those who surround her, for she has behaved just as her parents did before her. After further judgment, she is found to be more wicked than either one of her two sisters. The first sibling is Samaria (representing the ten northern tribes who entered into idolatry), and the second is Sodom (destroyed by fire). Disgrace and misery now replace the splendor that was once Jerusalem. Read verses 35–59 of Ezekiel chapter 16.

Her Restoration. God's holy character insures that He'll always maintain and uphold His part of the covenant. In spite of everything Jerusalem has done to disgrace herself, God forgives her and prophesies reestablishment of their relationship for the sake of the covenant. Sovereign God has determined that Jerusalem will be His.

> Nevertheless, I will [earnestly] remember My covenant with you in the days of your youth and I will establish with you an everlasting covenant. Then you will [earnestly] remember your ways and be ashamed and confounded when you shall receive your sisters, both your elder and your younger; I will give them to you as daughters, but not on account of your covenant [with Me]. And I will establish My covenant with you, and you shall know (understand and realize) that I am the Lord. That you may [earnestly] remember and be ashamed

and confounded and never open your mouth again because of your shame when I have forgiven you all that you have done, says the Lord god. (Ezekiel 16:60–63 AMP)

Prosperity is promised to those who love Jerusalem. Because God so loves this city, He wants everyone to be in love with her too. He evens promises the reward of prosperity to those who will join Him in His affection. David, the king who made Jerusalem the capital of the nation, was inspired to pen the words of Psalm 122 three thousand years ago:

> I was glad when they said to me, "Let us go to the house of the Lord." Our feet are standing Within your gates, O Jerusalem, Jerusalem, that is built As a city that is compact together; To which the tribes go up, even the tribes of the Lord- An ordinance for Israel- To give thanks to the name of the Lord. For there thrones were set for judgment, The thrones of the house of David. Pray for the peace of Jerusalem: "May they prosper who love you. May peace be within your walls, And prosperity within your palaces." For the sake of my brothers and my friends, I will now say, "May peace be within you." For the sake of the house of the Lord our God, I will seek your good. (Psalm 122 NASB)

The Lord personally appoints sentries to be stationed around the perimeter of Jerusalem. These unique watchmen are assigned to remain at their posts until the Lord's purpose for this city is fully accomplished. Included in that purpose is His promise to make Jerusalem into a place of praise throughout the earth. The Creator of the heavens and the earth intends for the entire world to praise Jerusalem. This is clearly a tall order because it means that at some future date the very name of Jerusalem will evoke only such responses as love and admiration, approval, and honor. Only good things will be said about the city. The contentious negotiations over her sovereignty and existence will be a thing of the past. Jerusalem will be lauded and celebrated. To this end, He has positioned vigilant lookouts to constantly remind Him of His promises pertaining to Jerusalem. These watchmen/sentries are the believers worldwide who have answered the call to take up the mandate to pray for the peace of Jerusalem. Although there is an actual medieval wall of stone surrounding the boundary of the Old City, the walls mentioned in the following verses are composed of human stones.

"I have set watchmen upon your walls, O Jerusalem, who will never hold their peace day or night; you who [are His servants and by your prayers] put the Lord in remembrance [of His promises], keep not silence, and give Him no rest until He establishes Jerusalem and makes her a praise in the earth" (Isaiah 62:6–7 AMP).

For centuries, the city of David has continued its existence more or less unchanged from the era of the Crusades. Less than a hundred years ago, most people might have hesitated to accept the scriptures from Isaiah 62 and Psalm 122 in a literal sense. Jerusalem—a place of praise in the earth? At that time, Jerusalem was not the capital of anything. It was a lackluster, partially broken-down, dismally dreary place located in the Judean hills of the decaying Ottoman Empire's Syrian province.

In the decades before and after World War I and the Balfour Declaration, the area known as Palestine began to change due to a steady migration of European Jews and the influx of Arabs coming from neighboring countries to find work. Even so, Jerusalem enjoyed no political autonomy because decisions continued to be made from Westminster. Under the existing mandate system, Great Britain held all final authority. Certainly Jerusalemites were not to be included among the movers and shakers of that geopolitical time period. In fact, most would have understood the injunction to pray for the peace of Moscow, Berlin, Washington DC, Paris, or London, but *Jerusalem?*

Today, people get it. Jerusalem is an international flash point, routinely mentioned in United Nations' debates and resolutions. Believers worldwide understand the necessity of praying for this city. Now, it is obvious that the command in Psalm 122 is not allegorical and that when the psalmist wrote about Jerusalem, he was actually referring to *literal* Jerusalem. What has happened that would cause Jerusalem to be thrust onto the current worldwide scene amidst such controversy? What has happened to cause Jerusalem to become *the* international hot potato? The twofold answer is simple: the Jewish state was born in 1948, and Jerusalem was recognized as its capital in 1967.

Jerusalem plays a major role in the end times. Now that the Jews are being re-gathered to their land and ancient Jerusalem has reemerged as the capital, circumstances have begun lining up for the culmination of the ages. As this is happening, there still exists a deadly foe who does not want to see this come to pass, for it spells his final demise. Therefore, Satan—that ancient adversary—doggedly and ferociously works to thwart the fulfillment of prophecy for Jerusalem.

God has determined to use this city as a focal point whereby the nations of the world will find themselves positioned in a confrontation from which only one victor will emerge. In pronouncing the following ominous decree, God used the prophet Zechariah as His mouthpiece: "Behold, I will make Jerusalem a cup of reeling unto all the peoples round about, and upon Judah also shall it be in the siege against Jerusalem. And it shall come to pass in that day, that I will make Jerusalem a burdensome stone for all the peoples; all that burden themselves with it shall be sore wounded;

and all the nations of the earth shall be gathered together against it" (Zechariah 12:2–3 ASV).

Jerusalem is likened to "a cup of reeling" in verse 2. This cup is identified as a drink that causes the one who swallows its content to become intoxicated and to drunkenly reel or stagger under the influence of the cup's potion. A cup of reeling is one that induces an otherwise stable and rational individual to behave in ways that would never be remotely considered under ordinary circumstances. This is the cup that renders its victim a stumbling, mad fool.

The prophecy goes on to compare Jerusalem to "a burdensome stone" in verse 3. Be forewarned, and do not proceed! The Lord chooses to fashion Jerusalem into a stone of such magnitude that all who surround it are troubled because of it. A warning is clearly issued that interference with Jerusalem will result in injury, the consequence of such action posted by God Himself. Beware, for guaranteed wounding is foretold for those who trifle with Jerusalem.

The nations take on Jerusalem at their own peril. As the world's pundits continue to bandy about the disputed status of Jerusalem, it is imperative for believers to keep God's viewpoint squarely before their eyes lest they risk being drawn off into a humanistic rationale. Scripture provides clear evidence that the status of Jerusalem has always been important to the Lord. That this city will continue to remain in the headlines as a focal point for worldwide political negotiation until Jesus returns is scarcely debatable. And because of Jerusalem's vital role in the return of the king, God issues the sternest of warnings against trespassing to the unwitting meddler.

Both Zechariah 14:4 and Acts 1:11-12 disclose the Mount of Olives as the actual site of the Lord's return. The itinerary plainly indicates that His first stop will be to the very spot from where He ascended, and, as the Mount of Olives is located within the city limits, it means He is returning to Jerusalem.

God jealously guards Jerusalem, and warns the nations against "burdening" themselves with it. In the following passages, notice how the battle against Jerusalem is tied to the appearance and subsequent recognition of the Messiah king. Notice that the citizens of Jerusalem will see Him, and then, after being confronted with the wounds that He still carries in His body, they will finally recognize Him as the Jesus of history. At this realization, their collective, heart-rending remorse will be as a parent's anguish at the death of an only child. Their eyes, which were blinded for the sake of the Gentiles, will be opened to Jesus as their very own redeemer.[8]

"And it shall be in that day that I will make it My aim to destroy all the nations that come against Jerusalem. And I will pour out upon the house of David and upon the inhabitants of Jerusalem the Spirit of grace or unmerited favor and supplication. And they shall look [earnestly] upon Me Whom they have pierced, and they shall mourn for Him as one mourns for his only son, and shall be in bitterness for Him as one who is in bitterness for his firstborn" (Zechariah 12:9–10 AMP).

"Then shall the Lord go forth and fight against those nations as when He fought in the day of battle. And His feet shall stand in that day upon the Mount of Olives, which lies before Jerusalem on the east, and the Mount of Olives shall be split in two from the east to the west by a very great valley; and half of the mountain shall remove toward the north and half of it toward the south" (Zechariah 14: 3–4 AMP).

"And it shall be in that day that living waters shall go out from Jerusalem, half of them to the eastern [Dead] Sea and half of them to the western [Mediterranean] Sea; in summer and in winter shall it be. And the Lord shall be King over all the earth; in that day the Lord shall be one [in the recognition and worship of men] and His name one" (Zechariah 14:8–9 AMP).

---

[8] For Paul's treatment of this mystery, see Roman 11:8–25.

"And everyone who is left of all the nations which came against Jerusalem shall even go up from year to year to worship the King, the Lord of hosts, and to keep the Feast of Tabernacles or Booths. And it shall be that whoso of the families of the earth shall not go up to Jerusalem to worship the King, the Lord of hosts, upon them there shall be no rain" (Zechariah 14:16-17 AMP).

The believer's bottom line. God chose Jerusalem. With an existence transcending time and space, the connection between the celestial city and its earthly counterpart is evidenced by the name's plural Hebrew ending, *im. Yerushalayim.* Traditionally, the city is referred to as *Yerushalayim shel Mata* (literally "Jerusalem of below") or *Yerushalayim shel Maalah* ("Jerusalem of above"). Thus the city is actually "compacted together," as earlier described by the author of Psalm 122. Having introduced Jerusalem in the first act of Genesis, the master playwright concludes His pageantry of revelation with the appearance of a radiant New Jerusalem in the magnificent finale known as the Revelation of John. From beginning to end, Jerusalem endures, and the redeemed of the Lord are assured an eternal home in Yerushalayim shel Maalah, the New Jerusalem.

"Then I saw a new heaven and a new earth, for the first heaven and the first earth had passed away, and the sea was no more. And I saw the holy city, new Jerusalem, coming down out of heaven from God, prepared as a bride adorned for her husband." (Revelation 21:1-2)

Chapter 11 Study Guide

1. Jerusalem is mentioned _____ times in the Bible.
2. Jerusalem has been Israel's capital since _____ BC.
3. Jerusalem has been Israel's capital for _____ years.
4. Jerusalem's origin is detailed in this scripture _____.
5. Jerusalem's founder is revealed in this scripture _____.
6. Yerushalayim shel Mata means _____.
7. Yerushalayim shel Maalah means _____.
8. The definition and meaning of Ha'Makom is _____.

_____

9. God's own predictions for Jerusalem:
   Spiritual capital of the world (locate the scripture) _____.
   "Cup of reeling" and "burdensome stone" (locate the scripture)
   _____.

"Pray for the peace of Jerusalem! May they prosper who love you!" (Psalm 122:6).

"I have set watchmen upon your walls, O Jerusalem, who will never hold their peace day or night; you who [are His servants and by your prayers] put the Lord in rememberance [of His promises], keep not silence, And give Him no rest until He establishes Jerusalem and makes her a praise in the earth." (Isaiah 62:6-7 AMP).

"And I heard a loud voice from the throne saying, 'Behold, the dwelling place of God is with man. He will dwell with them, and they will be his people, and God himself will be with them as their God'" (Revelation 21:3).

Chapter 12

Aliyah

Chapter 11 Recap: Jerusalem is God's idea and His favorite city in all of the earth. Jesus was crucified just outside of the city's walls, and it is to this place that He will return. Though once concealed as a secret within the heart of God, it has been appointed the capital of the world. Believers are commanded to pray for the city's peace. Meanwhile, amid controversy, violence, and combustible emotion, the status of this municipality occupies the international community. In the final analysis, however, Jerusalem—the city of gold, city of David, and capital of the State of Israel—is destined ultimately to become the designated residence of the supreme international ruler and great king of kings, Lord Jesus.

Aliyah. A remarkable thing is happening in the world today. After two thousand years of exile, Jews from every corner of the globe are returning to the land of Israel. A corner in the spiritual realm of the heavenlies has been turned as our present generation witnesses the fulfillment of God's promise to Abraham's descendants. Their return to the Promised Land is an extraordinary event like none other, and it is also an ongoing process orchestrated from the throne room of the universe.

In Hebrew, the word *aliyah* is translated as "to go up." Aliyah means "to ascend." During Bible times, the people of Israel were required to go up or ascend to Jerusalem three times a year: Passover, in the spring, Pentecost, in late spring/early summer, and Feast of Tabernacles, in the fall. A special group of the psalms, Psalms 120–134, is distinguished by the description, "songs of ascents." While eagerly anticipating the festivals in Jerusalem, pilgrims would sing these fifteen psalms as they traveled in groups from their villages. The fifteen Psalms are aptly named songs of ascents for two reasons. First, the people were actually going up, as Jerusalem is higher in elevation than most of Israel. And secondly, the people believed that they were also rising to a higher spiritual awareness as they entered the city.

Today, when a Jew immigrates to Israel, it is said that he or she has "made aliyah." Indeed, the prophets foretold of a time when the world's Jewish population would again take up permanent residence in the land. Speaking to the nations, God makes the following announcement: "Hear the word of the Lord, O nations, and declare it in the coastlands far away; say, 'He who scattered Israel will gather him, and will keep him as a shepherd keeps his flock'" (Jeremiah 31:10). This verse is saying that the people of Israel will be gathered and returned to their original pasture, where they will be guarded and protected by none other than God, their shepherd. With the fullness of their punishment of exile having come to term, God Himself is bringing them back from all the nations, never to be driven away again. For the past century and a half, the world has witnessed this most amazing phenomenon, namely, the return of the Jews to Israel. This previously foretold return is known as aliyah.

A second Exodus. "Therefore, behold, the days are coming, declares the Lord, when it shall no longer be said, 'As the Lord lives who brought up the people of Israel out of the land of Egypt,' but 'As the Lord lives who brought up the people of Israel out of the north country and out of all the countries where he had driven them.' For I will bring them back to their own land that I gave to their fathers" (Jeremiah 16:14–15).

Jeremiah makes five points.

1. The reader is reminded that the Lord executed the spectacular events of the Exodus.
2. Notification is given about a future grander exodus that will originate from the north and other countries.
3. The Lord Himself expelled His people from Israel.
4. The Lord Himself will also bring them back to Israel.
5. Finally, the scripture is a reminder that the Lord is not defaulting on promises made originally to their fathers, the three patriarchs. Jeremiah's words make it crystal clear that though God drove the children of Israel from the land, God will also be the one to bring them back to the land because of His promise to Abraham, Isaac, and Jacob.

Looking at a map, it can be seen that Moscow is approximately due north of Israel. Today, there are more than one million Jews who already have made aliyah from the former Soviet Union. In addition to these immigrants from the north are the Jews returning from the far corners of the earth, "out of all the countries where he had driven them." In keeping with His promise, God is currently bringing His previously dispersed people home to the land of Israel, and prophecy is being fulfilled before the eyes of all the nations.

Surely there must be a reason that aliyah is even a topic for discussion. If the Jews originally lived in the land given to them by God, then how is it that they came to be absent from that land so that they must now return to it? To answer that question, it is necessary to look into the conditions laid down by God concerning the original land lease. For instance, what exactly were the terms laid down for the people's expected behavior during their administration and stewardship of His land? Were those terms specifically outlined?

The land of Israel belongs to God. Beginning with the original instructions to Moses, God always specifies ownership of Eretz Israel as His alone. He is intentional about descriptions of the land, carefully reminding the Jews that as the chosen stewards of His real estate, the land in fact always belongs to Him.

- Leviticus 25:23 states, "The land shall not be sold in perpetuity, for **the land is mine** [emphasis added]. For you are strangers and sojourners with me."
- As evidenced in Ezekiel 36:5, God also expects the surrounding nations to acknowledge and respect His ownership of the land. "Therefore thus says the Lord God: Surely I have spoken in my hot jealousy against the rest of the nations and against all Edom, who gave **my land** [emphasis added] to themselves as a possession with wholehearted joy and utter contempt, that they might make its pasturelands a prey."

The original deed to Israel mandates that the land be maintained in holiness for the Lord. God issued the charge of responsibility for the land specifically to the nation of Israel and insisted that it reflect His own holiness. He also warned of dire consequences should the stewards shirk that duty.

- Leviticus 20:22 states, "You shall therefore keep all my statutes and all my rules and do them, that the land where I am bringing you to live may not vomit you out."
- Jeremiah 16:17–18 states, "For my eyes are on all their ways. They are not hidden from me, nor is their iniquity concealed from my eyes. But first I will doubly repay their iniquity and their sin, because they have polluted my land with the carcasses of their detestable idols, and have filled my inheritance with their abominations."

Diaspora. The repercussion for idolatry and not managing God's land according to His ways was expulsion and exile. Sure enough, in spite of repeated warnings, the people didn't uphold their part of the covenant. In the aftermath of the resulting judgment, Jews were scattered to the ends of the earth, and their descendants that now live outside of Israel became known collectively as the Diaspora. The following scriptures refer directly to the community of the Diaspora:

- Leviticus 26:33 states, "And I will scatter you among the nations, and I will unsheathe the sword after you, and your land shall be a desolation, and your cities shall be a waste."
- Ezekiel 36:16–20 states,

  The word of the Lord came to me: "Son of man, when the house of Israel lived in their own land, they defiled it by their ways and their deeds. Their ways before me were like the uncleanness of a woman in her menstrual impurity. So I poured out my wrath upon them for the blood that they had shed in the land, for the idols with which they had defiled it. I scattered them among the nations, and they were dispersed through the countries. In accordance with their ways and their deeds I judged them. But when they came to the nations, wherever they came, they profaned my holy name, in that people said of them, 'These are the people of the Lord, and yet they had to go out of his land.'"

By 722 BC, the northern kingdom had fallen to Assyria. Nearly a century and a half later, in 586 BC, the southern kingdom, or Judea, along with its capital of Jerusalem, was crumbling before Nebuchadnezzar's mighty Babylonian army. After another six hundred fifty years, Jerusalem was destroyed again in 70 AD by the Roman general, Titus. And finally, in 135 AD, the city was razed to the ground once more. With each of these defeats, much of the Jewish population was carried away to foreign lands. The Jewish people have indeed suffered horrific consequences for their disobedience and lack of care for God's land.

The pages of the Bible offer numerous examples of how the Jews failed in their responsibility to maintain their inheritance. They broke laws concerning basic care for the land, including a failure to let the fields lie fallow every seven years.[1] Idolatry crept in, and religion took the place of their relationship with the Lord. Just as men sin today, Israel sinned then. And in so doing, an entire nation, as well as its descendants, has endured the consequence of exile. But God! Because God is merciful, tenderhearted, long-suffering, willing to forgive, and full of compassion, the story does not stop there.

God's promise to Israel has never changed. The Old and New Testaments are replete with God's assurance that He is a covenant-keeping God. He is not a man that He should lie, and His promises are without even a hint of fraud. For the record, He is the original promise keeper. The following two scriptures (one from the Old Testament and one from the New Testament) underline this commitment to Israel in spite of her sin. In fact, the declaration states that as long as the sun, stars, and moon remain in orbit, God pledges to maintain His covenant with Israel. Furthermore, God reveals His plan herein for a new covenant and Israel's inclusion within that covenant as follows:

---

[1] Leviticus 25:1–7. Every seventh year is known as the *shmita,* or Sabbath year. During the seventh year, the land was supposed to lie fallow so that it could rest.

- Jeremiah 31:31–40 NIV states,

"The days are coming," declares the Lord, "when I will make a new covenant with the people of Israel and with the people of Judah. It will not be like the covenant I made with their ancestors when I took them by the hand to lead them out of Egypt, because they broke my covenant, though I was a husband to them," declares the Lord. "This is the covenant I will make with the people of Israel after that time," declares the Lord. "I will put my law in their minds and write it on their hearts. I will be their God, and they will be my people. No longer will they teach their neighbor, or say to one another, 'Know the Lord,' because they will all know me, from the least of them to the greatest," declares the Lord. "For I will forgive their wickedness and will remember their sins no more." This is what the Lord says, he who appoints the sun to shine by day, who decrees the moon and stars to shine by night, who stirs up the sea so that its waves roar-- the Lord Almighty is his name: "Only if these decrees vanish from my sight," declares the Lord, "will Israel ever cease being a nation before me." declares the Lord. This is what the Lord says: "Only if the heavens above can be measured and the foundations of the earth below be searched out will I reject all the descendants of Israel because of all they have done," "The days are coming," declares the Lord, "when this city will be rebuilt for me from the Tower of Hananel to the Corner Gate. The measuring line will stretch from there straight to the hill of Gareb and then turn to Goah. The whole valley where dead bodies and ashes are thrown, and all the terraces out to the Kidron Valley on the east as far as the corner of the Horse Gate, will be holy to the Lord. The city will never again be uprooted or demolished."

Hebrews 8:8–12 NIV states,

But God found fault with the people and said: "The days are coming, declares the Lord, when I will make a new covenant with the people of Israel and with the people of Judah. It will not be like the covenant I made with their ancestors when I took them by the hand to lead them out of Egypt, because they did not remain faithful to my covenant, and I turned away from them, declares the Lord. This is the covenant I will establish with the people of Israel after that time, declares the Lord. I will put my laws in their minds and write them on their hearts. I will be their God, and they will be my people. No longer will they teach their neighbor, or say to one another, 'Know the Lord,' because they will all know me, from the least of them to the greatest. For I will forgive their wickedness and will remember their sins no more."

Both scripture references are written to Jews, with the latter quoting directly from the former. Further, the book of Hebrews was written after Israel, as a nation, had rejected Jesus as Messiah. Therefore, the author of Hebrews is making the point that God's covenant with Israel still stands.

At the cross, the wall between Jew and Gentile was broken down once and for all. Both were made one in Christ. The two became one because of the last Adam's victory, and having the understanding of this mystical union was a foundational imperative for the first-generation Church. Otherwise, they could not have moved forward. Even though Hebrews 8:8–12 is reassurance to the Jewish believer about the new covenant, Gentile believers also needed to be educated about the "one new man."[2] With this on his heart, the proper relationship between Jew and Gentile is spelled out in Paul's letter to the congregation that met in Rome. Not surprisingly then, Jeremiah 31 is again quoted directly to that group. There is an interesting twist, however, regarding the letter to the Romans. This congregation was composed of both Jew *and* Gentile believers, and significant tension apparently existed between the two groups. It was therefore critical for the Gentile congregants to comprehend and accept the immutability of Jeremiah's message. The inclusion of the scripture from Jeremiah emphasizes the fact that the new covenant is intended for both Jew and Gentile. Three chapters in this letter (Romans 9, 10, and 11) deal expressly with the nation of Israel.

- Romans 9, 10, and 11. Bible teachers often refer to these three chapters as a "book within a book" because they specifically and thoroughly address the mystery of Israel. When taken out of context and left to stand alone, Romans 9:8 is the basis for replacement theology proponents.[3]

---

[2] The "one new man," God's masterpiece of recreation, is introduced in Ephesians 2:10–22.

[3] Romans 9:8 (NIV) reads, "In other words, it is not the children by physical descent who are God's children, but it is the children of the promise who are regarded as Abraham's offspring." Taken out of context, this verse has been used as verification for removing the Jews (children of physical DNA descent) as heirs of the covenant and replacing them with the Church (children of the promise) as the rightful heirs to the covenant promises. There is, however, an obvious downside to this horribly flawed interpretation, known as replacement theology. If God breaks covenant with Israel, He can also break covenant with Christians. In actuality, chapters 9, 10, and 11 are Paul's impassioned clarification of God's continuing covenant relationship with Israel. It is this author's opinion that every Christian should read these three chapters as though they are a parenthesis inserted between chapters 8 and 12.

However, when read within proper context, both chapters 9 and 10 speak to the "remnant" of Israel and to that remnant's faith. And finally, Paul maintains God's steadfast and unwavering call, as well as His plans for Israel, when he states, "But as regards election, they are beloved for the sake of their forefathers. For the gifts and the calling of God are irrevocable" (Romans 11:28–29). God will never revoke His covenant with Israel.

Writing to the Roman Church, Paul rhetorically voices this question, "I ask, then, has God rejected his people? By no means! For I myself am an Israelite, a descendant of Abraham, a member of the tribe of Benjamin" (Romans 11:1). Continuing with Paul's methodical, legal, and theological arguments throughout the remainder of chapter 11, the only possible conclusions to his case progressively emerge. Although Israel has been scattered throughout the earth generation after generation, it is still considered to be the root of the Church, *and* the Lord has never reneged upon His promise to bring the nation back to its land.

Furthermore, it appears that the term of punishment has been served because the land is currently in the process of welcoming its returning occupants. The God of Israel is currently executing His promise to bring His people back home.

God's heart is aliyah. The prophet Ezekiel lived a full six hundred years before Christ, yet his words thunder down through the corridors of time to the present generation of the Diaspora. He communicates to both the land of Israel and the nation of Israel. The following verses are the written record of God's encouragement to the land; they are not a message to human beings but a message for the land. Listen as Ezekiel records the Creator's words to the land.

Ezekiel 36:8–12 states,

> But you, O mountains of Israel,[4] shall shoot forth
> your branches and yield your fruit to my people
> Israel, for they will soon come home. For behold,
> I am for you, and I will turn to you, and you shall
> be tilled and sown. And I will multiply people on
> you, the whole house of Israel, all of it. The cities
> shall be inhabited and the waste places rebuilt. And
> I will multiply on you man and beast, and they shall
> multiply and be fruitful. And I will cause you to be
> inhabited as in your former times, and will do more
> good to you than ever before. Then you will know
> that I am the Lord. I will let people walk on you,
> even my people Israel. And they shall possess you,
> and you shall be their inheritance, and you shall no
> longer bereave them of children.

This is good news for the land that was so plaintively described by Mark Twain in *Innocents Abroad.* In the following verses, Ezekiel relays God's plan for His Jewish people once the long exile is finished. Here, He speaks only words of encouragement; they convey hope and are couched in tenderness. He declares that as Israel's punishment becomes a thing of the past, the nation will be rescued from exile and escorted home. God assures them that once back in their own land, He will heal and restore all that was previously broken. Finally, the people are given the promise of a brand new heart - one that beats in harmony with God's own heart.

---

[4] A chain of low-lying mountains runs the length of Israel from north to south. Along this geographical spine, known as the mountains of Israel, are the cities mentioned so often in the Bible: Shechem, Shilo, Bethel, Jerusalem, Bethany, Bethlehem, and Hebron. Repopulation of these ancient sites is tangible fulfillment of Ezekiel 36:8–12.

Listen to the next five verses as Ezekiel records the Creator's words to the people.

Ezekiel 36:24–28 states,

> I will take you from the nations and gather you from
> all the countries and bring you into your own land.
> I will sprinkle clean water on you, and you shall be
> clean from all your uncleannesses, and from all your
> idols I will cleanse you. And I will give you a new
> heart, and a new spirit I will put within you. And I
> will remove the heart of stone from your flesh and
> give you a heart of flesh. And I will put my Spirit
> within you, and cause you to walk in my statutes
> and be careful to obey my rules. You shall dwell in
> the land that I gave to your fathers, and you shall be
> my people, and I will be your God.

The valley of the dry bones. The familiar story of the valley of the dry bones is found in Ezekiel 37. The following verses shed light on the identity of the bones, bones that appear to be long dead and dry.

Ezekiel 37:11–14 states,

> Then he said to me, "Son of man, these bones are the
> whole house of Israel. Behold, they say, 'Our bones
> are dried up, and our hope is lost; we are indeed
> cut off.' Therefore prophesy, and say to them, Thus
> says the Lord God: Behold, I will open your graves
> and raise you from your graves, O my people. And I
> will bring you into the land of Israel. And you shall
> know that I am the Lord, when I open your graves,
> and raise you from your graves, O my people. And I

will put my Spirit within you, and you shall live, and
I will place you in your own land. Then you shall
know that I am the Lord; I have spoken, and I will
do it, declares the Lord."

The vast allegorical valley described by Ezekiel represents the
nations inhabited by the scattered children of Israel. Tragically for
the Jews, the nations are likened to a cemetery. Once driven from
their homes (although a remnant always remained in the land), the
majority of Abraham's descendants drifted from one country to
another for two thousand years. With a lasting security always just
beyond their grasp, the nations of their exile became the graveyard
for their dead bones. But chapter 37 reveals that God has a plan to
open the graves, extract His people, infuse them with life, and cause
them to return to their own land. Today, the bones that were dead
are coming to life and are in the process of being brought back to
their allotted patch of earth, Eretz Israel.

God intends that His people should know, beyond a shadow of
a doubt, that their God is the only God capable of delivering on all
of His promises. "When I bring them home from the lands of their
enemies, I will display my holiness among them for all the nations
to see. Then my people will know that I am the Lord their God,
because I sent them away to exile and brought them home again. I
will leave none of my people behind" (Ezekiel 39:27–28 NLT).

Aliyah from the nations. Isaiah 11:11 states, "In that day the
Lord will extend his hand yet a second time to recover the remnant
that remains of his people, from Assyria, from Egypt, from Pathros,
from Cush, from Elam, from Shinar, from Hamath, and from the
coastlands of the sea."

The Jewish return to the land of Israel over the past century
and a half is the "second time" mentioned in the previous verse;
never before had Jews returned from all the areas listed by Isaiah.
Likewise, the modern rebirth of Israel, as a nation, accompanied

by the steady influx of a Jewish repopulation, is that prophecy's fulfillment *in process*. In May 2015, 27,933 new Jewish immigrants celebrated their first independence day as Israelis.[5] During these recent years of aliyah, the returning Jews have come out of the very places referenced by Isaiah. Sections of four modern nations are located in the territory once occupied by ancient Assyria: Iraq, Iran, Syria, and Turkey. Upper Egypt (southern Egypt) is *Pathros*. Ethiopia is *Cush*. Western Iran is *Elam*. Iraq is *Shinar* and Syria is *Hamath*. The names for the nations during Isaiah's day may have changed, but God's word is steadfast and unaltered, and He continues to recover the remnant of His people. The return has begun.

Between the destruction of the temple in 70 AD and the current, large-scale return migration that began in the 1880s, Jews continued to maintain an intermittent homeward trek. In fact, their presence in Jerusalem was twice the size of their Muslim neighbors. William Seward, secretary of state under President Lincoln, traveled to the Holy Land in 1871. Describing Jerusalem, he wrote, "The Mohammedans are four thousand, and occupy the northeast quarter, including the whole area of the Mosque of Omar. The Jews are eight thousand, and have the southeast quarter."[6]

Although there has always been a Jewish presence in the land, the recent, *worldwide* migration of Jews back to their homeland can be catalogued into specific time periods. The numbers for this immigration, as well as the countries represented, are documented and preserved by more than one organization, for massive relocation on this scale necessitates a global endeavor. By

---

[5] Raphael Poch, *Worldwide Celebrations in Honor of Israel's Independence*, April 23, 2015, Breaking Israel News - Latest News, Biblical Perspective (http://www.breakingisraelnews.com/) accessed 4/23/2015.

[6] Lenny Ben-David, *Lincoln's Secretary of State's Jerusalem Visit*, August 21, 2015, www.israeldailypicture.com via Aish.com (www.Aish.com) Accessed 8/21/2015.

compiling information provided from these sources, the following thumbnail sketch of the major aliyah movements emerges.[7]

Aliyah during pre-World War I Ottoman rule.

- The earliest tentative foray toward permanent immigration by European Jews is known as the first aliyah (1882–1903). It began taking place in the last decades of the nineteenth century. This first aliyah was primarily composed of religious, European Chassidic Jews, although a small contingent from Yemen immigrated also at about the same time.[8] These pioneers would be responsible for the addition of approximately thirty-five thousand new residents into a land still governed by the Ottoman Empire.

- A second aliyah (1904–1919) brought another forty thousand newcomers some twenty years later. Theodore Herzl's budding Zionist movement was gaining momentum as evidenced by a flood of Russian immigrants. Escaping from Czarist pograms, many in this group were non-religious, and their socialist ideas formed the basis for a kibbutz system that would serve as the foundation for the early Jewish communities. Degania, the first of these collective farms, or kibbutzim, was soon established at the southern end of

---

[7] Information concerning histories, chronologies, and statistics relating to the different groups of aliyah is available from organizations such as International Christian Embassy Jerusalem (www.icej.org), The Jewish Federation of North America (www.jewishfederations.org), Operation Exodus, a Ministry of Ebenezer Emergency Fund International (www.operation-exodus.org), The Jewish Agency for Israel (www.jewishagency.org), and Shavei Israel (www.shavei.org). Other excellent web sites for this topic are: Jewish History.org, http://www.jewishhistory.org/ and Jewish Virtual Library, http://www.jewishvirtuallibrary.org/.

[8] Chassidic (or Hasidic) Jews belong to a branch of Orthodox Judaism known as Chassidism. The movement began in the 1700s in Eastern Europe. Followers are characterized by their distinctive black dress, their devotion to study, and a religiously pious lifestyle.

the Sea of Galilee. In 1915, as Israeli guides like to remind their groups, the famous general, Moshe Dayan, was born on the Degania kibbutz. During this aliyah, the coastal city of Tel Aviv was founded, and Hebrew was reintroduced as a modern, spoken language through the efforts of a Lithuanian immigrant who had arrived earlier, Eliezar Ben-Yehuda.

Aliyah during the British Mandate, post-World War I.

- The third aliyah (1919–1923) continued to draw Jews mostly from Eastern Europe and came about as a direct result of the Russian Revolution. About this same time, another series of pogroms in Poland and Hungary, along with the issuance of the Balfour Declaration, helped to spur large immigration numbers. Forty thousand immigrants arrived during these years. Marshlands in the Jezreel Valley were drained to accommodate major land reclamation, and the earlier agricultural settlements continued to grow.
- The fourth aliyah (1924–1929) was a large one and was composed of mainly middle-class Polish immigrants. Because this group arrived with the monetary wherewithal to invest, small businesses and industry increased. This aliyah reached eighty-two thousand before the end of 1929.
- The fifth aliyah (1929–1939) coincided with the rise of the Nazi Party in Germany. Those who could still escape began to flood out of Europe. Consisting mainly of educated professionals, this group eventually swelled to two hundred fifty thousand. During these years, Haifa was constructed as a modern seaport, and Israel's oil refining industry emerged. As a result of the massive Jewish population increase during this aliyah, the era was also marked by violent Arab attacks on settlements throughout the mandate. The period is also known as the 1936–1939 Arab Revolt. In an attempt to keep

the peace, Britain issued a new policy in 1939. Today, that policy is known as the infamous White Paper that capped Jewish immigration for the next five years to a maximum total of seventy-five thousand.

- Aliyah Bet (1939-1948) is the name given to the next wave of immigration, but the exact numbers are unknown, as this aliyah was an illegal one. From 1939 until statehood, desperate Jews continued their efforts to try to reach the safety of British-mandated Palestine. Best estimates for those arriving in the land after escaping from Nazi-occupied Europe point to around 110,000 or more. The majority of the refugees attempted to arrive by ship, in spite of British naval blockades, and it is also known that over a thousand from Syria clandestinely traveled overland. The saga of the *S.S. Exodus* and her human cargo of 4,500 is probably the best-known incident from this particularly tragic period.[9]

Aliyah to the State of Israel, 1948 to the present.

- With the establishment of the State of Israel in 1948, Jewish immigration entered a new phase as recent arrivals became known as *olim*. Olim is a distinctly Hebrew term used by native Israelis to identify immigrants. Some five hundred twelve thousand refugees arrived during the first three years of statehood, and the subsequent waves of aliyah began to take on decidedly biblical names. This was a less than subtle reminder to the rest of the world that the returning Jews were coming home to their ancient biblical origin.
- Operation Wings of Eagles (1949–1950) was carried out as a secret mission. Three hundred and eighty separate American and British transports successfully delivered forty-nine

---

[9] *S.S. Exodus* (see chapter 4).

thousand Jewish refugees to the new state during a period of fifteen months. Forty-seven thousand members of this group were Yemenite Jews with a smaller contingent being made up by Jews from Djibouti and Eritrea. "You yourselves have seen what I did to the Egyptians, and how I bore you on eagles' wings and brought you to myself" (Exodus 19:4). The aliyah is also known by its other name: Operation Magic Carpet.

- Operation Ezra and Nehemiah (1950–1952) was named for the two leaders credited with organizing the Jewish return from Babylon captivity. This aliyah came about as a result of a major crisis in Iraq. In the wake of the vote by the United Nations on Israel's statehood, along with the following War of Independence, Iraqi Jews began to fear for their lives. Outbreaks of violence and anti-Semitism burst to the surface in Baghdad. Forbidden from taking any of their personal jewelry, restricted to hand-carried luggage, and allowed less than one hundred dollars, between one hundred twenty thousand and one hundred thirty thousand of Iraq's ancient, twenty-five-hundred-year-old Jewish community were airlifted to Israel via Cypress and Iran.

- Operation Moses, Operation Joshua, Operation Solomon, and Operation Wings of Doves (1984–2013) are the names given to the successive missions focusing on rescuing "Beta Israel." Jews from Ethiopia are known as Beta Israel. According to tradition, Ethiopia's Jews are the descendants of Menelik I, son of King Solomon and the Queen of Sheba. This group was transported out of Ethiopia during a series of complex secret operations that required the combined efforts of the Israeli Defense Forces, the CIA, the Sudanese government, and a now defunct European airline, TEA. In spite of news leaks that could have sabotaged the first attempt, the operations were able to bring home over twenty-one thousand members of Beta Israel.

- Operation Exodus (1989–2002) came about in the aftermath of two separate events. A combination of the following situations had resulted in renewed anti-Semitism in Russia: the formal break in Soviet–Israeli diplomatic relations following the Six-Day War (1967) and a failed airplane hijacking in 1970 by a group of refuseniks.[10] The latter happened during a time when threats of arrest, imprisonment, and harassment dogged any Jew who signed up for an exit visa to make aliyah. When the would-be hijackers turned out to be Zionists, with plans to fly the plane to Israel, open anti-Semitism erupted, and Jews found themselves ostracized from the rest of the country's population. Since the dissolution of the former Soviet Union in 1991, however, approximately one million Russian Jews have flooded into Israel. This aliyah's very name is reminiscent of the earlier mass exodus from Egypt because Russian olim have poured into Israel in record numbers. It is also a reminder of Jeremiah's prophecy concerning an exodus that would come from the north.[11]

- Operation *Bnei-Menashe* (2013- present). This ongoing effort involves a group located in northeastern India and claiming descent from Manasseh, one of the ten lost tribes carried away into Assyrian captivity in 722 BC. Their oral tradition relates the tale of travels over the famed Silk Road before their eventual settling in India. Twenty-seven centuries later, in 2005, Israel's Sephardi chief rabbi, Shlomo Amar, declared

---

[10] "Refuseniks." Russian term used to refer to Soviet citizens wanting to immigrate to another country. Typically, the refuseniks were Jewish. A famous refusenik eventually making aliyah is Natan Shransky. Since immigrating, he has served in various positions in the Israeli government, as an elected member of the Knesset, and as chair of the executive of the Jewish Agency for Israel.

[11] "But it will be said, 'As surely as the Lord lives, who brought the Israelites up out of the land of the north and out of all the countries where he had banished them.' For I will restore them to the land I gave their ancestors" (Jeremiah 16:15 NIV).

their legal right to return to the land of their origin, Israel. With seventeen hundred Bnei-Menashe (Sons of Manasseh) having made aliyah, efforts are in place to help the more than seventy-two hundred who still remain in India.

Aliyah continues. While events continue to unfold in the arena of the Middle East—and Israel in particular—Jews continue to return to their hereditary home in record numbers. As foretold by the prophets, the land sworn to the patriarchs is undergoing a current population boom as the descendants from the original twelve tribes come back to their ancient homeland. In the last one hundred twenty years, well over 2.5 million Jews have made aliyah.[12]

The believer's bottom line. Christians also have a part in aliyah. "Thus says the Lord God: "Behold, I will lift up my hand to the nations, and raise my signal to the peoples; and they shall bring your sons in their arms, and your daughters shall be carried on their shoulders" (Isaiah 49:22). Just as truly as it was prophesized that God would restore His people to the land, it has also been prophesized that the nations, or Gentiles, would be included in this very special operation. Accordingly, a growing number of believers from the nations have begun partnering with the excellent organizations currently facilitating aliyah. How typically characteristic of the heavenly Father to include each branch of His family in this process of aliyah! The "dry bones" are coming to life, and the desert has begun to bloom again.

Once obsolete, Hebrew is now spoken by millions, and the hills of Judea and Samaria boast innovative industry, productive fields and vineyards, and exceptional flocks. The laughter of children is heard in the streets as aliyah is in full swing. As it is written, God has raised the signal, and Abraham's descendants are coming home to Israel.

---

[12] *"ALIYAH - bringing God's chosen people home"*; International Christian Embassy Jerusalem http://int.icej.org/aid/aliyah. Accessed 10/16/2014.

Chapter 12 Study Guide

1. The Hebrew word *aliyah* means _____.
2. Which psalms are the psalms of aliyah?_____.
3. Collectively, Jews living outside of Israel are part of the _____.
4. Explain replacement theology_____

   _____.

5. Summarize Romans 9, 10, and 11 (book within a book)

   _____

   _____.

6. Hebrews 8:8–12 directly quotes from what Old Testament scripture? _____.
7. When did the aliyah operations begin to be given Bible names?

   _____.

8. So far, the largest aliyah has come from this place: _____.
9. Isaiah 49:22 states that this group of people will assist the Jews to make aliyah _____.

"'I will bring my exiled people of Israel back from distant lands, and they will rebuild their ruined cities and live in them again. They will plant vineyards and gardens; they will eat their crops and drink their wine. I will firmly plant them there in their own land. They will never again be uprooted from the land I have given them,' says the Lord your God" (Amos 9:14–15 NLT).

Study Guide Key
(Answers for Chapter Study Guides)

Chapter 1
1. Yeshua, Salvation
2. Mashiach, anointed
3. Faith, sons, Abraham
4. Abraham, Gentiles
5. Abraham's offspring and heirs according to the promise
6. Jews, Greeks, Church of God
7. Old Testament or Hebrew Bible

Chapter 2
1. Seventy-five, land
2. Land, Abraham's descendants, forever
3. Land, river, of Egypt, Euphrates River
4. Isaac
5. Jacob
6. Land
7. Sun, moon, stars, and sea tides cease to exist
8. Irrevocable
9. Land

Chapter 3
A. Lebanon
B. Syria
C. Jordan

D. Saudi Arabia

E. Egypt

F. Dead Sea

G. Sea of Galilee

H. Mediterranean Sea

I. Golan Heights

J. West Bank/ Judea and Samaria

*1948

*Prince of God (see p 10)

Chapter 4

1. Babylon, 586 BC
2. Rome, 70 AD
3. Jerusalem, Israel
4. Crusades
5. Jews are confined to home during Easter; clothing patch identifies Jews
6. Edward I issues Edict of Expulsion, expelling Jews from England on the ninth of Av
7. Jews imprisoned and property confiscated; they are evicted from France by Phillippe IV.
8. Ferdinand and Isabella sign Alhambra Decree; the Jews are evicted from Spain on the ninth of Av.
9. Russian pograms, Dreyfus Affair in France, *Der Judenstaat* published, *Innocents Abroad* published.
10. First Zionist Conference in Basel, Switzerland. Theodor Herzl writes his fifty-year prophecy.
11. The Balfour Declaration is issued by Great Britain.
12. State of Israel declared on May 14, 1948.

Chapter 5

1. Ishmael
2. Islam

3. Arab, Muslim
4. House of Islam, House of War
5. Sunni
6. Shiite or Shia
7. Progressive Revelation

Psalm 83:

. Jordan

. Arabian peninsula, Arab nations(Ishmael)

. Jordan

. Bedouin of Arabia, Libya, Sinai, Jordan, Sudan

. Lebanon (Hezbollah)

. Jordan

. Negev, Arabia (Esau)

. Gaza (Hamas)

. Lebanon (Hezbollah)

. Parts of Iraq, Syria, Turkey (Sisera and Jabin)

. Northwest Arabia (from Keturah)

. Midian kings and princes (Arabia)

Chapter 6

1. Canaan
2. Israel
3. True
4. False
5. Aegean Sea region, Crete, Indo-European
6. Arab lands in mandated Palestine
7. After 1967 Six-Day War
8. Arabic
9. Islam
10. *The Palestine Post*

Chapter 7

1. "And there was evening and morning, the first day" (Genesis 1:5).
2. Sabbath or Shabbat, Genesis 2:1–3

3. Abib (Aviv), Nissan
4. Passover or the Exodus
5. Fixed time or season, appointed or ordained
6. Convocation or assembly, rehearsal
7. Leviticus 23

Chapter 8
1. Three
2. Passover
3. Feast of Unleavened Bread
4. Firstfruits

Chapter 9
1. Matan Torah, Giving of the Torah; Pentecost
2. Fifty
3. Holy Spirit coming to earth
4. Counting the omer
5. Wheat
6. Two loaves of leavened bread
7. Document/gift from the groom lists his promises and guarantees to the bride; unilateral
8. Negotiated deal with one who had legal right; he provided and protected and brought the bride into his household.
9. Two

Chapter 10
1. Peace-making, repentance, and preparation
2. Three, Tishrei
3. Yom Teruah, Yom HaZikaron, Rosh HaShanah
4. Day of Atonement
5. Feast of Tabernacles or booths
6. Stable
7. Succot, Feast of Tabernacles

Chapter 11
1. Over eight hundred times
2. 1000 BC
3. Three thousand years
4. Ezekiel 16
5. Psalm 87:1
6. Jerusalem below
7. Jerusalem above
8. The place, site of akeidah and the temple's Holy of Holies
9. Isaiah 2:2–4; Zechariah 12:2–3

Chapter 12
1. To go up
2. Psalms 121–134
3. Diaspora
4. God has replaced the Jews with the Church.
5. The Church's roots are in Israel; God's covenant with Israel is irrevocable.
6. Jeremiah 31
7. At the time that Israel became a modern state in 1948
8. Former Soviet Union (the country to the north)
9. The peoples, the nations (the Gentiles)

For Further Reading

Chapter One

Baron, David. *Israel in The Plan of God*. Grand Rapids: Kregel Publications, 1983.

Boskey, Avner. *Israel The Key to World Revival*. Nashville: David's Tent Publishing, 1999.

Cohen, Chuck and Karen. *Roots of Our Faith*. Jerusalem: CFI Jerusalem Publishing, 2002.

Halley, Henry H. *Halley's Bible Handbook*. Grand Rapids: Zondervan Publishing House, 1965.

Lash, Jamie. *A Kiss a Day-A Jewish Roots Devotional Commentary*. Fort Lauderdale, 2012.

Mears, Henrietta C. *What the Bible Is All About*. Ventura: Regal Books, 1983.

Parsons, John J. *A Year through the Torah*. Scottsdale: Hebrew Heart Publications, 2008.

Rasmussen, Carl G. *Zondervan NIV Atlas of the Bible*. Grand Rapids: Regency Reference Library, 1989.

Robinson, Thomas. *The Bible Timeline*. Nashville: Thomas Nelson Publishers, 1992.

Scherman, Nosson and Zlotowitz, Meir. *The Chumash (The ArtScroll Series/The Stone Edition)*. Brooklyn: Mesorah Publications, Ltd., 2000.

Teplinsky, Sandra. *Why Care About Israel?* Grand Rapids: Chosen Books, 2004.

Chapter Two

Archbold, Norma Parrish. *The Mountains of Israel.* Israel and USA: Phoebe's Song, 1996.

Blech, Benjamin. *The Complete Idiot's Guide to Jewish History and Culture,* New York: Alpha Books, 1999.

Bourke, Stephen. *The Middle East-The Cradle of Civilization Revealed.* Lane Cove: Global Book Publishing, 2008.

Woodrow, Martin and Sanders, E.P. *People from the Bible.* Wilton: Morehouse-Barlow, 1987.

Chapter Three

Anderson, Scott. *Lawrence in Arabia.* New York: Doubleday, 2013.

Bard, Mitchell G. *Myths and Facts.* Chevy Chase: American Israeli Cooperative Enterprise (AICE), 2001.

Catherwood, Christopher. *Churchill's Folly.* New York: Carroll & Graf Publishers, 2004.

Cohen, Chuck and Karen. *Grounded The Promised Land in the New Testament.* Jerusalem, http://shop.ifi.org.il/collections/books/products/grounded-the-promised-land-in-the-new-testament.

Cohen, Bruce. *Israel, Arabs,& The Middle East.* Wynnewood: Har Tavor Publishing Ltd., 1992.

Chapter Four

Duvernoy, Claude. *The Prince and the Prophet.* Branson: A Glorious Church Fellowship, Inc., 1979.

Herzog, Chaim. *The Arab-Israeli Wars.* New York: Vintage Books, 2005.

Ironside, H.A. *The Four Hundred Silent Years.* Neptune: Loizeaux Brothers, Inc., 1980.

Johnson, Matt and Goodenough, Nicola (editors). *Christians and Israel. Essays on Biblical Zionism and on Islamic Fundamentalism.* Jerusalem: International Christian Embassy Jerusalem, 1996.

Mackey, Sandra. *The Saudis: Inside the Desert Kingdom.* New York: W.W. Norton & Company, 2002.

Pierce, Larry and Marion. *Newton's Revised History of Ancient Kingdoms.* Green Forest, Master Books, 2009

Prince, Derek. *The Last Word on the Middle East.* Fort Lauderdale: DPM International, 1982.

Prince, Lydia. *Appointment in Jerusalem.* Waco: A Chosen Book, 1978.

Rubin, David. *God, Israel, & Shiloh.* Shiloh: Shiloh Israel Press, 2011.

Shachan, Avigdor. *In the Footsteps of the Lost Ten Tribes.* Jerusalem: Devora Publishing, 2007.

St. John, Robert. *Tongue of the Prophets.* North Hollywood: Wilshire Book Company, 1952.

Thornton, Bruce S. *The Wages of Appeasement.* New York: Encounter Books, 2011.

Chapter Five

Boskey, Avner. *A Perspective on Islam.* Nashville: Final Frontier Ministries, 2001.

Gilbert, Lela. *Saturday People, Sunday People.* New York: Encounter Books, 2012.

Gilbert, Martin. *In Ishmael's House: A History of Jews in Muslim Lands.* New Haven: Yale University Press, 2011

Gabriel, Brigitte. *Because They Hate.* New York: St. Martin's Press, 2006.

Gabriel, Mark A. *Islam and the Jews.* Lake Mary: Charisma House, 2003.

Little, Gene. *The Mystery of Islam.* Jasper: 2003.

Rubin, David. *The Islamic Tsunami.* Shiloh: Shiloh Israel Press, 2010.

White, Andrew. *The Vicar of Baghdad.* Oxford: Monarch Books, 2009.

Ye'or, Bat. *The Dhimmi.* London: Associated University Presses, 1985.

Zacharias, Ravi. *Light in the Shadow of Jihad.* Sisters: Multnomah Publishers, Inc., 2002.

Chapter Six

Ben-Haim, Eliyahu. *Setting the Record Straight.* Jerusalem, http://shop.ifi.org.il/collections/books/products/setting-the-record-straight.

Bard, Mitchell. *The Complete Idiot's Guide To Middle East Conflict.* Indianapolis: Alpha Books, 1999.

Davis, David. *The Elijah Legacy.* Haifa: 2003.

Gilbert, Martin. *The Routledge Atlas of Jewish History.* London: Routledge, 2010.

Katz, Samuel. *Battleground: Fact & Fantasy in Palestine.* New York: Taylor Productions LTD., 2002.

Levy, Raanan (Rani), *Land for Peace: A Century of Failure.* Springfield: 21st Century Press, 2010.

Oren, Michael B. *Six Days of War.* New York: Random House Publishing Group, 2003.

Peters, Joan. *From Time Immemorial.* Chicago: JKAP Publications, 2002.

Rosenberg, Joel. *Inside the Revolution.* Carol Stream: Tyndale, 2011.

Sharon, Moshe. *Jihad Islam Against Israel and the West.* Jerusalem, 2007.

Twain, Mark. *The Innocents Abroad.* New York: A Signet Classic, 1980.

Chapters Seven, Eight, Nine, and Ten

Cantrell, Ron. *The Feasts of the Lord.* Jerusalem, 1999.

Garr, John D. *Living Emblems.* Atlanta: Restoration Foundation, 2000.

Hedding, Malcolm. *The Celebration of the Feast of Tabernacles.* Jerusalem: International Christian Embassy Jerusalem, 2004.

Howard, Kevin and Rosenthal, Marvin. *The Feasts of the Lord.* Nashville: Thomas Nelson, Inc., 1997.

Levitt, Zola. The Seven Feasts of Israel. Dallas: ZOLA, 1979.

Michas, Peter A., Vander Maten, Robert, and Michas, Christie D. *The Rod of an Almond Tree in God's Master Plan.* Mukilteo: WinePress Publishing, 1997.

Shannon, Jill. *A Prophetic Calendar The Feasts of Israel.* Shippensburg: Destiny Image Publishers, Inc., 2009.

Scarlata, Robin & Pierce, Linda. *A Family Guide to the Biblical Holidays.* Woodbridge: Heart of Wisdom Publishing, 1999.

Stone, Perry. *Breaking the Code of the Feasts.* Cleveland: Voice of Evangelism, 2007.

Chapter Eleven

Ariel, Israel and Richman, Chaim. *Carta's Illustrated Encyclopedia of The Holy Temple in Jerusalem.* Jerusalem: The Temple Institute and Carta, 2005.

Brim, Billye. *Jerusalem, Above and Below.* Branson: A Glorious Church Fellowship, Inc.

Collins, Larry and LaPierre Dominique. *O Jerusalem!* New York: Touchstone Book, 1972.

Conner, Kevin J. *The Tabernacle of David.* Portland: City Bible Publishing, 1976.

Edersheim, Alfred. *The Temple, Its Ministry and Services.* Peabody: Hendrickson Publishers, Inc., 1994.

Hagee, John. *Jerusalem Countdown.* Lake Mary: Frontline, 2006.

Hess, Tom. *The Watchmen.* Charlotte: Morningstar Publications, 1998.

Hess, Tom. *Pray for the Peace of Jerusalem.* Jerusalem: Progressive Vision International, 2000.

Kaplan, Aryeh. *Jerusalem, The Eye of the Universe.* New York: The National Conference of Synagogue Youth, 1976.

Kitson, Hugh. *Jerusalem the Covenant City.* West Sussex: Hatikvah Ltd., 2000.

Lambert, Lance. *The Battle of the Ages.* Corona: Two-fish Publications, 2014.

Mitchell, Chris. *Dateline Jerusalem.* Nashville: Nelson Books, 2013.

Montefiore, Simon Sebag. *Jerusalem. The Biography.* New York: Alfred A. Knopf, 2011.

van der Hoeven, Jan Willem. *Babylon or Jerusalem?* Shippensburg: Destiny Image, 1993.

Chapter Twelve

Bierman, Dominiquae. *Sheep Nations.* Tel Aviv: Kad-esh MAP Ministries International, 2003.

Gottier, Richard F. *Aliyah: God's Last Great Act of Redemption.* Tonbridge: Sovereign World Ltd., 2002.

Lightle, Steve. *Exodus II: Let My People Go!* Kingwood: Hunter Books, 1983.

Insightful news and information are found on the following websites:

Breaking Israel News - Latest News, Biblical Perspective: http://www.breakingisraelnews.com

Dateline Jerusalem, http://www1.cbn.com/video/dateline-jerusalem.

Gatestone Institute, http://www.gatestoneinstitute.org.

ICEJ News, http://int.icej.org/media/icej-media.

Israel Hayom,http://www.israelhayom.com.

JerusalemOnline, http://www.jerusalemonline.com.

Maoz Israel Report, http://www.maozisrael.org/site/PageServer?pagename=maoz_report.

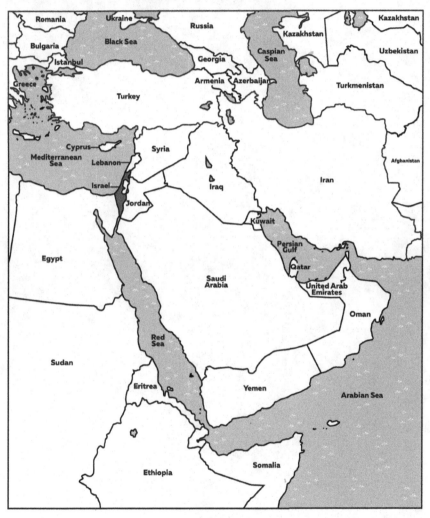

The Middle East

The Middle East

Printed in the United States
By Bookmasters